RESEARCH DESIGN

FIFTH EDITION

I dedicate this book to all of my mentees and former students over the years who have engaged in this fascinating process of research and who have welcomed my suggestions for improving their scholarly works. I also welcome my son, J. David Creswell, a noted psychologist and researcher at Carnegie Mellon University, as my coauthor.

Sara Miller McCune founded SAGE Publishing in 1965 to support the dissemination of usable knowledge and educate a global community. SAGE publishes more than 1000 journals and over 800 new books each year, spanning a wide range of subject areas. Our growing selection of library products includes archives, data, case studies and video. SAGE remains majority owned by our founder and after her lifetime will become owned by a charitable trust that secures the company's continued independence.

Los Angeles | London | New Delhi | Singapore | Washington DC | Melbourne

RESEARCH DESIGN

Qualitative, Quantitative, and Mixed Methods Approaches

FIFTH EDITION

John W. Creswell
Department of Family Medicine
University of Michigan

J. David Creswell
Department of Psychology
Carnegie Mellon University

Los Angeles | London | New Delhi
Singapore | Washington DC | Melbourne

FOR INFORMATION:

SAGE Publications, Inc.
2455 Teller Road
Thousand Oaks, California 91320
E-mail: order@sagepub.com

SAGE Publications Ltd.
1 Oliver's Yard
55 City Road
London EC1Y 1SP
United Kingdom

SAGE Publications India Pvt. Ltd.
B 1/I 1 Mohan Cooperative Industrial Area
Mathura Road, New Delhi 110 044
India

SAGE Publications Asia-Pacific Pte. Ltd.
3 Church Street
#10-04 Samsung Hub
Singapore 049483

Printed in the United States of America

Library of Congress Cataloging-in-Publication Data

Names: Creswell, John W., author. | Creswell, J. David, author.

Title: Research design : qualitative, quantitative, and mixed methods approaches / John W. Creswell, PhD, Department of Family Medicine, University of Michigan, and J. David Creswell, PhD, Department of Psychology, Carnegie Mellon University.

Description: Fifth edition. | Los Angeles : SAGE, [2018] | Includes bibliographical references and index.

Identifiers: LCCN 2017044644 | ISBN 978-1-5063-8670-6 (pbk. : alk. paper)

Subjects: LCSH: Social sciences—Research—Methodology. | Social sciences—Statistical methods.

Classification: LCC H62 .C6963 2018 | DDC 300.72/1—dc23
LC record available at https://lccn.loc.gov/2017044644

Acquisitions Editor: Helen Salmon
Content Development Editor: Chelsea Neve
Editorial Assistant: Megan O'Heffernan
Production Editor: David C. Felts
Copy Editor: Amy Marks
Typesetter: C&M Digitals (P) Ltd.
Proofreader: Eleni-Maria Georgiou
Indexer: Stepping Stones Indexing Services
Cover Designer: Janet Kiesel
Marketing Manager: Shari Countryman

17 18 19 20 21 10 9 8 7 6 5 4 3 2 1

Brief Contents

Detailed Contents

Analytic Contents of Research Techniques

Chapter 1. The Selection of a Research Approach

- Determining your research approach
- Identifying a worldview with which you are most comfortable
- Defining the three types of research approaches
- Using quantitative, qualitative, and mixed methods designs and methods

Chapter 2. Review of the Literature

- Assessing whether your topic is researchable
- Using steps in conducting a literature review
- Using computerized databases available for reviewing the literature
- Developing a priority for types of literature to review
- Designing a literature map
- Writing a good abstract of a research study
- Using important elements of a style manual
- Defining terms
- Employing a model for writing a literature review

Chapter 3. The Use of Theory

- Testing causal claims in quantitative research
- Identifying variables in a quantitative study
- Defining the nature of a quantitative theory
- Using a script to write a theoretical perspective into a quantitative study
- Considering the types of theories used in qualitative research

- Using a script for writing a quantitative purpose statement

- Considering how the script would change depending on your quantitative design

- Using a script for writing a mixed methods purpose statement

- Considering how the script would change depending on your mixed methods design

Chapter 7. Research Questions and Hypotheses

- Writing a script for a qualitative central question

- Considering how this script would change depending on the qualitative design

- Writing a script for quantitative research questions and hypotheses

- Considering how this script would change depending on the quantitative design and the different types of hypotheses

- Using a model for descriptive and inferential quantitative questions and hypotheses

- Writing scripts for different forms of research questions for a mixed methods study

Chapter 8. Quantitative Methods

- Using a checklist for survey research to form topic sections of a survey procedure

- Employing steps in analyzing data for a survey procedure

- Writing a complete survey methods discussion

- Using a checklist for experimental research to form sections for an experimental procedure

- Identifying the type of experimental procedure that best fits your proposed study

- Drawing a diagram of experimental procedures

- Identifying the potential internal validity and external validity threats to your proposed study

Chapter 9. Qualitative Methods

- Using a checklist for qualitative research to form topic sections of a procedure

- Stating the basic characteristics of qualitative research

- Determining how reflexivity will be included in a proposed study

- Weighing the different types of data collected in qualitative research

- Employing steps in the qualitative data analysis process

- Establishing validity in qualitative research

Chapter 10. Mixed Methods Procedures

- Stating a definition and the characteristics of mixed methods research

- Using a convergent mixed methods design

- Using an explanatory sequential mixed methods design

- Employing an exploratory sequential mixed methods design

- Using one of the complex mixed methods designs

- Choosing which design is best for a mixed methods study

Preface

Purpose

This book advances a framework, a process, and compositional approaches for designing a proposal or research project for qualitative, quantitative, and mixed methods research in the human, health, and social sciences. The ascendency of qualitative research, the emergence of mixed methods approaches, and the growth of quantitative designs have created a need for this book's unique comparison of the three approaches to inquiry. This comparison begins with preliminary consideration of philosophical assumptions for all three approaches, a review of the literature, an assessment of the use of theory and conceptual frameworks in research approaches, and reflections about the importance of writing and ethics in scholarly inquiry. The book then addresses the key elements in the process of designing and conducting a research project: writing an introduction; stating a purpose or research aims for the study; identifying research questions and hypotheses; and advancing methods and procedures for data collection, analysis, and interpretation. At each step in this process, the reader is taken through qualitative, quantitative, and mixed methods approaches.

Audience

This book is intended for students and faculty who seek assistance in preparing a plan, proposal, or research project for a scholarly journal article, a dissertation, a thesis, or an application for funding. At a broader level, the book may be useful as both a reference book and a textbook for courses in research methods. To best take advantage of the design features in this book, the reader needs a basic familiarity with qualitative and quantitative research; however, terms will be explained and defined and recommended strategies advanced for those needing introductory assistance in the design process. Highlighted terms in the text and a glossary of the terms at the back of the book provide a working language for understanding research. This book also is intended for a broad audience in the human, health, and social sciences. Readers' comments from the past four editions suggest that individuals using the book come from many disciplines and fields. We hope that researchers in fields such as marketing, management, criminal justice, communication studies, psychology, sociology, K–12 education, higher and postsecondary education, nursing, family medicine, health services research, global health, behavioral health, urban studies, family research, and other fields of study will find this fifth edition useful.

Format
....

In each chapter, we share examples drawn from varied disciplines. These examples are drawn from books, journal articles, dissertation proposals, and dissertations. Though our primary specialization is in educational psychology, the health sciences, and in psychology, the illustrations are intended to be inclusive of many fields. They reflect issues in social justice and examples of studies with marginalized individuals in our society as well as the traditional samples and populations studied by researchers. Inclusiveness also extends to methodological pluralism in research today, and the discussion incorporates alternative philosophical ideas, diverse modes of inquiry, and numerous procedures.

This book is not a detailed method text; instead, we highlight the essential features of research design. We have attempted to reduce research to its essential core ideas so that researchers can plan a thorough and thoughtful study. The coverage of research designs is limited to frequently used forms: surveys and experiments in quantitative research; narrative research, phenomenology, grounded theory, ethnography, and case studies in qualitative research; and convergent, explanatory sequential, and exploratory sequential designs in mixed methods research. Although students preparing a dissertation proposal should find this book helpful, topics related to the politics of presenting and negotiating a study with review committees are addressed thoroughly in other texts.

Consistent with accepted conventions of scholarly writing, we have tried to eliminate any words or examples that convey a discriminatory (e.g., sexist or ethnic) orientation. Examples were selected to provide a full range of gender and cultural orientations. Throughout the text we do not favor either qualitative or quantitative research. Indeed, we have intentionally altered the order of qualitative and quantitative examples throughout the book. Readers should also note that in the longer examples cited in this book, many references are made to other writings. Only the reference to the work we use in the illustration will be cited, not the entire list of references embedded within any particular example. As with earlier editions, we have maintained features to enhance the readability and understandability of the material: bullets to emphasize key points, numbered points to stress key steps in a process, and longer examples of complete passages with annotations to highlight key research ideas that are being conveyed by the authors.

In this fifth edition of the book, new features have been added in response to developments in research and reader feedback:

- In this edition, we shape the discussion not only around designing a *proposal* for a *research project* but also around the steps in designing a *research study*. Thus, the emphasis on designing a research study (as opposed to focusing only on a proposal) is slightly larger for this edition than in past editions.

- We have added more information about the epistemological and ontological assumptions as they relate to research questions and methods.

- In the worldview section, we now include more on the transformative worldview.

- In the methods discussion, we have added more on specific approaches such as case studies, participatory action research, and visual methods in qualitative research.

- Also in the qualitative methods, we have added information about social media and online qualitative methods. Also, we have added more information on memoing and on reflexivity.

- In the mixed methods, we now incorporate information about action research (participatory research) and program evaluation.

- In the respective methods chapters, we have included more on qualitative and quantitative data analysis software.

- In the theory section, we have added information about causality, and then incorporated its relationship to statistics in the quantitative methods.

- For our quantitative, qualitative, and mixed methods sections, we have incorporated sections on writing discussion sections into each of these methodologies.

- We have incorporated new information into all of our methods chapters—quantitative, qualitative, and mixed methods. Our mixed methods chapter now reflects the latest advances in the field.

- Throughout the book, we have cited updated editions of research methods books that have emerged since the last edition and added current references and additional readings.

Outline of Chapters

This book is divided into two parts. Part I consist of steps that researchers need to consider *before* they develop their proposals or plans for research. Part II discusses the various sections used to develop a scholarly research proposal for a thesis, dissertation, or a research report.

Part I. Preliminary Considerations

This part of the book discusses preparing for the design of a scholarly study. It contains Chapters 1 through 4.

Chapter 1. The Selection of a Research Approach

In this chapter, we begin by defining quantitative, qualitative, and mixed methods approaches. We then discuss how philosophy, designs, and methods intersect when one uses one of these approaches. We review different philosophical stances; advanced types of qualitative, quantitative, and mixed methods designs; and then discuss the methods associated with each design. We also consider the factors that go into the choice of an approach to research. Thus, this chapter should help proposal developers decide whether a qualitative, quantitative, or mixed methods approach is suitable for their proposed research project.

Chapter 2. Review of the Literature

It is important to extensively review the literature on your topic before you design your proposal. Thus, you need to begin with a researchable topic and then explore the literature using the steps advanced in this chapter. This calls for setting a priority for selecting material from the literature, drawing a visual map of studies that relate to your topic, writing good abstracts, employing skills learned from using style manuals, and defining key terms. This chapter should help researchers thoughtfully consider relevant literature on their topics and start compiling and writing literature reviews.

Chapter 3. The Use of Theory

Theories serve different purposes in the three approaches inquiry. In quantitative research, they provide a proposed explanation for the relationship among variables being tested by the investigator. In qualitative research, they may often serve as a lens for the inquiry or they may be generated during the study. In mixed methods studies, researchers employ them in many ways, including those associated with quantitative and qualitative approaches. This chapter helps researchers consider and plan how theory might be incorporated into their studies.

Chapter 4. Writing Strategies and Ethical Considerations

It is helpful to have an overall outline of the topics to be included in a proposal or research study before you begin writing. Thus, this chapter begins with different outlines for writing proposals. The outlines can be used as models depending on whether your proposed study is qualitative, quantitative, or mixed methods. Then we convey several ideas about the actual writing of the proposal, such as developing a habit of writing, and grammar ideas that have been helpful to us in improving our scholarly writing. Finally, we turn to ethical issues and discuss these not as abstract ideas, but as considerations that need to be anticipated in multiple phases of the research process.

Part II. Designing Research

In Part II, we turn to the components of designing the research proposal. Chapters 5 through 10 address steps in this process.

Chapter 5. The Introduction

It is important to properly introduce a research study. We provide a model for writing a good scholarly introduction to your proposal. The chapter begins with designing an abstract for a study. This is followed by developing an introduction to include identifying the research problem or issue, framing this problem within the existing literature, pointing out deficiencies in the literature, and targeting the study for an audience. This chapter provides a systematic method for designing a scholarly introduction to a proposal or study.

Chapter 6. The Purpose Statement

At the beginning of research proposals or projects, authors mention the central purpose or intent of the study. This passage is the most important statement in the entire research process, and an entire chapter is devoted to this topic. In this chapter, you learn how to write this statement for quantitative, qualitative, and mixed methods studies, and you will be provided with scripts that help you design and write these statements.

Chapter 7. Research Questions and Hypotheses

The questions and hypotheses addressed by the researcher serve to narrow and focus the purpose of the study. As a major signpost in a project, the set of research questions and hypotheses needs to be written carefully. In this chapter, you will learn how to write both qualitative and quantitative research questions and hypotheses, as well as how to employ both forms in writing mixed methods questions and hypotheses. Numerous examples serve as scripts to illustrate these processes.

Chapter 8. Quantitative Methods

Quantitative methods involve the processes of collecting, analyzing, interpreting, and writing the results of a study. Specific methods exist in both survey and experimental research that relate to identifying a sample and population, specifying the type of design, collecting and analyzing data, presenting the results, making an interpretation, and writing the research in a manner consistent with a survey or experimental study. In this chapter, the reader learns the specific procedures for designing survey or experimental methods that need to go into a research proposal. Checklists provided in the chapter help to ensure that all steps are included.

Chapter 9. Qualitative Methods

Qualitative approaches to data collection, analysis, interpretation, and report writing differ from the traditional, quantitative approaches. Purposeful sampling, collection of open-ended data, analysis of text or images (e.g., pictures), representation of information in figures and tables, and personal interpretation of the findings all inform qualitative methods. This chapter advances steps in designing qualitative procedures into a research proposal, and it also includes a checklist for making sure that you cover important procedures. Ample illustrations provide examples from narrative studies, phenomenology, grounded theory, ethnography, and case studies.

Chapter 10. Mixed Methods Procedures

Mixed methods involves the collection and "mixing" or integration of both quantitative and qualitative data in a study. It is not enough to only analyze your qualitative and quantitative data. Further analysis consists of integrating the two databases for additional insight into research problems and questions. Mixed methods research has increased in popularity in recent years, and this chapter highlights important developments and provides an introduction to the use of this design. This chapter begins by defining mixed methods research and the core characteristics that describe it. Then the three core designs in mixed methods research—(a) convergent, (b) explanatory sequential, and (c) exploratory sequential—are detailed in terms of their characteristics, data collection and analysis features, and approaches for interpreting and validating the research. Further, these core designs are employed within other designs (e.g., experiments), within theories (e.g., feminist research), and within methodologies (e.g., evaluation procedures). Finally, we discuss the decisions needed to determine which one of the designs would be best for your mixed methods project. We provide examples of the core designs and include a checklist to review to determine whether you incorporated all of the essential steps in your proposal or project.

Designing a study is a difficult and time-consuming process. This book will not necessarily make the process easier or faster, but it can provide specific skills useful in research, knowledge about the steps involved in the process, and a practical guide to composing and writing scholarly research. Before the steps of the process unfold, we recommend that proposal developers think through their approaches to research, conduct literature reviews on their topics, develop an outline of topics to include in a proposal design, and begin anticipating potential ethical issues that may arise in the research. Part I begins with these topics.

Companion Website

The SAGE edge companion site for *Research Design*, Fifth Edition, is available at https://edge.sagepub.com/creswellrd5e

SAGE edge for Students provides a personalized approach to help students accomplish their coursework goals.

- **Mobile-friendly quizzes** test understanding of the concepts from each chapter

- **Videos featuring John W. Creswell** and others curated from **the SAGE Research Methods platform** expand on important topics in research design

- **SAGE Journal articles** plus accompanying exercises provide opportunities to apply concepts from each chapter

- **Sample research proposals and templates** offer further guidance on research design

SAGE edge for Instructors supports teaching by making it easy to integrate quality content and create a rich learning environment.

- **Sample syllabi** assist in structuring and preparing a course

- **Editable, chapter-specific PowerPoint® slides** offer ease and flexibility in creating a multimedia presentation

- A diverse range of prewritten and editable **test questions** help **assess** progress and understanding

- **Lecture notes** highlight key concepts from each chapter and provide a helpful reference and teaching tool

- **Chapter-specific writing and peer review exercises** emphasize critical thinking and application of the concepts

- **Discussion questions and group activities** launch classroom interaction and encourage students to engage further with the material

- All **figures and tables** from the book available for download

Acknowledgments

••

This book could not have been written without the encouragement and ideas of the hundreds of students in the doctoral-level Proposal Development course that John taught at the University of Nebraska-Lincoln for over 30 years. Specific former students and editors were instrumental in its development: Dr. Sharon Hudson, Dr. Leon Cantrell, the late Nette Nelson, Dr. De Tonack, Dr. Ray Ostrander, and Diane Wells. Since the publication of the first edition, John has also become indebted to the students in his introductory research methods courses and to individuals who have participated in his qualitative and mixed methods seminars. These courses have been his laboratories for working out ideas, incorporating new ones, and sharing his experiences as a writer and researcher. In addition, John wants to thank his staff over the years in the Office of Qualitative and Mixed Methods Research at the University of Nebraska-Lincoln who have helped to conceptualize content in this book and now those in the Department of Family Medicine at the University of Michigan. John is especially indebted to the scholarly work of Dr. Vicki Plano Clark, Dr. Ron Shope, Dr. Kim Galt, Dr. Yun Lu, Dr. Sherry Wang, Amanda Garrett, and Dr. Alex Morales.

In addition, we are grateful for the insightful suggestions provided by the reviewers for SAGE. We also could not have produced this book without the generous support and encouragement of our friends at SAGE. SAGE is and has been a first-rate publishing house. We especially owe much to our former editor and mentor, C. Deborah Laughton (now of Guilford Press), and to Lisa Cuevas-Shaw and Vicki Knight. Now we are working under the talented guidance of Helen Salmon, who has been most supportive of our work and who has encouraged us throughout the process. Lastly, we want to thank all of the SAGE staff with whom we have had the pleasure to work. We have grown together and helped to develop research methods as a distinguished, worldwide field. At SAGE, we have also benefited from the contributions of reviewers to this fifth edition: Clare Bennett, University of Worcester; Kelly Kennedy, Chapman University; Therese A.G. Lewis, Northumbria University; Andrew Ryder, University of North Carolina Wilmington; Tiffany J. Davis, University of Houston; Lora L. Wolff, Western Illinois University; Laura Meyer, University of Denver; Andi Hess, Arizona State University; and Audrey Cund, University of the West of Scotland.

About the Authors

John W. Creswell, PhD, is a professor of family medicine and co-director of the Michigan Mixed Methods Research and Scholarship Program at the University of Michigan. He has authored numerous articles and 28 books on mixed methods research, qualitative research, and research design. While at the University of Nebraska-Lincoln, he held the Clifton Endowed Professor Chair, served as director of a mixed methods research office, founded SAGE's *Journal of Mixed Methods Research*, and was an adjunct professor of family medicine at the University of Michigan and a consultant to the Veterans Administration health services research center. He was a Senior Fulbright Scholar to South Africa in 2008 and to Thailand in 2012. In 2011, he co-led a national working group on mixed methods practices at the National Institutes of Health, served as a visiting professor at Harvard's School of Public Health, and received an honorary doctorate from the University of Pretoria, South Africa. In 2014, he was the president of the Mixed Methods International Research Association. In 2015, he joined the staff of Family Medicine at the University of Michigan. John has been teaching research methods courses for the past 40 years.

J. David Creswell, PhD, is an associate professor of psychology and director of the Health and Human Performance laboratory at Carnegie Mellon University. Much of his research is quantitative in nature, and focuses on understanding what makes people resilient under stress. He has published over 50 peer-reviewed articles, co-edited the *Handbook of Mindfulness* (2015, Guilford), and received early career awards for his research from the Association for Psychological Science (2011), the American Psychological Association (2014), and the American Psychosomatic Society (2017). These research contributions came from a childhood and early adulthood of discussing research methodology with his dad, so this book now extends a collaboration going back many years! David has been teaching research methods courses for the past 9 years.

Preliminary Considerations

This book is intended to help researchers develop a plan or proposal for a research study. Part I addresses several preliminary considerations that are necessary before designing a proposal or a plan for a study. These considerations relate to selecting an appropriate research approach, reviewing the literature to position the proposed study within the existing literature, deciding on whether to use a theory in the study, and employing—at the outset—good writing and ethical practices.

The Selection of a Research Approach

Research approaches are plans and the procedures for research that span the steps from broad assumptions to detailed methods of data collection, analysis, and interpretation. This plan involves several decisions, and they need not be taken in the order in which they make sense to us and the order of their presentation here. The overall decision involves which approach should be used to study a topic. Informing this decision should be the philosophical assumptions the researcher brings to the study; procedures of inquiry (called **research designs**); and specific **research methods** of data collection, analysis, and interpretation. The selection of a research approach is also based on the nature of the **research problem** or issue being addressed, the researchers' personal experiences, and the audiences for the study. Thus, in this book, *research approaches, research designs,* and *research methods* are three key terms that represent a perspective about research that presents information in a successive way from broad constructions of research to the narrow procedures of methods.

The Three Approaches to Research

In this book, three research approaches are advanced: (a) qualitative, (b) quantitative, and (c) mixed methods. Unquestionably, the three approaches are not as discrete as they first appear. Qualitative and quantitative approaches should not be viewed as rigid, distinct categories, polar opposites, or dichotomies. Instead, they represent different ends on a continuum (Creswell, 2015; Newman & Benz, 1998). A study *tends* to be more qualitative than quantitative or vice versa. **Mixed methods research** resides in the middle of this continuum because it incorporates elements of both qualitative and quantitative approaches.

Often the distinction between **qualitative research** and **quantitative research** is framed in terms of using words (qualitative) rather than numbers (quantitative), or better yet, using closed-ended questions and responses (quantitative hypotheses) or open-ended questions and responses (qualitative interview questions). A more complete way to view the gradations of differences between them is in the basic philosophical assumptions researchers bring to the study, the types of research strategies used in the research (e.g., quantitative experiments or qualitative **case studies**), and the specific methods employed in conducting these strategies (e.g., collecting data quantitatively on instruments versus collecting qualitative data through observing a setting). Moreover, there is a historical evolution to both approaches—with the quantitative approaches dominating the forms of research in the social sciences from the late 19th century up until the mid-20th century. During the latter half of the 20th century, interest in qualitative research increased and along with it, the development of mixed methods research. With this background, it should prove helpful to view definitions of these three key terms as used in this book:

- *Qualitative research* is an approach for exploring and understanding the meaning individuals or groups ascribe to a social or human problem. The process of research involves emerging questions and procedures, data typically collected in the participant's setting, data analysis inductively building from particulars to general themes, and the researcher making interpretations of the meaning of the data. The final written report has a flexible structure. Those who engage in this form of inquiry support a way of looking at research that honors an inductive style, a focus on individual meaning, and the importance of reporting the complexity of a situation.

- *Quantitative research* is an approach for testing objective **theories**by examining the relationship among variables. These variables, in turn, can be measured, typically on instruments, so that numbered data can be analyzed using statistical procedures. The final written report has a set structure consisting of introduction, literature and theory, methods, results, and discussion. Like qualitative researchers, those who engage in this form of inquiry have assumptions about testing theories deductively, building in protections against bias, controlling for alternative or counterfactual explanations, and being able to generalize and replicate the findings.

- *Mixed methods research* is an approach to inquiry involving collecting both quantitative and qualitative data, integrating the two forms of data, and using distinct designs that may involve philosophical assumptions and theoretical frameworks. The core assumption of this form of inquiry is that the integration of qualitative and quantitative data yields additional insight beyond the information provided by either the quantitative or qualitative data alone.

These definitions have considerable information in each one of them. Throughout this book, we will discuss the parts of the definitions so that their meanings will become clear to you as you read ahead.

Three Components Involved in an Approach

Two important components in each definition are that the approach to research involves philosophical assumptions as well as distinct methods or procedures. The broad research approach is the *plan or proposal to conduct research*, involves the intersection of philosophy, research designs, and specific methods. A framework that we use to explain the interaction of these three components is seen in Figure 1.1. To reiterate, in planning a study,

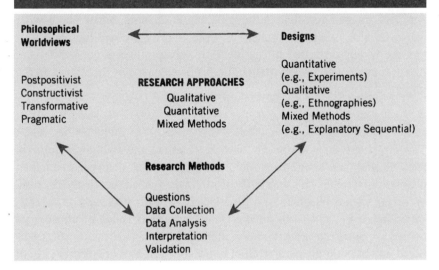

Philosophical Worldviews

Postpositivist
Constructivist
Transformative
Pragmatic

RESEARCH APPROACHES

Qualitative
Quantitative
Mixed Methods

Designs

Quantitative
(e.g., Experiments)
Qualitative
(e.g., Ethnographies)
Mixed Methods
(e.g., Explanatory Sequential)

Research Methods

Questions
Data Collection
Data Analysis
Interpretation
Validation

researchers need to think through the philosophical worldview assumptions that they bring to the study, the research design that is related to this worldview, and the specific methods or procedures of research that translate the approach into practice.

Philosophical Worldviews

Although philosophical ideas remain largely hidden in research (Slife & Williams, 1995), they still influence the practice of research and need to be identified. We suggest that individuals preparing a research proposal or plan make explicit the larger philosophical ideas they espouse. This information will help explain why they chose qualitative, quantitative, or mixed methods approaches for their research. In writing about worldviews, a proposal might include a section that addresses the following:

- The philosophical worldview proposed in the study

- A definition of basic ideas of that worldview

- How the worldview shaped their approach to research

We have chosen to use the term *worldview* as meaning "a basic set of beliefs that guide action" (Guba, 1990, p. 17). Others have called them *paradigms* (Lincoln, Lynham, & Guba, 2011; Mertens, 2010); *epistemologies* and *ontologies* (Crotty, 1998), or *broadly conceived research methodologies* (Neuman, 2009). We see worldviews as a general philosophical orientation about the world and the nature of research that a researcher brings to a study. Individuals develop worldviews based on their discipline orientations and research communities, advisors and mentors, and past research experiences. The types of beliefs held by individual researchers based on these factors will often lead to embracing a strong qualitative, quantitative, or mixed methods approach in their research. Although there is ongoing debate about what worldviews or beliefs researchers bring to inquiry, we will highlight four that are widely discussed in the literature: postpositivism, constructivism, transformative, and **pragmatism**. The major elements of each position are presented in Table 1.1.

The Postpositivist Worldview

The postpositivist assumptions have represented the traditional form of research, and these assumptions hold true more for quantitative research than qualitative research. This worldview is sometimes called the *scientific method,* or doing *science research.* It is also called *positivist/postpositivist research, empirical science,* and *postpositivism.* This last term is called postpositivism because it represents the thinking after positivism, challenging the traditional notion of the absolute truth of knowledge (Phillips & Burbules, 2000) and recognizing that we cannot be absolutely positive about our claims of knowledge when studying the behavior and actions of humans. The postpositivist tradition comes from 19th-century writers, such as Comte, Mill, Durkheim, Newton, and Locke (Smith, 1983) and more recently from writers such as Phillips and Burbules (2000).

Postpositivists hold a deterministic philosophy in which causes (probably) determine effects or outcomes. Thus, the problems studied by postpositivists reflect the need to identify and assess the causes that influence outcomes, such as those found in experiments. It is also reductionistic in that the intent is to reduce the ideas into a small, discrete set to test, such as the variables that comprise hypotheses and research questions.

Table 1.1 Four Worldviews	
Postpositivism	**Constructivism**
• Determination • Reductionism • Empirical observation and measurement • Theory verification	• Understanding • Multiple participant meanings • Social and historical construction • Theory generation
Transformative	**Pragmatism**
• Political • Power and justice oriented • Collaborative • Change-oriented	• Consequences of actions • Problem-centered • Pluralistic • Real-world practice oriented

The knowledge that develops through a postpositivist lens is based on careful observation and measurement of the objective reality that exists "out there" in the world. Thus, developing numeric measures of observations and studying the behavior of individuals becomes paramount for a postpositivist. Finally, there are laws or theories that govern the world, and these need to be tested or verified and refined so that we can understand the world. Thus, in the scientific method—the accepted approach to research by postpositivists—a researcher begins with a theory, collects data that either supports or refutes the theory, and then makes necessary revisions and conducts additional tests.

In reading Phillips and Burbules (2000), you can gain a sense of the key assumptions of this position, such as the following:

1. Knowledge is conjectural (and antifoundational)—absolute truth can never be found. Thus, evidence established in research is always imperfect and fallible. It is for this reason that researchers state that they do not prove a hypothesis; instead, they indicate a failure to reject the hypothesis.

2. Research is the process of making claims and then refining or abandoning some of them for other claims more strongly warranted. Most quantitative research, for example, starts with the test of a theory.

3. Data, evidence, and rational considerations shape knowledge. In practice, the researcher collects information on instruments based on measures completed by the participants or by observations recorded by the researcher.

4. Research seeks to develop relevant, true statements, ones that can serve to explain the situation of concern or that describe the causal relationships of interest. In quantitative studies, researchers advance the relationship among variables and pose this in terms of questions or hypotheses.

5. Being objective is an essential aspect of competent inquiry; researchers must examine methods and conclusions for bias. For example, standard of validity and reliability are important in quantitative research.

The Constructivist Worldview

Others hold a different worldview. Constructivism or social constructivism (often combined with interpretivism) is such a perspective, and it is typically seen as an approach to qualitative research. The ideas came from Mannheim and from works such as Berger and Luckmann's (1967) *The Social Construction of Reality* and Lincoln and Guba's (1985) *Naturalistic Inquiry*. More recent writers who have summarized this position are Lincoln and colleagues (2011), Mertens (2010), and Crotty (1998), among others. **Social constructivists** believe that individuals seek understanding of the world in which they live and work. Individuals develop subjective meanings of their experiences—meanings directed toward certain objects or things. These meanings are varied and multiple, leading the researcher to look for the complexity of views rather than narrowing meanings into a few categories or ideas. The goal of the research is to rely as much as possible on the participants' views of the situation being studied. The questions become broad and general so that the participants can construct the meaning of a situation, typically forged in discussions or interactions with other persons. The more open-ended the questioning, the better, as the researcher listens carefully to what people say or do in their life settings. Often these subjective meanings are negotiated socially and historically. They are not simply imprinted on individuals but are formed through interaction with others (hence social constructivism) and through historical and cultural norms that operate in individuals' lives. Thus, constructivist researchers often address the processes of interaction among individuals. They also focus on the specific contexts in which people live and work in order to understand the historical and cultural settings of the participants. Researchers recognize that their own backgrounds shape their interpretation, and they position themselves in the research to acknowledge how their interpretation flows from their personal, cultural, and historical experiences. The researcher's intent is to make sense of (or interpret) the meanings others have about the world. Rather than starting with a theory (as in postpositivism), inquirers generate or inductively develop a theory or pattern of meaning.

For example, in discussing constructivism, Crotty (1998) identified several assumptions:

1. Human beings construct meanings as they engage with the world they are interpreting. Qualitative researchers tend to use open-ended questions so that the participants can share their views.

2. Humans engage with their world and make sense of it based on their historical and social perspectives—we are all born into a world of meaning bestowed upon us by our culture. Thus, qualitative researchers seek to understand the context or setting of the participants through visiting this context and gathering information personally. They also interpret what they find, an interpretation shaped by the researcher's own experiences and background.

3. The basic generation of meaning is always social, arising in and out of interaction with a human community. The process of qualitative research is largely inductive; the inquirer generates meaning from the data collected in the field.

The Transformative Worldview

Another group of researchers holds to the philosophical assumptions of the transformative approach. This position arose during the 1980s and 1990s from individuals who felt that the postpositivist assumptions imposed structural laws and theories that did not fit marginalized individuals in our society or issues of power and social justice, discrimination, and oppression that needed to be addressed. There is no uniform body of literature characterizing this worldview, but it includes groups of researchers that are critical theorists; participatory action researchers; Marxists; feminists; racial and ethnic minorities; persons with disabilities; indigenous and postcolonial peoples; and members of the lesbian, gay, bisexual, transsexual, and queer communities. Historically, the transformative writers have drawn on the works of Marx, Adorno, Marcuse, Habermas, and Freire (Neuman, 2009). Fay (1987), Heron and Reason (1997), Kemmis and Wilkinson (1998), Kemmis and McTaggart (2000), and Mertens (2009, 2010) are additional writers to read for this perspective.

In the main, these inquirers felt that the constructivist stance did not go far enough in advocating for an action agenda to help marginalized peoples. A **transformative worldview** holds that research inquiry needs to be intertwined with politics and a political change agenda to confront social oppression at whatever levels it occurs (Mertens, 2010). Thus, the research contains an action agenda for reform that may change lives of the participants, the institutions in which individuals work or live, and the researcher's life. Moreover, specific issues need to be addressed that speak to important social issues of the day, issues such as empowerment, inequality, oppression, domination, suppression, and alienation. The researcher often begins with one of these issues as the focal point of the study. This research also assumes that the inquirer will proceed collaboratively so as to not further marginalize the participants as a result of the inquiry. In this sense, the participants may help design questions, collect data, analyze information, or reap the rewards of the research. Transformative research provides a voice for these participants, raising their consciousness or advancing an agenda for change to improve their lives. It becomes a united voice for reform and change.

This philosophical worldview focuses on the needs of groups and individuals in our society that may be marginalized or disenfranchised. Therefore, theoretical perspectives may be integrated with the philosophical assumptions that construct a picture of the issues being examined, the people to be studied, and the changes that are needed, such as feminist perspectives, racialized discourses, critical theory, queer theory, and disability theory—theoretical lens to be discussed more in Chapter 3.

Although these are diverse groups and our explanations here are generalizations, it is helpful to view the summary by Mertens (2010) of key features of the transformative worldview or paradigm:

- It places central importance on the study of lives and experiences of diverse groups that have traditionally been marginalized. Of special interest for these diverse groups is how their lives have been constrained by oppressors and the strategies that they use to resist, challenge, and subvert these constraints.

- In studying these diverse groups, the research focuses on inequities based on gender, race, ethnicity, disability, sexual orientation, and socioeconomic class that result in asymmetric power relationships.

- The research in the transformative worldview links political and social action to these inequities.

- Transformative research uses a program theory of beliefs about how a program works and why the problems of oppression, domination, and power relationships exist.

The Pragmatic Worldview

Another position about worldviews comes from the pragmatists. Pragmatism derives from the work of Peirce, James, Mead, and Dewey (Cherryholmes, 1992). Other writers include Murphy (1990), Patton (1990), and Rorty (1990). There are many forms of this philosophy, but for many, pragmatism as a worldview arises out of actions, situations, and consequences rather than antecedent conditions (as in postpositivism). There is a concern with applications—what works—and solutions to problems (Patton, 1990). Instead of focusing on methods, researchers emphasize the research problem and question and use all approaches available to understand the problem (see Rossman & Wilson, 1985). As a philosophical underpinning for mixed methods studies, Morgan (2007), Patton (1990), and Tashakkori and Teddlie (2010) convey its importance for focusing attention on the research problem in social science research and then using pluralistic approaches to derive knowledge about the problem. Using Cherryholmes (1992), Morgan (2007), and our own views, pragmatism provides a philosophical basis for research:

- Pragmatism is not committed to any one system of philosophy and reality. This applies to mixed methods research in that inquirers draw liberally from both quantitative and qualitative assumptions when they engage in their research.

- Individual researchers have a freedom of choice. In this way, researchers are free to choose the methods, techniques, and procedures of research that best meet their needs and purposes.

- Pragmatists do not see the world as an absolute unity. In a similar way, mixed methods researchers look to many approaches for collecting and analyzing data rather than subscribing to only one way (e.g., quantitative or qualitative).

- Truth is what works at the time. It is not based in a duality between reality independent of the mind or within the mind. Thus, in mixed methods research, investigators use both quantitative and qualitative data because they work to provide the best understanding of a research problem.

- The pragmatist researchers look to the *what* and *how* to research based on the intended consequences—where they want to go with it. Mixed methods researchers need to establish a purpose for their mixing, a rationale for the reasons why quantitative and qualitative data need to be mixed in the first place.

- Pragmatists agree that research always occurs in social, historical, political, and other contexts. In this way, mixed methods studies may include a postmodern turn, a theoretical lens that is reflective of social justice and political aims.

- Pragmatists have believed in an external world independent of the mind as well as that lodged in the mind. But they believe that we need to stop asking questions about reality and the laws of nature (Cherryholmes, 1992). "They would simply like to change the subject" (Rorty, 1990, p. xiv).

- Thus, for the mixed methods researcher, pragmatism opens the door to multiple methods, different worldviews, and different assumptions, as well as different forms of data collection and analysis.

Research Designs

The researcher not only selects a qualitative, quantitative, or mixed methods study to conduct; the inquirer also decides on a type of study within these three choices. Research designs are types of inquiry within qualitative, quantitative, and mixed methods approaches that provide specific direction for procedures in a research study. Others have called them *strategies of inquiry* (Denzin & Lincoln, 2011). The designs available to the researcher have grown over the years as computer technology has advanced our data analysis and ability to analyze complex models, and as individuals have articulated new procedures for conducting social science research. Select types will be emphasized in the methods of Chapters 8, 9, and 10—designs that are frequently used in the social sciences. Here we introduce those that are discussed later and that are cited in examples throughout the book. An overview of these designs is shown in Table 1.2.

Quantitative Designs

During the late 19th and throughout the 20th century, strategies of inquiry associated with quantitative research were those that invoked the postpositivist worldview and that originated mainly in psychology. These include *true*

Table 1.2 Alternative Research Designs

Quantitative	Qualitative	Mixed Methods
• Experimental designs • Nonexperimental designs, such as surveys • Longitudinal designs	• Narrative research • Phenomenology • Grounded theory • Ethnographies • Case study	• Convergent • Explanatory sequential • Exploratory sequential • Complex designs with embedded core designs

experiments and the less rigorous experiments called *quasi-experiments* (see, an original, early treatise on this, Campbell & Stanley, 1963). An additional experimental design is *applied behavioral analysis or single-subject experiments* in which an experimental treatment is administered over time to a single individual or a small number of individuals (Cooper, Heron, & Heward, 2007; Neuman & McCormick, 1995). One type of nonexperimental quantitative research is *causal-comparative research* in which the investigator compares two or more groups in terms of a cause (or independent variable) that has already happened. Another nonexperimental form of research is the *correlational design* in which investigators use the correlational statistic to describe and measure the degree or association (or relationship) between two or more variables or sets of scores (Creswell, 2012). These designs have been elaborated into more complex relationships among variables found in techniques of structural equation modeling, hierarchical linear modeling, and logistic regression. More recently, quantitative strategies have involved complex experiments with many variables and treatments (e.g., factorial designs and repeated measure designs). Designs often employ longitudinal data collection over time to examine the development of ideas and trends. Designs have also included elaborate structural equation models that incorporate causal paths and the identification of the collective strength of multiple variables. Rather than discuss all of these quantitative approaches, we will focus on two designs: surveys and experiments.

• **Survey research** provides a quantitative or numeric description of trends, attitudes, or opinions of a population by studying a sample of that population. It includes cross-sectional and longitudinal studies using questionnaires or structured interviews for data collection—with the intent of generalizing from a sample to a population (Fowler, 2008).

• **Experimental research** seeks to determine if a specific treatment influences an outcome. The researcher assesses this by providing a specific treatment to one group and withholding it from another and then determining how both groups scored on an outcome. Experiments include true experiments, with the random assignment of subjects to treatment conditions, and quasi-experiments that use nonrandomized assignments (Keppel, 1991). Included within quasi-experiments are single-subject designs.

Qualitative Designs

In qualitative research, the numbers and types of approaches have also become more clearly visible during the 1990s and into the 21st century. The historic origin for qualitative research comes from anthropology, sociology, the humanities, and evaluation. Books have summarized the various types, and complete procedures are now available on specific qualitative inquiry approaches (Creswell & Poth, 2018). For example, Clandinin and Connelly (2000) constructed a picture of what narrative researchers do. Moustakas (1994) discussed the philosophical tenets and the procedures of the phenomenological method; Charmaz (2006), Corbin and Strauss (2007; 2015), and Strauss and Corbin (1990, 1998) identified the procedures of **grounded theory**. Fetterman (2010) and Wolcott (2008) summarized ethnographic procedures and the many faces and research strategies of **ethnography**, and Stake (1995) and Yin (2009, 2012, 2014) suggested processes involved in case study research. In this book, illustrations are drawn from the following strategies, recognizing that approaches such as participatory action research (Kemmis & McTaggart, 2000), discourse analysis (Cheek, 2004), and others not mentioned are also viable ways to conduct qualitative studies:

- **Narrative research** is a design of inquiry from the humanities in which the researcher studies the lives of individuals and asks one or more individuals to provide stories about their lives (Riessman, 2008). This information is then often retold or restoried by the researcher into a narrative chronology. Often, in the end, the narrative combines views from the participant's life with those of the researcher's life in a collaborative narrative (Clandinin & Connelly, 2000).

- **Phenomenological research** is a design of inquiry coming from philosophy and psychology in which the researcher describes the lived experiences of individuals about a phenomenon as described by participants. This description culminates in the essence of the experiences for several individuals who have all experienced the phenomenon. This design has strong philosophical underpinnings and typically involves conducting interviews (Giorgi, 2009; Moustakas, 1994).

- Grounded theory is a design of inquiry from sociology in which the researcher derives a general, abstract theory of a process, action, or interaction grounded in the views of participants. This process involves using multiple stages of data collection and the refinement and interrelationship of categories of information (Charmaz, 2006; Corbin & Strauss, 2007, 2015).

- Ethnography is a design of inquiry coming from anthropology and sociology in which the researcher studies the shared patterns of behaviors, language, and actions of an intact cultural group in a natural setting over a prolonged period of time. Data collection often involves observations and interviews.

- Case studies are a design of inquiry found in many fields, especially evaluation, in which the researcher develops an in-depth analysis of a case, often a program, event, activity, process, or one or more individuals. Cases are bounded by time and activity, and researchers collect detailed information using a variety of data collection procedures over a sustained period of time (Stake, 1995; Yin, 2009, 2012, 2014).

Mixed Methods Designs

Mixed methods involves combining or integration of qualitative and quantitative research and data in a research study. Qualitative data tends to be open-ended without predetermined responses while quantitative data usually includes closed-ended responses such as found on questionnaires or psychological instruments. The field of mixed methods research, as we know it today, began in the middle to late 1980s. Its origins, however, go back further. In 1959, Campbell and Fisk used multiple methods to study psychological traits—although their methods were only quantitative measures. Their work prompted others to begin collecting multiple forms of data, such as observations and interviews (qualitative data) with traditional surveys (Sieber, 1973). Early thoughts about the value of multiple methods—called mixed methods—resided in the idea that all methods had bias and weaknesses, and the collection of both quantitative and qualitative data neutralized the weaknesses of each form of data. Triangulating data sources—a means for seeking convergence across qualitative and quantitative methods—was born (Jick, 1979). By the early 1990s, mixed methods turned toward the systematic *integration* of quantitative and qualitative data, and the idea of ways to combine the data through different types of research designs emerged. These types of designs were extensively discussed in a major handbook addressing the field in 2003 and reissued in 2010 (Tashakkori & Teddlie, 2010). Procedures for expanding mixed methods developed such as follows:

- Ways to integrate the quantitative and qualitative data, such as one database, could be used to check the accuracy (validity) of the other database.

- One database could help explain the other database, and one database could explore different types of questions than the other database.

- One database could lead to better instruments when instruments are not well-suited for a sample or population.

- One database could build on other databases, and one database could alternate with another database back and forth during a longitudinal study.

Further, the designs were developed and notation was added to help the reader understand the designs; challenges to working with the designs emerged (Creswell & Plano Clark, 2011, 2018). Practical issues are being widely discussed today in terms of examples of "good" mixed methods studies and evaluative criteria, the use of a team to conduct this model of inquiry, and the expansion of mixed methods to other countries and disciplines. Although many designs exist in the mixed methods field, this book will focus on the three primary designs found in the social and health sciences today:

- **Convergent mixed methods** is a form of mixed methods design in which the researcher converges or merges quantitative and qualitative data in order to provide a comprehensive analysis of the research problem. In this design, the investigator typically collects both forms of data at roughly the same time and then integrates the information in the interpretation of the overall results. Contradictions or incongruent findings are explained or further probed in this design.

- **Explanatory sequential mixed methods** is one in which the researcher first conducts quantitative research, analyzes the results and then builds on the results to explain them in more detail with qualitative research. It is considered explanatory because the initial quantitative data results are explained further with the qualitative data. It is considered sequential because the initial quantitative phase is followed by the qualitative phase. This type of design is popular in fields with a strong quantitative orientation (hence the project begins with quantitative research), but it presents challenges of identifying the quantitative results to further explore and the unequal sample sizes for each phase of the study.

- **Exploratory sequential mixed methods** is the reverse sequence from the explanatory sequential design. In the exploratory sequential approach the researcher first begins with a qualitative research phase and explores the views of participants. The data are then analyzed, and the information used to build into a second, quantitative phase. The qualitative phase may be used to build an instrument that best fits the sample under study, to identify appropriate instruments to use in the follow-up quantitative phase, to develop an intervention for an experiment, to design an app or website, or to specify variables that need to go into a follow-up quantitative study. Particular challenges to this design reside in focusing in on the appropriate qualitative findings to use and the sample selection for both phases of research.

- These basic or core designs then can be used in more complex mixed methods strategies. The core designs can augment an experiment by, for example, collecting qualitative data after the experiment to help explain the quantitative outcome results. The core designs can be used within a case study framework to deductively document cases or to generate cases for further analysis. These basic designs can inform a theoretical study drawn from social justice or power (see Chapter 3) as an overarching perspective within a design that contains both quantitative and qualitative data. The core designs can also be used in the different phases of an evaluation procedure that spans from a needs assessment to a test of a program or experimental intervention.

Research Methods

The third major element in the framework is the specific research methods that involve the forms of data collection, analysis, and interpretation that researchers propose for their studies. As shown in Table 1.3, it is useful to consider the full range of possibilities of data collection and to organize these methods, for example, by their degree of predetermined nature, their use of closed-ended versus open-ended questioning, and their focus on numeric versus nonnumeric data analysis. These methods will be developed further in Chapters 8 through 10.

Researchers collect data on an instrument or test (e.g., a set of questions about attitudes toward self-esteem) or gather information on a behavioral checklist (e.g., observation of a worker engaged in a complex skill). On the other end of the continuum, collecting data might involve visiting a research site and observing the behavior of individuals without predetermined questions or conducting an interview in which the individual is allowed to talk openly about a topic, largely without the use of specific questions. The choice of methods turns on whether the intent is to specify the type of information to be collected in advance of the study or to allow it to emerge from participants in the project. Also, the type of data analyzed may be numeric information gathered on scales of instruments or text information recording and reporting the voice of the participants. Researchers make interpretations of the statistical results, or they interpret the themes or patterns that emerge from the data. In some forms of research, both quantitative and qualitative data are collected, analyzed, and interpreted. Instrument data may be augmented with open-ended observations, or census data may be followed by in-depth exploratory interviews. In this case of mixing methods, the researcher makes inferences across both the quantitative and qualitative databases.

Table 1.3 Quantitative, Mixed, and Qualitative Methods		
Quantitative Methods	**Mixed Methods**	**Qualitative Methods**
Pre-determined	Both predetermined and emerging methods	Emerging methods
Instrument based questions	Both open- and closed-ended questions	Open-ended questions
Performance data, attitude data, observational data, and census data	Multiple forms of data drawing on all possibilities	Interview data, observation data, document data, and audiovisual data
Statistical analysis	Statistical and text analysis	Text and image analysis
Statistical interpretation	Across databases interpretation	Themes, patterns interpretation

Research Approaches as
Worldviews, Designs, and Methods
....

The worldviews, the designs, and the methods all contribute to a research approach that *tends* to be quantitative, qualitative, or mixed. Table 1.4 creates distinctions that may be useful in choosing an approach. This table also includes practices of all three approaches that are emphasized in remaining chapters of this book.

Typical scenarios of research can illustrate how these three elements combine into a research design.

- *Quantitative approach:* Postpositivist worldview, experimental design, and pretest and posttest measures of attitudes

  In this scenario, the researcher tests a theory by specifying narrow hypotheses and the collection of data to support or refute the hypotheses. An experimental design is used in which attitudes are assessed both before and after an experimental treatment. The data are collected on an instrument that measures attitudes, and the information is analyzed using statistical procedures and hypothesis testing.

- *Qualitative approach:* Constructivist worldview, ethnographic design, and observation of behavior

  In this situation, the researcher seeks to establish the meaning of a phenomenon from the views of participants. This means identifying a culture-sharing group and studying how it develops shared patterns of behavior over time (i.e., ethnography). One of the key elements of collecting data in this way is to observe participants' behaviors during their engagement in activities.

- *Qualitative approach:* Transformative worldview, narrative design, and open-ended interviewing

  For this study, the inquirer seeks to examine an issue related to oppression of individuals. To study this, stories are collected of individual oppression using a narrative approach. Individuals are interviewed at some length to determine how they have personally experienced oppression.

- *Mixed methods approach:* Pragmatic worldview, collection of both quantitative and qualitative data sequentially in the design

  The researcher bases the inquiry on the assumption that collecting diverse types of data best provides a more complete understanding of a research problem than either quantitative or qualitative data alone. The study begins with a broad survey in order to generalize results to a population and then, in a second phase, focuses on qualitative, open-ended interviews to collect detailed views from participants to help explain the initial quantitative survey.

Table 1.4 Qualitative, Quantitative, and Mixed Methods Approaches

Tend to or Typically . . .	Qualitative Approaches	Quantitative Approaches	Mixed Methods Approaches
• Use these philosophical assumptions • Employ these strategies of inquiry	• Constructivist/transformative knowledge claims • Phenomenology, grounded theory, ethnography, case study, and narrative	• Postpositivist knowledge claims • Surveys and experiments	• Pragmatic knowledge claims • Sequential, convergent, and transformative
• Employ these methods	• Open-ended questions, emerging approaches, text or image data	• Closed-ended questions, predetermined approaches, numeric data (may include some open-ended questions)	• Both open- and closed-ended questions, both emerging and predetermined approaches, and both quantitative and qualitative data and analysis
• Use these practices of research as the researcher	• Positions him- or herself • Collects participant meanings • Focuses on a single concept or phenomenon • Brings personal values into the study • Studies the context or setting of participants • Validates the accuracy of findings • Makes interpretations of the data • Creates an agenda for change or reform • Collaborates with the participants • Employs text analysis procedures	• Tests or verifies theories or explanations • Identifies variables to study • Relates variables in questions or hypotheses • Uses standards of validity and reliability • Observes and measures information numerically • Uses unbiased approaches • Employs statistical procedures	• Collects both quantitative and qualitative data • Develops a rationale for mixing • Integrates the data at different stages of inquiry • Presents visual pictures of the procedures in the study • Employs the practices of both qualitative and quantitative research

Criteria for Selecting a
Research Approach

Given the possibility of qualitative, quantitative, or mixed methods approaches, what factors affect a choice of one approach over another for the design of a proposal? Added to worldview, design, and methods would be the research problem, the personal experiences of the researcher, and the audience(s) for whom the report will be written.

The Research Problem and Questions

A research problem, more thoroughly discussed in Chapter 5, is an issue or concern that needs to be addressed (e.g., the issue of racial discrimination). The problem comes from a void in the literature, and conflict in research results in the literature, topics that have been neglected in the literature; a need to lift up the voice of marginalized participants; and "real-life" problems found in the workplace, the home, the community, and so forth.

Certain types of social research problems call for specific approaches. For example, if the problem calls for (a) the identification of factors that influence an outcome, (b) the utility of an intervention, or (c) understanding the best predictors of outcomes, then a quantitative approach is best. It is also the best approach to use to test a theory or explanation. On the other hand, if a concept or phenomenon needs to be explored and understood because little research has been done on it or because it involves an understudied sample, then it merits a qualitative approach. Qualitative research is especially useful when the researcher does not know the important variables to examine. This type of approach may be needed because the topic is new, the subject has never been addressed with a certain sample or group of people, and existing theories do not apply with the particular sample or group under study (Morse, 1991). A mixed methods design is useful when the quantitative or qualitative approach, each by itself, is inadequate to best understand a research problem and the strengths of both quantitative and qualitative research (and its data) can provide the best understanding. For example, a researcher may want to both generalize the findings to a population as well as develop a detailed view of the meaning of a phenomenon or concept for individuals. In this research, the inquirer first explores generally to learn what variables to study and then studies those variables with a large sample of individuals. Alternatively, researchers may first survey a large number of individuals and then follow up with a few participants to obtain their specific views and their voices about the topic. In these situations, collecting both closed-ended quantitative data and open-ended qualitative data proves advantageous.

Personal Experiences

Researchers' own personal training and experiences also influence their choice of approach. An individual trained in technical, scientific writing, statistics, and computer statistical programs and familiar with quantitative journals in the library would most likely choose the quantitative design. On the other hand, individuals who enjoy writing in a literary way or conducting personal interviews or making up-close observations may gravitate to the qualitative approach. The mixed methods researcher is an individual familiar with both quantitative and qualitative research. This person also has the time and resources to collect and analyze both quantitative and qualitative data.

Since quantitative studies are the traditional mode of research, carefully worked out procedures and rules exist for them. Researchers may be more comfortable with the highly systematic procedures of quantitative research. Also, for some individuals, it can be uncomfortable to challenge accepted approaches among some faculty by using qualitative and transformative approaches to inquiry. On the other hand, qualitative approaches allow room to be innovative and to work more within researcher-designed frameworks. They allow more creative, literary-style writing, a form that individuals may like to use. For those researchers undertaking social justice or community involvement, a qualitative approach is typically best, although this form of research may also incorporate mixed methods designs.

For the mixed methods researcher, the project will take extra time because of the need to collect and analyze both quantitative and qualitative data. It fits a person who enjoys and has the skills in both quantitative and qualitative research.

Audience

Finally, researchers write for audiences that will accept their research. These audiences may be journal editors and readers, faculty committees, conference attendees, or colleagues in the field. Students should consider the approaches typically supported and used by their advisers. The experiences of these audiences with quantitative, qualitative, or mixed methods studies can shape the decision made about the choice of design.

SUMMARY

In planning a research project, researchers need to identify whether they will employ a qualitative, quantitative, or mixed methods approach. This approach is based on bringing together a worldview or assumptions about research, a specific design, and research methods. Decisions about choice of an approach are further influenced by the research problem or issue being studied, the personal experiences of the researcher, and the audience for whom the researcher writes.

1. Identify a research question in a journal article and discuss what approach would be best to study the question and why.

2. Take a topic that you would like to study, and using the four combinations of worldviews, designs, and research methods in Figure 1.1, discuss a project that brings together a worldview, designs, and methods. Identify whether this would be quantitative, qualitative, or mixed methods research. Use the typical scenarios that we have advanced in this chapter as a guide.

3. What distinguishes a quantitative study from a qualitative study? Mention three characteristics.

Additional Readings

Cherryholmes, C. H. (1992, August–September). Notes on pragmatism and scientific realism. *Educational Researcher, 14,* 13–17.

Cleo Cherryholmes discusses pragmatism as a contrasting perspective from scientific realism. The strength of this article lies in the numerous citations of writers about pragmatism and a clarification of one version of pragmatism. Cherryholmes's version points out that pragmatism is driven by anticipated consequences, reluctance to tell a true story, and the idea that there is an external world independent of our minds. Also included in this article are numerous references to historical and recent writers about pragmatism as a philosophical position.

Crotty, M. (1998). *The foundations of social research: Meaning and perspective in the research process.* Thousand Oaks, CA: Sage.

Michael Crotty offers a useful framework for tying together the many epistemological issues, theoretical perspectives, methodology, and methods of social research. He interrelates the four components of the research process and shows in a table a representative sampling of topics of each component. He then goes on to discuss nine different theoretical orientations in social research, such as postmodernism, feminism, critical inquiry, interpretivism, constructionism, and positivism.

Kemmis, S., & Wilkinson, M. (1998). Participatory action research and the study of practice. In B. Atweh, S. Kemmis, & P. Weeks (Eds.), *Action research in practice: Partnerships for social justice in education* (pp. 21–36). New York: Routledge.

Stephen Kemmis and Mervyn Wilkinson provide an excellent overview of participatory research. In particular, they note the six major features of this inquiry approach and then discuss how action research is practiced at the individual, the social, or at both levels.

Lincoln, Y. S., Lynham, S. A., & Guba, E. G. (2011). Paradigmatic controversies, contradictions, and emerging confluences revisited. In N. K. Denzin & Y. S. Lincoln, *The SAGE handbook of qualitative research* (4th ed., pp. 97–128). Thousand Oaks, CA: Sage.

Yvonna Lincoln, Susan Lynham, and Egon Guba have provided the basic beliefs of five alternative inquiry paradigms in social science research: (a) positivism, (b) postpositivism, (c) critical theory, (d) constructivism, and (e) participatory. These extend the earlier analysis provided in the first and second editions of the handbook. Each is presented in terms of ontology (i.e., nature of reality), epistemology (i.e., how we know what we know), and methodology (i.e., the process of research). The participatory paradigm adds another alternative paradigm to those originally advanced in the first edition. After briefly presenting these five approaches, they contrast them in terms of seven issues, such as the nature of knowledge, how knowledge accumulates, and goodness or quality criteria.

Mertens, D. (2009). *Transformative research and evaluation*. New York: Guilford.

Donna Mertens has devoted an entire text to advancing the transformative paradigm and the process of transformative research. She discusses the basic features of the transformative paradigm as an umbrella term, provides examples of groups affiliated with this paradigm, and links the paradigm to quantitative, qualitative, and mixed methods approaches. In this book she also discusses the research procedures of sampling, consent, reciprocity, data collection methods and instruments, data analysis and interpretation, and reporting.

Phillips, D. C., & Burbules, N. C. (2000). *Postpositivism and educational research*. Lanham, MD: Rowman & Littlefield.

D. C. Phillips and Nicholas Burbules summarize the major ideas of postpostivist thinking. Through two chapters, "What is Postpositivism?" and "Philosophical Commitments of Postpositivist Researchers," the authors advance major ideas about postpositivism—especially those that differentiate it from positivism. These include knowing that human knowledge is conjectural rather than unchallengeable and that our warrants for knowledge can be withdrawn in light of further investigations.

ⓈSAGE edge™

https://edge.sagepub.com/creswellrd5e

Students and instructors, please visit the companion website for videos featuring John W. Creswell, full-text SAGE journal articles, quizzes and activities, plus additional tools for research design.

CHAPTER

2

Review of the Literature

B esides selecting a quantitative, qualitative, or mixed methods approach, the proposal or study designer also needs to review the literature about a **topic**. This literature review helps to determine whether the topic is worth studying, and it provides insight into ways in which the researcher can limit the scope to a needed area of inquiry.

This chapter continues the discussion about preliminary considerations before launching into a proposal or project. It begins with a discussion about selecting a topic and writing this topic down so that the researcher can continually reflect on it. At this point, researchers also need to consider whether the topic *can* and *should* be researched. Then the discussion moves into the actual process of reviewing the literature; addressing the general purpose for using literature in a study; and then turning to principles helpful in designing literature into qualitative, quantitative, and mixed methods studies.

The Research Topic

Before considering what literature to use in a project, first identify a topic to study and reflect on whether it is practical and useful to undertake the study. The topic is the subject or subject matter of a proposed study, such as "faculty teaching," "organizational creativity," or "psychological stress." Describe the topic in a few words or in a short phrase. The topic becomes the central idea to learn about or to explore.

There are several ways that researchers gain some insight into their topics when they are initially planning their research (our assumption is that the topic is chosen by the researcher and not by an adviser or committee member). One way is to draft a brief working title to the study. We are surprised at how often researchers fail to draft a title early in the development of their projects. In our opinion, the working or draft title becomes a major road sign in research—a tangible idea that the researcher can keep refocusing on and changing as the project goes on (see Glesne, 2015; Glesne & Peshkin, 1992). It becomes an orienting device. We find that, in our research, this topic grounds us and provides a sign of what we are studying, as well as a sign useful for conveying to others the central notion of the study. When students first provide their research project ideas to us, we often ask them to supply a working title if they do not already have one written down on paper.

How would this working title be written? Try completing this sentence: "My study is about . . ." A response might be, "My study is about at-risk children in the junior high," or "My study is about helping college faculty become better researchers." At this stage in the design, frame the answer to the question so that another scholar might easily grasp the meaning of the project. A common shortcoming of beginning researchers is that they frame their study in complex and erudite language. This perspective may result from reading published articles that have undergone numerous revisions before being set in print. Good, sound research projects begin with straightforward, uncomplicated thoughts that are easy to read and understand. Think about a journal article that you have read recently. If it was easy and quick to read, it was likely written in general language that many readers could easily identify with in a way that was straightforward and simple in overall design and conceptualization. As a project develops it will become more complicated.

Wilkinson (1991) provided useful advice for creating a title: Be brief and avoid wasting words. Eliminate unnecessary words, such as "An Approach to . . . ," "A Study of . . . ," and so forth. Use a single title or a double title. An example of a double title would be "An Ethnography: Understanding a Child's Perception of War." In addition to Wilkinson's thoughts, consider a title no longer than 12 words, eliminate most articles and prepositions, and make sure that it includes the focus or topic of the study.

Another strategy for topic development is to pose the topic as a brief question. What question needs to be answered in the proposed study? A researcher might ask, "What treatment is best for depression?" "What does it mean to be Arabic in U.S. society today?" "What brings people to tourist sites in the Midwest?" When drafting questions such as these, focus on the key topic in the question as the major signpost for the study. Consider how this question might be expanded later to be more descriptive of your study (see Chapters 6 and 7 on the purpose statement and research questions and hypotheses).

Actively elevating this topic to a research study calls for reflecting on whether the topic can and should be researched. A topic *can* be researched if a researcher has participants willing to serve in the study. It also can be researched if the investigator has resources such as collecting data over a sustained period of time and using available computer programs to help in the analysis of data.

The question of *should* is a more complex matter. Several factors might go into this decision. Perhaps the most important are whether the topic adds to the pool of research knowledge in the literature available on the topic, replicates past studies, lifts up the voices of underrepresented groups or individuals, helps address social justice, or transforms the ideas and beliefs of the researcher.

A first step in any project is to spend considerable time in the library examining the research on a topic (strategies for effectively using the library and library resources appear later in this chapter). This point cannot be overemphasized. Beginning researchers may advance a great study that is complete in every way, such as in the clarity of research questions, the comprehensiveness of data collection, and the sophistication of statistical analysis. But the researcher may garner little support from faculty committees or conference planners because the study does not add anything new to the body of research. Ask, "How does this project contribute to the literature?" Consider how the study might address a topic that has yet to be examined, extend the discussion by incorporating new elements, or replicate (or repeat) a study in new situations or with new participants. Contributing to the literature may also mean how the study adds to an understanding of a theory or extends a theory (see Chapter 3), or how the study provides a new perspective or "angle" to the existing literature, for example, by

- Studying an unusual location (e.g., rural America)

- Examining an unusual group of participants (e.g., refugees)

- Taking a perspective that may not be expected and reverses the expectation (e.g., why marriages do work rather than do not work)

- Providing novel means of collecting data (e.g., collect sounds)

- Presenting results in unusual ways (e.g., graphs that depict geographical locations)

- Studying a timely topic (e.g., immigration issues) (Creswell, 2016)

The issue of *should* the topic be studied also relates to whether anyone outside of the researcher's own immediate institution or area would be interested in the topic. Given a choice between a topic that might be of limited regional interest or one of national interest, we would opt for the latter because it would have wide appeal to a much broader audience. Journal editors, committee members, conference planners, and funding agencies all appreciate research that reaches a broad audience. Finally, the *should* issue also relates to the researcher's personal goals. Consider the time it takes to complete a project, revise it, and disseminate the results. All researchers should consider how the study and its heavy commitment of time will pay off in enhancing career goals, whether these goals relate to doing more research, obtaining a future position, or advancing toward a degree.

Before proceeding with a proposal or a study, one needs to weigh these factors and ask others for their reaction to a topic under consideration. Seek reactions from colleagues, noted authorities in the field, academic advisers, and faculty committee members. We often have students bring to us a one-page sketch of their proposed project that includes the problem or issue leading to a need for the study, the central research question they plan on asking, the types of data they will collect, and the overall significance of their study.

The Literature Review

Once the researcher identifies a topic that can and should be studied, the search can begin for related literature on the topic. The literature review accomplishes several purposes. It shares with the reader the results of other studies that are closely related to the one being undertaken. It relates a study to the larger, ongoing dialogue in the literature, filling in gaps and extending prior studies (Cooper, 2010; Marshall & Rossman, 2016). It provides a framework for establishing the importance of the study as well as a benchmark for comparing the results with other findings. All or some of these reasons may be the foundation for writing the scholarly literature into a study (see Boote & Beile, 2005, for a more extensive discussion of purposes for compiling a literature review in research). Studies need to add to the body of literature on a topic, and literature sections in proposals are generally shaped from the larger problem to the narrower issue that leads directly into the methods of a study.

The Use of the Literature

Beyond the question of why literature is used is the additional issue of how it is used in research and proposals. It can assume various forms. Our best advice is to seek the opinion of your adviser or faculty members as to how they would like to see the literature addressed. We generally recommend to our advisees that the literature review in a proposal or project be brief and provide a summary of the major studies on the research problem; it does not need to be fully developed and comprehensive at this point, since faculty may ask for major changes in the study at the proposal meeting. In this model, the literature review is shorter—say 20 to 30 pages in length—and tells the reader that the student is aware of the literature on the topic and the latest writings. Another approach is to develop a detailed outline of the topics and potential references that will later be developed into an entire chapter, usually the second, titled "Literature Review," which might run from 20 to 60 pages or so.

The literature review in a journal article is an abbreviated form of that found in a dissertation or master's thesis. It typically is contained in a section called "Related Literature" and follows the introduction to a study. This is the pattern for quantitative research articles in journals. For qualitative research articles, the literature review may be found in a separate section, included in the introduction, or threaded throughout the study. Regardless of the form, another consideration is how the literature might be reviewed, depending on whether a qualitative, quantitative, or mixed methods approach has been selected.

In general, the literature review can take several forms. Cooper (2010) discussed four types: literature reviews that (a) integrate what others have done and said, (b) criticize previous scholarly works, (c) build bridges between related topics, and (d) identify the central issues in a field. With the exception of criticizing previous scholarly works, most dissertations and theses serve to integrate the literature, organize it into a series of related topics (often from general topics to narrower ones), and summarize the literature by pointing out the central issues.

In *qualitative* research, inquirers use the literature in a manner consistent with the assumptions of learning from the participant, not prescribing the questions that need to be answered from the researcher's standpoint. One of the chief reasons for conducting a qualitative study is that the study is exploratory. This usually means that not much has been written about the topic or the population being studied, and the researcher seeks to listen to participants and build an understanding based on what is heard.

However, the use of the literature in qualitative research varies considerably. In theoretically oriented studies, such as ethnographies or critical ethnographies, the literature on a cultural concept or a critical theory is introduced early in the report or proposal as an orienting framework. In grounded theory, case studies, and phenomenological studies, literature is less often used to set the stage for the study.

With an approach grounded in learning from participants and variation by type, there are several models for incorporating the literature review into a qualitative study. We offer three placement locations, and it can be used in any or all of these locations. As shown in Table 2.1, the researcher might include the literature review in the introduction. In this placement, the literature provides a useful backdrop for the problem or issue that has led to the need for the study, such as who has been writing about it, who has studied it, and who has indicated the importance of studying the issue. This framing of the problem is, of course, contingent on available studies. One can find illustrations of this model in many qualitative studies employing different types of inquiry strategy.

Table 2.1   Using Literature in a Qualitative Study

Use of the Literature	Criteria	Examples of Suitable Strategy Types
The literature is used to frame the problem in the introduction to the study.	There must be some literature available.	Typically, literature is used in all qualitative studies, regardless of type.
The literature is presented in a separate section as a review of the literature.	This approach is often acceptable to an audience most familiar with the traditional postpositivist approach to literature reviews.	This approach is used with those studies employing a strong theory and literature background at the beginning of a study, such as ethnographies and critical theory studies.
The literature is presented in the study at the end; it becomes a basis for comparing and contrasting findings of the qualitative study.	This approach is most suitable for the inductive process of qualitative research; the literature does not guide and direct the study but becomes an aid once patterns or categories have been identified.	This approach is used in all types of qualitative designs, but it is most popular with grounded theory, where one contrasts and compares a theory with other theories found in the literature.

A second form is to review the literature in a separate section, a model typically used in quantitative research, often found in journals with a quantitative orientation. In theory-oriented qualitative studies, such as ethnography, critical theory, or with a transformative aim, the inquirer might locate the theory discussion and literature in a separate section, typically toward the beginning of the write-up. Third, the researcher may incorporate the related literature in the final section, where it is used to compare and contrast with the results (or themes or categories) to emerge from the study. This model is especially popular in grounded theory studies, and we recommend it because it uses the literature inductively.

Quantitative research, on the other hand, includes a substantial amount of literature at the beginning of a study to provide direction for the research questions or hypotheses. It is also used to introduce a problem or to describe in detail the existing literature in a section titled "Related Literature" or "Review of Literature," or some other similar phrase. Also, the literature review can introduce a theory—an explanation for expected relationships (see Chapter 3)—describe the theory that will be used, and suggest why it is a useful theory to examine. At the end of a study, the researcher then revisits the literature and makes a comparison between the results with the existing findings in the literature. In this model, the quantitative researcher uses the literature deductively as a framework for the research questions or hypotheses.

In a *mixed methods* study, the researcher uses either a qualitative or a quantitative approach to the literature, depending on the type of strategy being used. In a sequential approach, the literature is presented in each phase in a way consistent with the method being used. For example, if the study begins with a quantitative phase, then the investigator is likely to include a substantial literature review that helps to establish a rationale for the research questions or hypotheses. If the study begins with a qualitative phase, then the literature is substantially less, and the researcher may incorporate it more into the end of the study—an inductive approach. If the research advances a convergent study with an equal weight and emphasis on both qualitative and quantitative data, then the literature may take either qualitative or quantitative forms. The decision as to which form to use is based on the audience for the study and what they would be most receptive to as well as to the students' graduate committees and their orientation. To recap, the literature used in a mixed methods project will depend on the strategy and the relative weight given to the qualitative or quantitative research in the study.

Our suggestions for using the literature in planning a qualitative, quantitative, or mixed methods study are as follows:

- In a qualitative study, use the literature sparingly in the beginning in order to convey an inductive design unless the design type requires a substantial literature orientation at the outset.

- Consider the most appropriate place for the literature in a qualitative study, and base the decision on the audience for the project. Keep in mind the options: placing it at the beginning to frame the problem, placing it in a separate section, and using it at the end to compare and contrast with the findings.

- Use the literature in a quantitative study deductively—as a basis for advancing research questions or hypotheses.

- In a quantitative study plan, use the literature to introduce the study, advance a theory, describe related literature in a separate section, and compare findings.

- In a mixed methods study, use the literature in a way that is consistent with the major type of strategy and the qualitative or quantitative approach most prevalent in the design.

- Regardless of the type of study, consider the type of literature review to conduct, such as an integrative, critical, building bridges among topics or the identification of central issues.

Design Techniques

Regardless of the type of study, several steps are useful in conducting a literature review.

Steps in Conducting a Literature Review

A literature review means locating and summarizing the studies about a topic. Often these are research studies (since you are conducting a research study), but they may also include conceptual articles or opinion pieces that provide frameworks for thinking about topics. There is no single way to conduct a literature review, but many scholars proceed in a systematic fashion to capture, evaluate, and summarize the literature. Here is the way we recommend:

1. Begin by identifying key words, which is useful in locating materials in an academic library at a college or university. These key words may emerge in identifying a topic or may result from preliminary readings.

2. With these key words in mind, use your home computer to begin searching the databases for holdings (i.e., journals and books). Most major libraries have computerized databases, and we suggest you focus initially on journals and books related to the topic. General databases, including Google Scholar, Web of Science, EBSCO, ProQuest, and JSTOR, cover a broad range of disciplines. Other databases, such as ERIC, Sociofile, or PsycINFO, are based on particular disciplines.

3. Initially, try to locate about 50 reports of research in articles or books related to research on your topic. Set a priority on the search

for journal articles and books because they are easy to locate and obtain. Determine whether these articles and books exist in your academic library or whether you need to send for them by interlibrary loan or purchase them through a bookstore.

4. Skim this initial group of articles or chapters, and collect those that are central to your topic. Throughout this process, simply try to obtain a sense as to whether the article or chapter will make a useful contribution to your understanding of the literature.

5. As you identify useful literature, begin designing a **literature map** (to be discussed more fully later). This is a visual picture (or figure) of groupings of the literature on the topic that illustrates how your particular study will add to the existing literature and position your study within the larger body of research.

6. As you put together the literature map, also begin to draft summaries of the most relevant articles. These summaries are combined into the final literature review that you write for your proposal or research study. Include precise references to the literature using an appropriate style guide, such as the *Publication Manual of the American Psychological Association* (American Psychological Association [APA], 2010) so that you have a complete reference to use at the end of the proposal or study.

7. After summarizing the literature, assemble the literature review, structuring it thematically or organizing it by important concepts. End the literature review with a summary of the major themes and suggest how your particular study further adds to the literature and addresses a gap in the themes. This summary should also point toward the methods (i.e., data collection and data analysis) that need to be undertaken to add to the literature. It is at this point as well that you could advance a critique of the past literature and point out deficiencies in it and issues in its methods (see Boote & Beile, 2005).

Searching Computerized Databases

To ease the process of collecting relevant material, there are some techniques useful in accessing the literature quickly through databases. **Computer databases of the literature** are now available through the Internet, and they provide easy access to thousands of journals, conference papers, and materials on many different topics. Academic libraries at major universities have purchased commercial databases as well as obtained databases in the public domain. Only a few of the major databases available will be reviewed here, but they are the major sources to journal articles and documents that you should consult to determine what literature is available on your topic.

ERIC is a free online digital library of education research and information sponsored by the Institute of Education Sciences (IES) of the U.S.

Department of Education. This database can be found at www.eric.ed.gov, and ERIC provides a search of 1.2 million items indexed since 1966. The collection includes journal articles, books, research syntheses, conference papers, technical reports, policy papers, and other education-related materials. ERIC indexes more than hundreds of journals, and links are available to full-text copies of many of the materials. To best utilize ERIC, it is important to identify appropriate descriptors for your topic, the terms used by indexers to categorize articles or documents. Researchers can search through the *Thesaurus of ERIC Descriptors* (ERIC, 1975) or browse the online thesaurus. A **research tip** in conducting an ERIC search is to locate recent journal articles and documents on your topic. This process can be enhanced by conducting a preliminary search using descriptors from the online thesaurus and locating a journal article or document which is on your topic. Then look closely at the descriptors used in this article and document and run another search using these terms. This procedure will maximize the possibility of obtaining a good list of articles for your literature review.

Another free database to search is Google Scholar. It provides a way to broadly search for literature across many disciplines and sources, such as peer-reviewed papers, theses, books, abstracts, and articles from academic publishers, professional societies, universities, and other scholarly organizations. The articles identified in a Google Scholar search provide links to abstracts, related articles, electronic versions of articles affiliated with a library you specify, web searches for information about this work, and opportunities to purchase the full text of the article.

Researchers can obtain abstracts to publications in the health sciences through the free-access PubMed. This database is a service of the U.S. National Library of Medicine, and it includes over 17 million citations from MEDLINE and life science journals for biomedical articles going back to the 1950s (www.ncbi.nlm.nih.gov). PubMed includes links to full-text articles (located in academic libraries) and other related resources. To search PubMed, the researcher uses MeSH (Medical Subject Headings) terms, the U.S. National Library of Medicine's controlled vocabulary thesaurus used for indexing articles for MEDLINE/PubMed. This MeSH terminology provides a consistent way to retrieve information about topics that may be described using different terms.

On the Internet you can also go to other literature search programs. One typically available is ProQuest (http://proquest.com), which enables a researcher to search many different databases, and it is one of the largest online content repositories in the world. Another would be EBSCO publishing, a for-fee online research service, including full-text databases, subject indexes, point-of-care medical reference, historical digital archives, and e-books. The company provides more than 350 databases and nearly 300,000 e-books. Also at academic libraries you can search ERIC, PsycINFO, Dissertation Abstracts, Periodicals Index, Health and Medical Complete, and many more specialized databases (e.g., International Index to Black Periodicals). Because EBSCO taps into many different databases, it can be one search tool to use before using more specialized databases.

Another commercially licensed database found in many academic libraries is Sociological Abstracts (Cambridge Scientific Abstracts, www.csa.com). This database indexes over 2,000 journals; conference papers; relevant dissertation listings; book reviews; and selected books in sociology, social work, and related disciplines. For literature in the field of psychology and related areas, consult another commercial database: PsycINFO (www.apa.org). This database indexes 2,150 journal titles, books, and dissertations from many countries. It covers the field of psychology as well as psychological aspects of physiology, linguistics, anthropology, business, and law. It has a Thesaurus of Psychological Index Terms to locate useful terms in a literature search.

Psychological Abstracts (American Psychological Association [APA], 1927–) and PsycINFO (apa.org) represent important sources for locating research articles on topics broadly related to psychology. The PsycINFO database is available through libraries and may be accessed through another service, such as EBSCO, Ovid, or ProQuest. PsycINFO indexes nearly 2,500 journals in 22 major categories and it provides bibliographic citations, abstracts for psychological journal articles, dissertations, technical reports, books, and book chapters published worldwide. Similar to an ERIC record, a summary from PsycINFO includes key phrase *identifiers* as well as the author, title, source, and a brief abstract of the article.

Another commercial database available in libraries is the Social Sciences Citation Index (SSCI) (Web of Knowledge, Thomson Scientific [http://isiwebof knowledge.com]). It indexes 1,700 journals spanning 50 disciplines and selectively indexes relevant items from over 3,300 scientific and technical journals. It can be used to locate articles and authors who have conducted research on a topic. It is especially useful in locating studies that have referenced an important study. The SSCI enables you to trace all studies since the publication of the key study that have cited the work. Using this system, you can develop a chronological list of references that document the historical evolution of an idea or study. This chronological list can be most helpful in tracking the development of ideas about your literature review topic.

In summary, our **research tips** for searching computer databases are to do the following:

- Use both the free, online literature databases as well as those available through your academic library.

- Search several databases, even if you feel that your topic is not strictly education, as found in ERIC, or psychology, as found in PsycInfo. Both ERIC and PsycInfo view education and psychology as broad terms for many topics.

- Use guides to terms to locate your articles, such as a thesaurus, when available.

- Locate an article that is close to your topic; then look at the terms used to describe it, and use these terms in your search.

- Use databases that provide access to full-text copies of your articles (through academic libraries, your Internet connection to a library, or for a fee) as much as possible so that you can reduce the amount of time searching for copies of your articles.

A Priority for Selecting Literature Material

We recommend that you establish a priority in a search of the literature. What types of literature might be reviewed and in what priority? Consider the following:

1. Especially if you are examining a topic for the first time and unaware of the research on it, start with broad syntheses of the literature, such as overviews found in encyclopedias (e.g., Aikin, 1992; Keeves, 1988). You might also look for summaries of the literature on your topic presented in journal articles or abstract series (e.g., *Annual Review of Psychology*, 1950–).

2. Next, turn to journal articles in respected national journals—especially those that report research studies. By *research*, we mean that the author or authors pose a question or hypothesis, collect data, and try to answer the question or hypothesis. There are journals widely read in your field, and typically they are publications with a high-quality editorial board consisting of individuals from around the United States or abroad. By turning to the first few pages, you can determine if an editorial board is listed and whether it is made up of individuals from around the country or world. Start with the most recent issues of the journals, and look for studies about your topic and then work backward in time. Follow up on references at the end of the articles for more sources to examine.

3. Turn to books related to the topic. Begin with research monographs that summarize the scholarly literature. Then consider entire books on a single topic by a single author or group of authors or books that contain chapters written by different authors.

4. Follow this search by looking for recent conference papers. Look for major national conferences and the papers delivered at them. Often, conference papers report the latest research developments. Most major conferences either require or request that authors submit their papers for inclusion in computerized indices. Make contact with authors of pertinent studies. Seek them out at conferences. Write or phone them, asking if they know of studies related to your area of interest and inquire also if they have an instrument that might be used or modified for use in your study.

5. If time permits, scan the entries in *Dissertation Abstracts* (University Microfilms, 1938–). Dissertations vary immensely in quality, and one needs to be selective in choosing those to review. A search of the *Abstracts* might result in one or two relevant dissertations, and you can request copies of them through interlibrary loans or through the University of Michigan Microfilm Library.

6. The web also provides helpful materials for a literature review. The easy access and ability to capture entire articles makes this source of material attractive. However, screen these articles carefully for quality and be cautious about whether they represent rigorous, thoughtful, and systematic research suitable for use in a literature review. Online journals, on the other hand, often include articles that have undergone rigorous reviews by editorial boards. You might check to see if the journal has a refereed editorial board that reviews manuscripts and has published standards for accepting manuscripts in an editorial statement.

In summary, we place refereed journal articles high on the list because they are the easiest to locate and duplicate. They also report research about a topic. Dissertations are listed lower in priority because they vary considerably in quality and are the most difficult reading material to locate and reproduce. Caution should be used in choosing journal articles on the web unless they are part of refereed online journals.

A Literature Map of the Research

One of the first tasks for a researcher working with a new topic is to organize the literature. As mentioned earlier, this organization enables a person to understand how the proposed study adds to, extends, or replicates research already completed.

A useful approach for this step is to design a literature map. This is an idea that we developed several years ago, and it has been a useful tool for students to use when organizing their review of the literature for making presentations to graduate committees, summarizing the literature for a scholarly presentation, or composing an article for journal publication.

This map is a visual summary of the research that has been conducted by others, and it is typically represented in a figure. Maps are organized in different ways. One could be a hierarchical structure with a top-down presentation of the literature, ending at the bottom with the proposed study. Another might be similar to a flowchart in which the reader understands the literature as unfolding from left to right with the farthest right-hand section advancing a proposed study. A third model might be a series of circles; each circle represents a body of literature and the intersection of the circles as the place in which the future research is indicated. We have seen examples of all of these possibilities and found them all effective.

The central idea is that the researcher begins to build a visual picture of existing research about a topic. This literature map presents an overview of existing literature. Figure 2.1 is an illustration of a map that shows the literature found on procedural justice in organizational studies (Janovec, 2001). Janovec's map illustrates a hierarchical design, and she used several principles of good map design:

- She placed her topic in the box at the top of the hierarchy.

- Next, she took the studies that she found in computer searches, located copies of these studies, and organized them into three broad subtopics (i.e., Justice Perceptions Formation, Justice Effects, and Justice in Organizational Change). For another map, the researcher may have more or fewer than three major categories, depending on the extent and publications on the topic.

- Within each box are labels that describe the nature of the studies in the box (i.e., outcomes).

- Also within each box are references to major citations illustrating its content. It is useful to use references that are current and illustrative of the topic of the box and to briefly state the references in an appropriate style, such as APA (APA, 2010).

- Consider several levels for the literature map. In other words, major topics lead to subtopics and then to sub-subtopics.

- Some branches of the chart are more developed than others. This development depends on the amount of literature available and the depth of the exploration of the literature by the researcher.

- After organizing the literature into a diagram, Janovec (2001) next considered the branches of the figure that provided a springboard for her proposed study. She placed a "Need to Study" (or proposed study) box at the bottom of the map, she briefly identified the nature of this proposed study (Procedural Justice and Culture), and she then drew lines to past literature that her project would *extend*. She proposed this study based on ideas written by other authors in the future research sections of their studies.

- Include quantitative, qualitative, and mixed methods studies in your literature map.

- Write a narrative description of your literature map for your committee or for presentation that begins with your topic (the heading box at the top), the databases you have reviewed, the division of the literature into broad topics in the map, the specific topic that you plan to study (at the bottom box of the map), and how your topic relates to various branches in the literature (the connecting lines— what literature your study builds on and how it builds).

Composing a literature map can be challenging. Individuals seeing this map may not be familiar with this approach to organizing the literature and making a case for your study. They need to be told the intent of such a map. It takes time to develop such a map and locate literature to put into the map. For a preliminary map, we consider collecting maybe 25 studies. For a full literature map for a dissertation or thesis, we would consider developing a map with at least 100 studies. Figuring out how your study adds to the literature takes some time. It may add to several threads in your literature map. We would refrain from tying it to all of your subdivisions; select one or two subdivisions. It is also challenging to figure out what the broad topic might be for the top of the map. This is the topic to which your literature map adds. Ask others who know about your literature, see how the research studies group according to some synthesis of the literature, and continually ask yourself what body of literature your study will contribute to. You may also have to develop several versions of your map before it comes together. Develop your map, write the discussion, and check it out with others.

Abstracting Studies

When researchers write reviews of the literature for proposed studies, they locate articles and develop brief abstracts of the articles that comprise the review. An **abstract** is a brief review of the literature (typically a short paragraph) that summarizes major elements to enable a reader to understand the basic features of the article (see Example 2.1). In developing an abstract, researchers need to consider what material to extract and summarize. This is important information when reviewing perhaps dozens, if not hundreds, of studies. A good summary of a research study reported in a journal might include the following points:

- Mention the problem being addressed.
- State the central purpose or focus of the study.
- Briefly state information about the sample, population, or subjects.
- Review key results that relate to the proposed study.
- If it is a critique or methods review (Cooper, 2010), point out technical and methodological flaws in the study.

When examining a study to develop a summary, there are places to look for these parts. In well-crafted journal articles, the problem and purpose statements are clearly stated in the introduction. Information about the sample, population, or subjects is found midway through in a method (or procedure) section, and the results are often reported toward the end. In the

Figure 2.1   An Example of a Literature Map

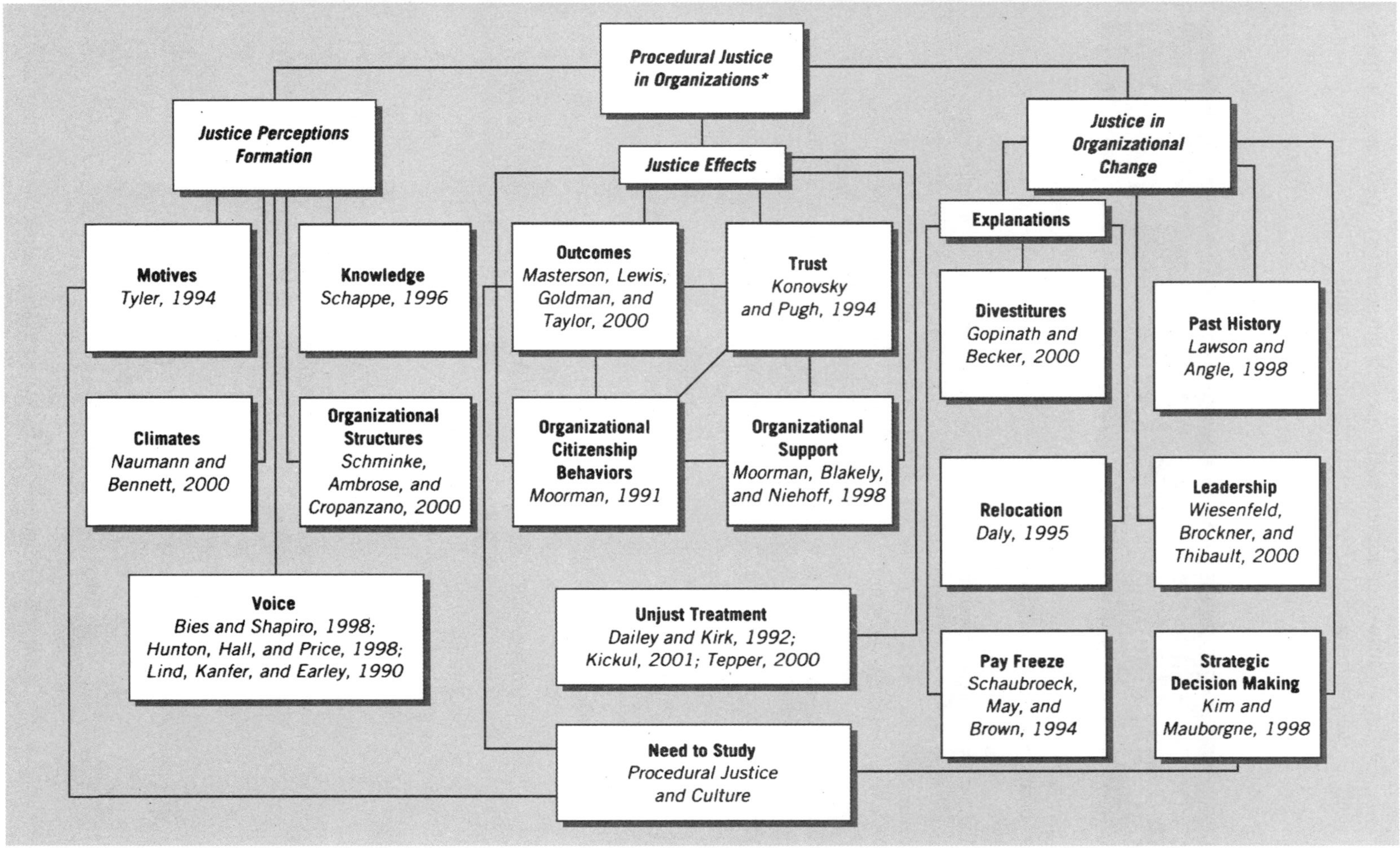

*Employees' concerns about the fairness of and the making of managerial decisions

Source: Janovec (2001). Reprinted by permission.

37

results sections, look for passages in which the researchers report information to answer or address each research question or hypothesis. For book-length research studies, look for the same points.

Example 2.1 Literature Review Abstract in a Quantitative Study

The paragraph that follows summarizes the major components of a quantitative study (Creswell, Seagren, & Henry, 1979), much like the paragraph might appear in a review of the literature section of a dissertation or a journal article. In this passage, we have chosen key components to be abstracted.

Creswell and colleagues (1979) tested the Biglan model, a three-dimensional model clustering 36 academic areas into hard or soft, pure or applied, life or nonlife areas, as a predictor of chairpersons'

professional development needs. Eighty department chairpersons located in four state colleges and one university of a midwestern state participated in the study. Results showed that chairpersons in different academic areas differed in terms of their professional development needs. Based on the findings, the authors recommended that those who develop inservice programs needed to consider differences among disciplines when they plan for programs.

Creswell and colleagues began with an in-text reference in accord with the format in the APA *Publication Manual* (APA, 2010). Next, we reviewed the central purpose of the study, followed by information about the data collection. The abstract ended by stating the major results and presenting the practical implications of these results.

How are essays, opinions, typologies, and syntheses of past research abstracted, since these are not research studies? The material to be extracted from these non-empirical studies would be as follows:

- Mention the problem being addressed by the article or book.

- Identify the central theme of the study.

- State the major conclusions related to this theme.

- If the review type is methodological, mention flaws in reasoning, logic, force of argument, and so forth.

Example 2.2 illustrates the inclusion of these aspects.

Example 2.2 Literature Review Abstract in a Study Advancing a Typology

Sudduth (1992) completed a quantitative dissertation in political science on the topic of the use of strategic adaptation in rural hospitals. He reviewed the literature in several chapters at the beginning of the study. In an example of summarizing a single study advancing a typology, Sudduth summarized the problem, the theme, and the typology:

> Ginter, Duncan, Richardson, and Swayne (1991) recognize the impact of the external environment on a hospital's ability to adapt to change. They advocate a process that they call environmental analysis, which allows the organization to strategically determine the best responses to change occurring in the environment. However, after examining the multiple techniques used for environmental analysis, it appears that no comprehensive conceptual scheme or computer model has been developed to provide a complete analysis of environmental issues (Ginter et al., 1991). The result is an essential part of strategic change that relies heavily on a non-quantifiable and judgmental process of evaluation. To assist the hospital manager to carefully assess the external environment, Ginter et al. (1991) have developed the typology given in Figure 2.1. (p. 44)

In this example, the authors referenced the study with an in-text reference, mentioned the problem ("a hospital's ability to adapt to change"), identified the central theme ("a process that they call environmental analysis"), and stated the conclusions related to this theme (e.g., "no comprehensive conceptual model," "developed the typology").

Style Manuals

In both examples, we have introduced the idea of using appropriate APA style for referencing the article at the beginning of the abstract. **Style manuals** provide guidelines for creating a scholarly style of a manuscript, such as a consistent format for citing references, creating headings, presenting tables and figures, and using nondiscriminatory language. A basic tenet in reviewing the literature is to use an appropriate and consistent reference style throughout. When identifying a useful document, make a complete reference to the source using an appropriate style. For dissertation proposals, graduate students should seek guidance from faculty, dissertation committee members, or department or college officials about the appropriate style manual to use for citing references.

The *Publication Manual of the American Psychological Association* (APA, 2010) is the most popular style manual used in the fields of education and psychology. *The Chicago Manual of Style* (University of Chicago Press, 2010) is also used but less widely than the APA style in the social sciences. Some journals have developed their own variations of the popular styles. We recommend identifying a style that is acceptable for your writing audiences and adopting it early in the planning process.

The most important style considerations involve in-text, end-of-text, heading, and figures and tables use. Some suggestions for using style manuals for scholarly writing are these:

- When writing in-text references, keep in mind the appropriate form for types of references and pay close attention to the format for multiple citations.

- When writing the end-of-text references, note whether the style manual calls for them to be alphabetized or numbered. Also, crosscheck that each in-text reference is included in the end-of-text list.

- The headings are ordered in a scholarly paper in terms of levels. First, note how many levels of headings you will have in your research study. Then, refer to the style manual for the appropriate format for each. Typically, research proposals or projects contain between two and four levels of headings.

- If footnotes are used, consult the style manual for their proper placement. Footnotes are used less frequently in scholarly papers today than a few years ago. If you include them, note whether they go at the bottom of the page, the end of each chapter, or at the end of the paper.

- Tables and figures have a specific form in each style manual. Note such aspects as bold lines, titles, and spacing in the examples given.

In summary, the most important aspect of using a style manual is to be consistent in the approach throughout the manuscript.

The Definition of Terms

Another topic related to reviewing the literature is the identification and **definition of terms** that readers will need in order to understand a proposed research project. A definition of terms section may be found separate from the literature review, included as part of the literature review, or placed in different sections of a proposal.

Define terms that individuals outside the field of study may not understand and that go beyond common language (Locke, Spirduso, & Silverman, 2013). Clearly, whether a term should be defined is a matter of judgment, but define a term if there is any likelihood that readers will not know its meaning. Also, define terms when they first appear so that a reader does not read ahead in the proposal operating with one set of definitions only to find out later that the author is using a different set. As Wilkinson (1991) commented, "scientists have sharply defined terms with which to think clearly about their research and to communicate their findings and ideas accurately" (p. 22). Defining terms also adds precision to a scientific study, as Firestone (1987) stated this:

> The words of everyday language are rich in multiple meanings. Like other symbols, their power comes from the combination of meaning in a specific setting. . . . Scientific language ostensibly strips this multiplicity of meaning from words in the interest of precision. This is the reason common terms are given "technical meanings" for scientific purposes. (p. 17)

With this need for precision, one finds terms stated early in the introduction to articles. In dissertations and thesis proposals, terms are typically defined in a special section of the study. The rationale is that in formal research, students must be precise in how they use language and terms. The need to ground thoughts in authoritative definitions constitutes good science. Define terms introduced in all sections of the research plan:

- The title of the study

- The problem statement

- The purpose statement

- The research questions, hypotheses, or objectives

- The literature review

- The theory base of the study

- The methods section

Special terms that need to be defined appear in all three types of studies: (a) qualitative, (b) quantitative, and (c) mixed methods.

- In qualitative studies, because of the inductive, evolving methodological design, inquirers may define few terms at the beginning though they may advance tentative definitions. Instead, themes (or perspectives or dimensions) may emerge through the data analysis. In the procedure section, authors define these terms in the procedure section as they surface during the process of research. This approach is to delay the definition of terms until they appear in the study, and it makes such definitions difficult to specify in advance in research proposals. For this reason, qualitative proposals often do not include separate sections for a definition of terms. Instead, writers pose tentative, qualitative definitions before entry into the field.

- On the other hand, quantitative studies—operating more within the deductive model of fixed and set research objectives—include extensive definitions early in the research proposal. Investigators may place them in separate sections and precisely define them. The researchers try to comprehensively define all relevant terms at the beginning of studies and to use accepted definitions found in the literature.

- In mixed methods studies, the approach to definitions might include a separate section if the study begins with a first phase of quantitative data collection. If it begins with qualitative data collection, then the terms may emerge during the research, and they are defined in the findings or results section of the final report. If both quantitative and qualitative data collection occurs at the same time, then the priority given to one or the other will govern the approach for definitions. However, in all mixed methods studies, there are terms that may be unfamiliar to readers—for example, the definition of a mixed methods study itself, in a procedural discussion (see Chapter 10). Also, clarify terms related to the strategy of inquiry used, such as concurrent or sequential, and the specific name for a strategy (e.g., convergent parallel design, as discussed in Chapter 10).

No one approach governs how one defines the terms in a study, but several suggestions follow (see also Locke et al., 2013):

- Define a term when it first appears in the proposal. In the introduction, for example, a term may require a definition to help the reader understand the research problem and questions or hypotheses in the study.

- Write definitions at a specific operational or applied level. Operational definitions are written in specific language rather than abstract, conceptual definitions. Since the definition section in a dissertation provides an opportunity for the author to be specific about the terms used in the study, a preference exists for operational definitions.

- Do not define the terms in everyday language; instead, use accepted language available in the research literature. In this way, the terms are grounded in the literature and not invented (Locke et al., 2013). It is possible that the precise definition of a term is not available in the literature and everyday language will need to be used. In this case, provide a definition and use the term consistently throughout the plan and the study (Wilkinson, 1991).

- Researchers might define terms so that they accomplish different goals. A definition may describe a common language word (e.g., organization). It may also be paired with a limitation (e.g., the curriculum may be limited). It may establish a criterion (e.g., high grade point average), and it could also define a term operationally (e.g., reinforcement will refer to listing).

- Although no one format exists for defining terms, one approach is to develop a separate section, called the "Definition of Terms," and clearly set off the terms and their definitions by highlighting the term. In this way, the word is assigned an invariant meaning (Locke et al., 2013). Typically, this separate section is not more than two to three pages in length.

Examples 2.3 and 2.4 illustrate varied structures for defining terms in a research study.

Example 2.3   Terms Defined in an Independent Variables Section

This set of two examples illustrates an abbreviated form of writing definitions for a study. The first illustrates a specific operational definition of a key term and the second the procedural definition of a key term. Vernon (1992) studied how divorce in the middle generation impacts grandparents' relationships with their grandchildren. These definitions were included in a section on independent variables:

Kinship Relationship to the Grandchild

Kinship relationship to the grandchild refers to whether the grandparents are maternal grandparents or paternal grandparents. Previous research (e.g., Cherlin & Furstenberg, 1986) suggests that maternal grandparents tend to be closer to their grandchildren.

Sex of Grandparent

Whether a grandparent is a grand*mother* or grand*father* has been found to be a factor in the grandparent/grandchild relationship (i.e., grandmothers tend to be more involved than grandfathers, which is thought to be related to the kinkeeping role of women within the family (e.g., Hagestad, 1988, pp. 35–36).

Example 2.4   Terms Defined in a Mixed Methods Dissertation

This example illustrates a lengthy definition of terms presented in a mixed methods study in a separate section of the first chapter that introduces the study. VanHorn-Grassmeyer (1998) studied how 119 new professionals in student affairs in colleges and universities engage in reflection—either individually or collaboratively. She both surveyed the new professionals and conducted in-depth interviews with them. Because she studied individual and collaborative reflection among student affairs professionals, she provided detailed definitions of these terms in the beginning of the study. We illustrate two of her terms next. Notice how she referenced her definitions in meanings formed by other authors in the literature:

(Continued)

(Continued)

Individual Reflection

Schon (1983) devoted an entire book to concepts he named reflective thinking, reflection-in-action, and reflective practice; this after an entire book was written a decade earlier with Argyris (Argyris & Schon, 1978) to introduce the concepts. Therefore, a concise definition of this researcher's understanding of individual reflection that did justice to something that most aptly had been identified as an intuitive act was difficult to reach. However, the most salient characteristics of individual reflection for the purposes of this study were these three: (a) an "artistry of practice" (Schon, 1983), (b) how one practices overtly what one knows intuitively, and (c) how a professional enhances practice through thoughtful discourse within the mind.

Student Affairs Professional

A professional has been described in many ways. One description identified an individual who exhibited "a high degree of independent judgment, based on a collective, learned body of ideas, perspectives, information, norms, and habits [and who engage(d) in professional knowing]" (Baskett & Marsick, 1992, p. 3). A student affairs professional has exhibited such traits in service to students in a higher education environment, in any one of a number of functions which support academic and co-curricular success (pp. 11–12).

A Quantitative or Mixed Methods Literature Review

When composing a review of the literature, it is difficult to determine how much literature to review. In order to address this problem, we have developed a model that provides parameters around the literature review, especially as it might be designed for a quantitative or mixed methods study that employs a standard literature review section. For a qualitative study, the literature review might explore aspects of the central phenomenon being addressed and divide it into topical areas. But the literature review for a qualitative study, as discussed earlier, can be placed in a proposal in several ways (e.g., as a rationale for the research problem, as a separate section, as something threaded throughout the study, as compared with the results of a project).

For a quantitative study or the quantitative strand of a mixed methods study, write a review of the literature that contains sections about the literature related to major independent variables, major dependent variables, and studies that relate the independent and dependent variables (more on variables in Chapter 3). This approach seems appropriate for dissertations and for conceptualizing the literature to be introduced in a journal article. Consider a literature review to be composed of five components: (a) an introduction, (b) Topic 1 (about the independent variable), (c) Topic 2 (about the dependent variable), (d) Topic 3, (studies that address both the independent and dependent variables), and (e) a summary. Here is more detail about each section:

1. Introduce the review by telling the reader about the sections included in it. This passage is a statement about the organization of the section.

2. Review Topic 1, which addresses the scholarly literature about the *independent* variable or variables. With several independent variables, consider subsections or focus on the single most important variable. Remember to address only the literature about the independent variable; keep the literature about the independent and dependent variables separate in this model.

3. Review Topic 2, which incorporates the scholarly literature about the *dependent* variable or variables. With multiple dependent variables, write subsections about each variable or focus on a single important one.

4. Review Topic 3, which includes the scholarly literature that relates the independent variable(s) to the dependent variable(s). Here we are at the crux of the proposed study. Thus, this section should be relatively short and contain studies that are extremely close in topic to the proposed study. Perhaps nothing has been written on the topic. Construct a section that is as close as possible to the topic or review studies that address the topic at a more general level.

5. Provide a summary that highlights the most important studies, captures major themes, suggests why more research is needed on the topic, and advances how the proposed study will fill this need.

This model focuses the literature review, relates it closely to the variables in the research questions and hypotheses, and sufficiently narrows the study. It becomes a logical point of departure for the research questions and the method section.

SUMMARY

Before searching the literature, identify your topic, using such strategies as drafting a brief title or stating a central research question. Also consider whether this topic can and should be researched by reviewing whether there is access to participants and resources and whether the topic will add to the literature, be of interest to others, and be consistent with personal goals.

Researchers use the scholarly literature in a study to present results of similar studies, to relate the present study to an ongoing dialogue in the literature, and to provide a framework for comparing results of a study with other studies. For qualitative, quantitative, and mixed methods designs, the literature serves different purposes. In qualitative research, the literature helps substantiate the research problem, but it does not constrain the views of participants. A popular approach is to include more literature at the end of a qualitative study than at the beginning. In quantitative research, the literature not only helps to substantiate the problem but it also suggests possible questions or hypotheses that need to be addressed. A separate literature review section is typically found in quantitative studies. In mixed methods research, the use of literature will depend on the type of design and weight given to the qualitative and quantitative aspects.

When conducting a literature review, identify key words for searching the literature. Then search the online databases, such as ERIC, EBSCO, ProQuest, Google Scholar, PubMed, and more specialized databases, such as PsycINFO, Sociofile, and SSCI. Then, locate articles or books based on a priority of searching first for journal articles and then books. Identify references that will make a contribution to your literature review. Group these studies into a literature map that shows the major categories of studies and positions of your proposed study within those categories. Begin writing summaries of the studies, noting complete references according to a style manual (e.g., APA, 2010) and extracting information about the research that includes the research problem, the questions, the data collection and analysis, and the final results.

Define key terms, and possibly develop a definition of terms section for your proposal or include them within your literature review. Finally, consider the overall structure for organizing these studies. One quantitative research model is to divide the review into sections according to major variables (a quantitative approach) or major subthemes of the central phenomenon (a qualitative approach) that you are studying.

Writing Exercises

1. Develop a literature map of the studies on your topic. Include in the map the proposed study and draw lines from the proposed study to branches of studies in the map so that a reader can easily see how yours will extend existing literature.

2. Organize a review of the literature for a quantitative study, and follow the model for delimiting the literature to reflect the variables in the study. As an alternative, organize a review of literature for a qualitative study and include it in an introduction as a rationale for the research problem in the study.

3. Practice using an online computer database to search for the literature on your topic. Conduct several searches until you find an article that is as close as possible to your research topic. Then conduct a second search using descriptors mentioned in this article. Locate 10 articles that you would select and abstract for your literature review.

4. Based on your search results from Exercise 3, write one quantitative and one qualitative abstract of two research studies found in your online search. Use the guidelines provided in this chapter for the elements to include in your literature abstracts.

Additional Readings

American Psychological Association. (2010). *Publication Manual of the American Psychological Association* (6th ed.). Washington, DC: Author.

The latest APA style manual is a must for every researcher's shelf. It provides an entire chapter offering examples of how to cite works in a reference list. The examples are extensive—from journals (or periodicals) to patents. Further guidelines for presenting tables and figures are available with good examples that you can use. This manual also has chapters on scholarly writing and the mechanics of style used in this type of writing. For those planning on publishing, it provides useful information about the standard elements of a manuscript as well as ethical issues to consider.

Boote, D. N., & Beile, P. (2005). Scholars before researchers: On the centrality of the dissertation literature review in research preparation. *Educational Researcher, 34*(6), 3–15.

David Boote and Penny Beile discuss the importance of dissertation students to compile sophisticated literature reviews. To this end, they advance five criteria that should be in a rigorous literature review. The author should justify the inclusion and exclusion of literature (coverage), critically examine the state of the field, situate the topic in the broader literature, examine the history of the topic, note ambiguities in definitions and the literature, and offer new perspectives (synthesis). It should also critique the research methods (methodology), as well as the practical and scholarly significance of the research (significance), and be written well in a coherent fashion (rhetoric).

Locke, L. F., Spirduso, W. W., & Silverman, S. J. (2010). *Proposals that work: A guide for planning dissertations and grant proposals* (6th ed.) Thousand Oaks, CA: Sage.

Lawrence Locke, Waneen Spirduso, and Stephen Silverman describe several stages for reviewing the literature: develop the concepts that provide a rationale for the study, develop subtopics for each major concept, and add the most important references that support each concept. They also provide five rules for defining terms in a scholarly study: (a) never invent words, (b) provide definitions early in a proposal, (c) do not use common language forms of words, (d) define words when they are first introduced, and (e) use specific definitions for words.

Punch, K. F. (2014). *Introduction to social research: Quantitative and qualitative approaches* (3rd ed.). Thousand Oaks, CA: Sage.

Keith Punch provides a guide to social research that equally addresses quantitative and qualitative approaches. His conceptualizations of central issues that divide the two approaches address key differences. Punch notes that when writing a proposal or report, the point at which to concentrate on the literature varies in different styles of research. Factors that affect that decision include the style of research, the overall research strategy, and how closely the study will follow the directions of the literature.

The Use of Theory

One component of reviewing the literature is to determine what theories might be used to explore the questions in a scholarly study. In *quantitative research*, researchers often test hypotheses stemming from theories. In a quantitative dissertation, an entire section of a research proposal might be devoted to presenting the broader theory guiding the study hypotheses. In *qualitative research*, the use of theory is much more varied. The inquirer may generate a theory as the final outcome of a study and place it at the end of a project, such as in grounded theory. In other qualitative studies, it comes at the beginning and provides a lens that shapes what is looked at and the questions asked, such as in ethnographies or in participatory–social justice research. In mixed methods research, researchers may both test theories and generate them. Moreover, mixed methods research may contain a theoretical framework within which both quantitative and qualitative data are collected. These frameworks can be drawn from feminist, racial, class, or other perspectives and they flow through different parts of a mixed methods study.

Theories can be used in quantitative, qualitative, and mixed methods studies. We begin this chapter by focusing on theory use in a quantitative study. We review a definition of a theory, the use of variables in a quantitative study, the placement of theory, and the alternative forms it might assume in a written plan. Procedures in identifying a theory are next presented, followed by a script of a theoretical perspective section of a quantitative research proposal. Then the discussion moves to the use of theory in a qualitative study. Qualitative inquirers use different terms for theories, such as *patterns, theoretical lens,* or *naturalistic generalizations,* to describe the broader explanations used or developed in their studies. Examples in this chapter illustrate the alternatives available to qualitative researchers. Finally, the chapter turns to the use of theories in mixed methods research and the use of social science and participatory–social justice theories in such research.

Quantitative Theory Use

Testing Causal Claims in Quantitative Research

Prior to discussing variables, their types, and their use in quantitative research, we first need to visit the concept of *causality* in quantitative research. A leading writer in this area has been Blalock (1991). Causality means that we would expect variable X to cause variable Y. As a simple example, does drinking one glass of red wine daily *cause* you to have a reduced risk for a heart attack? In this case, daily wine consumption is the X variable, and a heart attack event would be the Y variable. One critically important consideration in evaluating causal claims (like this red wine consumption example) is whether an unmeasured third variable (Z) may be the cause of the outcome you are measuring. For example, there may be a Z variable (such as daily exercise) that is positively associated with both moderate red wine consumption and with heart attacks, and may be the causal factor for reducing heart attacks (not moderate red wine consumption!). In quantitative research this third variable is called a *confounding variable*, and can become quite problematic for establishing causality if it is not measured in a study. We would not want to mistakenly infer that moderate red wine consumption promotes heart health if it plays no causal role in reducing heart attacks. If you aim to test a causal claim about the relationship between two or more variables in your quantitative study, your best choice is to conduct a true experiment, which will provide more control over potential confounding variables (see Chapter 8). If you are less interested in testing a causal claim or if you cannot conduct an experiment, then survey methods can be used to test claims about hypothesized associations between variables (see Chapter 8)—for example, you may be interested in first establishing if a positive association exists between moderate daily red wine consumption and clinical markers of heart disease risk in a correlation analysis. Indeed, a number of epidemiological health science studies highlight a positive association between moderate daily red wine consumption (1–2 drinks per day) and a 20% reduction in risk for heart disease (e.g., Szmitko & Verma, 2005).

Variables in Quantitative Research

Before discussing quantitative theories, it is important to understand variables and the types that are used in forming theories. A **variable** refers to a characteristic or attribute of an individual or an organization that can be measured or observed and that varies among the people or organization being studied. Variables often measured in studies include gender; age; socioeconomic status (SES); and attitudes or behaviors such as racism, social control, political power, or leadership. Several texts provide detailed discussions about the types of variables one can use and their scales of measurement (e.g., Isaac & Michael, 1981; Keppel, 1991; Kerlinger, 1979; Thompson, 2006; Thorndike, 1997). Variables are distinguished by two characteristics: (a) *temporal order* and (b) their measurement (or observation).

Temporal order means that one variable precedes another in time. Because of this time ordering, it is said that one variable affects or predicts another variable. Temporal order also means that quantitative researchers think about variables in an order from "left to right" (Punch, 2014) and order the variables in purpose statements, research questions, and visual models into left-to-right, cause-and-effect type presentations. Types of variables include the following:

- *Independent variables* are those that influence, or affect outcomes in experimental studies. They are described as "independent" because they are variables that are manipulated in an experiment and thus independent of all other influences. Using the earlier example, you may decide to run an eight-week experimental study where you ask some participants to drink one glass of red wine daily (red wine group), whereas other participants in a comparison group are instructed to maintain their normal consumption patterns (control group). You are systematically manipulating red wine consumption, and thus moderate red wine consumption is an independent variable in this study. Independent variables are also commonly referred to as *treatment* or *manipulated* variables in experimental studies.

- *Dependent variables* are those that depend on the independent variables; they are the outcomes or results of the influence of the independent variables. We recommend that one aim to measure multiple dependent measures in experimental studies, and in the red wine example a researcher might consider measuring dependent variables such as heart attack incidence, strokes, and/or the amount of arterial atherosclerotic plaque formations.

- *Predictor variables* (also called *antecedent* variables) are variables that are used to predict an outcome of interest in survey method studies. Predictor variables are similar to independent variables in that they are hypothesized to affect outcomes in a study, but dissimilar because the researcher is not able to systematically manipulate a predictor variable. It may not be possible or feasible to assign individuals to a red wine consumption or control group (as an independent variable) but it may be possible to measure naturally occurring red wine consumption in a community sample as a predictor variable.

- *Outcome variables* (also called *criterion* or *response* variables) are variables that are considered outcomes or results of predictor variables in survey method studies. They share the same properties as dependent variables (described above).

Other types of variables provide a supporting cast in quantitative research, and we recommend that you make efforts to identify and measure these variables in your quantitative research study:

- *Intervening* or *mediating* variables(*Intervening or mediating variables*) stand between the independent and dependent variables, and they transmit the effect of an independent variable on a dependent variable (for a review, see MacKinnon, Fairchild, & Fritz, 2007). A mediating variable can be tested using different kinds of statistical mediation analyses (see MacKinnon et al., 2007, for some examples), and provides a quantitative assessment of how the independent variable is exerting its effects on the dependent variable (or in the case of survey method studies how a predictor variable may be exerting its effects on an outcome variable of interest). One leading idea is that the polyphenol compounds in red wine are what is driving the health benefits of moderate red wine consumption (e.g., Szmitko & Verma, 2005), so one possibility could be to measure the amount of polyphenols occurring in a red wine consumption study as a mediating variable. Researchers use statistical procedures (e.g., analysis of covariance [ANCOVA]) to control for these variables.

- *Moderating variables* are predictor variables that affect the direction and/or the strength of the relationship between independent and dependent variables, or between predictor and outcome variables (Thompson, 2006). These variables act on or intersect with the independent variables, and then together in combination with the independent variables influence the dependent variables. Moderating variables are powerful in that they can identify potential boundary conditions (e.g., participant gender; are the effects of moderate red wine consumption on heart attacks much larger for males compared to females?) of the effect of interest.

In a quantitative research study, variables are related to answer a research question, and while we have focused our discussion on the simple red wine–heart disease relationship, these variables and links can be extended to a multitude of other phenomena that we care to understand (e.g., "How does self-esteem influence the formation of friendships among adolescents?" "Does number of overtime hours worked cause higher burnout among nurses?"). Specifically, we use our theories and specification of variables to generate hypotheses. A *hypothesis* is a prediction about a specific event or relationship between variables.

Definition of a Theory in Quantitative Research

With this background on variables, we can proceed to the use of quantitative theories. In quantitative research, some historical precedent exists for viewing a theory as a scientific prediction or explanation for what the researcher expects to find (see Thomas, 1997, for different ways of conceptualizing theories and how they might constrain thought). For example, Kerlinger's (1979) definition of a theory seems still valid today. He said that a theory is "a set of interrelated constructs (variables), definitions, and propositions that presents a systematic view of phenomena by specifying relations among variables, with the purpose of explaining natural phenomena" (p. 64).

In this definition, a **theory in quantitative research** is an interrelated set of constructs (or variables) formed into propositions, or hypotheses, that specify the relationship among variables (typically in terms of magnitude or direction). A theory might appear in a research study as an argument, a discussion, a figure, a rationale, or a conceptual framework, and it helps to explain (or predict) phenomena that occur in the world. Labovitz and Hagedorn (1971) added to this definition the idea of a *theoretical rationale,* which they defined as "specifying how and why the variables and relational statements are interrelated" (p. 17). Why would an independent variable, X, influence or affect a dependent variable, Y? The theory would provide the explanation for this expectation or prediction. A discussion about this theory would appear in a section of a proposal on the literature review or in a separate section called the *theory base,* the theoretical rationale, or the *theoretical perspective* or the *conceptual framework.*. We prefer the term *theoretical perspective* because it has been popularly used as a required section for proposals for research when one submits an application to present a paper at the American Educational Research Association conference.

The metaphor of a rainbow can help to visualize how a theory operates. Assume that the rainbow *bridges* the independent and dependent variables (or constructs) in a study. This rainbow ties together the variables and provides an overarching explanation for *how* and *why* one would expect the independent variable to explain or predict the dependent variable. Theories develop when researchers test a prediction over and over.

For example, here is how the process of developing a theory works. Investigators combine independent, mediating, and dependent variables into questions based on different forms of measures. These questions provide information about the type of relationship (positive, negative, or unknown) and its magnitude (e.g., high or low). Forming this information into a predictive statement (hypothesis), a researcher might write, "The greater the centralization of power in leaders, the greater the disenfranchisement of the followers." When researchers test hypotheses such as this over and over in different settings and with different populations (e.g., the Boy Scouts, a Presbyterian church, the Rotary Club, and a group of high school students), a theory emerges, and someone gives it a name (e.g., a theory of attribution). Thus, theory develops as an explanation to advance knowledge in particular fields (Thomas, 1997).

Another aspect of theories is that they vary in their breadth of coverage. Neuman (2009) reviewed theories at three levels: (a) micro-level, (b) meso-level, and (c) macro-level. Micro-level theories provide explanations limited to small slices of time, space, or numbers of people, such as Goffman's theory of face work, which explains how people engage in rituals during face-to-face interactions. Meso-level theories link the micro and macro levels. These are theories of organizations, social movement, or communities, such as Collins's theory of control in organizations. Macro-level theories explain larger aggregates, such as social institutions, cultural systems, and whole societies. Lenski's macro-level theory of social stratification, for example, explains how the amount of surplus a society produces increases with the development of the society.

Theories are found in the social science disciplines of psychology, sociology, anthropology, education, and economics, as well as within many subfields. To locate and read about these theories requires searching literature databases (e.g., *Psychological Abstracts, Sociological Abstracts*) or reviewing guides to the literature about theories (e.g., see Webb, Beals, & White, 1986).

Forms of Theories in Quantitative Research

Researchers state their theories in research proposals in several ways, such as a series of hypotheses, if-then logic statements, or visual models. First, some researchers state theories in the form of interconnected hypotheses. For example, Hopkins (1964) conveyed his theory of influence processes as a series of 15 hypotheses. Some of the hypotheses are as follows (these have been slightly altered to remove the gender-specific pronouns):

1. The higher one's rank, the greater one's centrality.

2. The greater one's centrality, the greater one's observability.

3. The higher one's rank, the greater one's observability.

4. The greater one's centrality, the greater one's conformity.

5. The higher one's rank, the greater one's conformity.

6. The greater one's observability, the greater one's conformity.

7. The greater one's conformity, the greater one's observability.
   (p. 51)

A second way is to state a theory as a series of if-then statements that explain why one would expect the independent variables to influence or cause the dependent variables. For example, Homans (1950) explained a theory of interaction:

> If the frequency of interaction between two or more persons increases, the degree of their liking for one another will increase, and vice versa. . . . Persons who feel sentiments of liking for one another will express those sentiments in activities over and above the activities of the external system, and these activities may further strengthen the sentiments of liking. The more frequently persons interact with one another, the more alike in some respects both their activities and their sentiments tend to become. (pp. 112, 118, 120)

Third, an author may present a theory as a visual model. It is useful to translate variables into a visual picture. Blalock (1969, 1985, 1991) advocated causal modeling and recast verbal theories into causal models so that a reader could visualize the interconnections of variables. Two simplified examples are presented here. As shown in Figure 3.1, three independent variables influence a single dependent variable, mediated by the influence of two intervening variables. A diagram such as this one shows the possible causal sequence among variables leading to modeling through path analysis and more advanced analyses using multiple measures of variables as found in structural equation modeling (see Kline, 1998). At an introductory level, Duncan (1985) provided useful suggestions about the notation for constructing these visual causal diagrams:

- Position the dependent variables on the right in the diagram and the independent variables on the left.

- Use one-way arrows leading from each determining variable to each variable dependent on it.

- Indicate the strength of the relationship among variables by inserting valence signs on the paths. Use positive or negative valences that postulate or infer relationships.

- Use two-headed arrows connected to show unanalyzed relationships between variables not dependent upon other relationships in the model.

More complicated causal diagrams can be constructed with additional notation. This one portrays a basic model of limited variables, such as typically found in a survey research study.

A variation on this theme is to have independent variables in which control and experimental groups are compared on one independent variable in terms of an outcome (dependent variable). As shown in Figure 3.2, two groups on variable X are compared in terms of their influence on Y, the dependent variable. This design is a between-groups experimental design (see Chapter 8). The same rules of notation previously discussed apply.

Figure 3.1   Three Independent Variables Influence a Single Dependent Variable Mediated by Two Intervening Variables

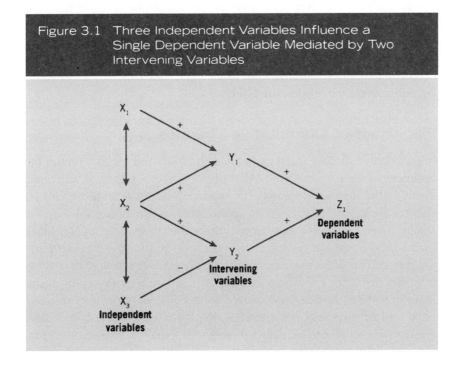

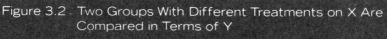

Figure 3.2   Two Groups With Different Treatments on X Are
             Compared in Terms of Y

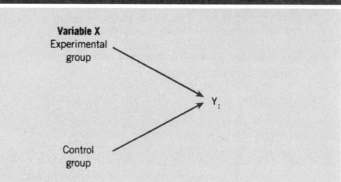

Source: Jungnickel (1990). Reprinted with permission.

These two models are meant only to introduce possibilities for connecting independent and dependent variables to build theories. More complicated designs employ multiple independent and dependent variables in elaborate models of causation (Blalock, 1969, 1985, 1991). For example, Jungnickel (1990), in a doctoral dissertation proposal about research productivity among faculty in pharmacy schools, presented a complex visual model, as shown in Figure 3.3. Jungnickel asked what factors influence a faculty member's scholarly research performance. After identifying these factors in the literature, he adapted a theoretical framework found in nursing research (Megel, Langston, & Creswell, 1987) and developed a visual model portraying the relationship among these factors, following the rules for constructing a model introduced earlier. He listed the independent variables on the far left, the intervening variables in the middle, and the dependent variables on the right. The direction of influence flowed from the left to the right, and he used plus and minus signs to indicate the hypothesized direction.

Placement of Quantitative Theories

In quantitative studies, one uses theory deductively and places it toward the beginning of the proposed study. With the objective of testing or verifying a theory rather than developing it, the researcher advances a theory, collects data to test it, and reflects on its confirmation or disconfirmation by the results. The theory becomes a framework for the entire study, an organizing model for the research questions or hypotheses and for the data collection procedure. The deductive model of thinking used in a quantitative study is shown in Figure 3.4. The researcher tests or verifies a theory by examining hypotheses or questions derived from it. These hypotheses or questions contain variables (or constructs) that the researcher needs to define. Alternatively, an acceptable definition might be found in the literature. From here, the investigator locates an instrument to use in measuring or observing attitudes or behaviors of participants in a study. Then the investigator collects scores on these instruments to confirm or disconfirm the theory.

Figure 3.3 A Visual Model of a Theory of Faculty Scholarly Performance

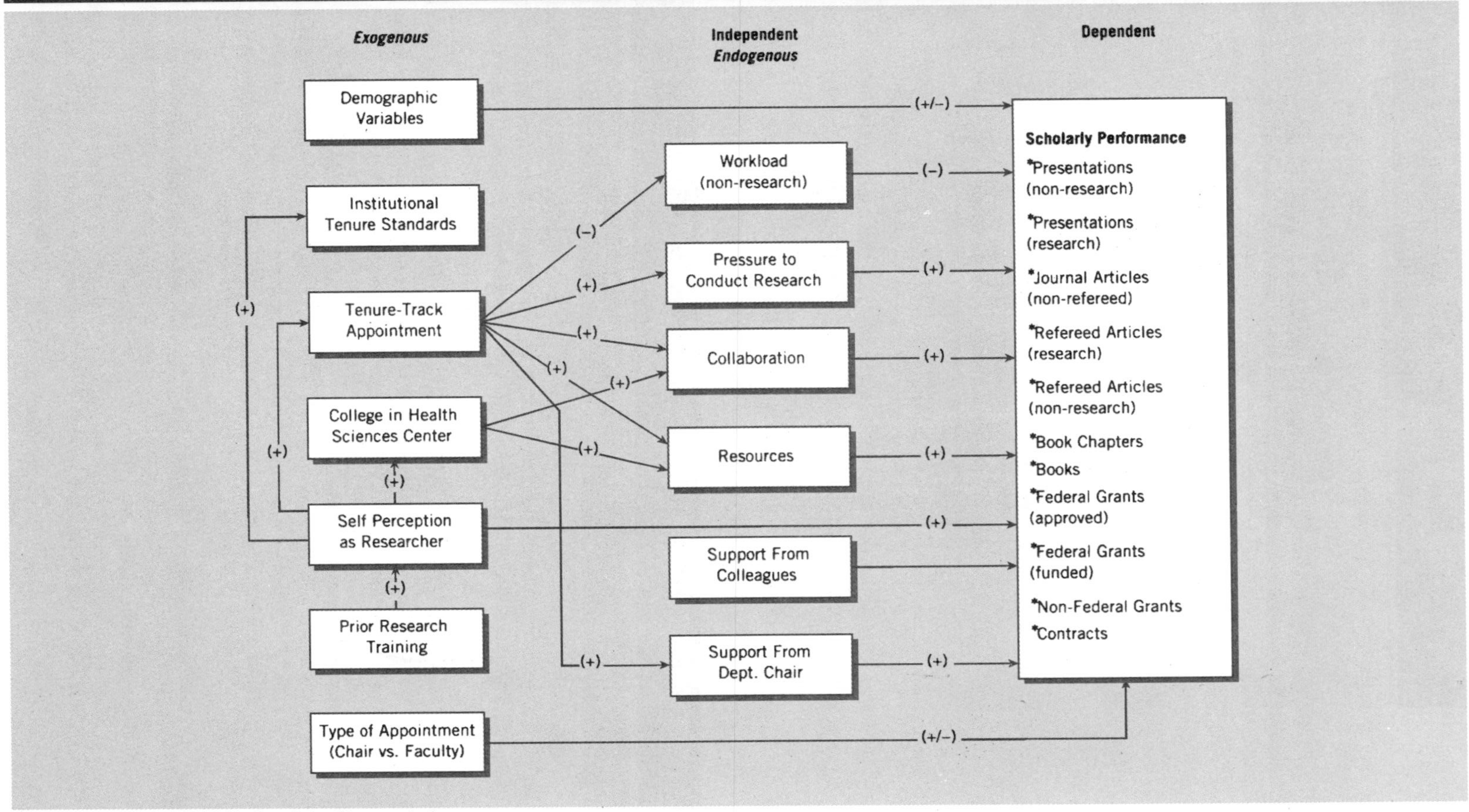

Source: Jungnickel (1990). Reprint with permission.

Figure 3.4 The Deductive Approach Typically Used in Quantitative Research

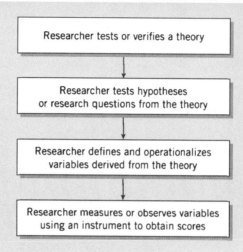

This deductive approach to research in the quantitative approach has implications for the *placement of a theory* in a quantitative research study (see Table 3.1).

A general guide is to introduce the theory early in a plan or study: in the introduction, in the literature review section, immediately after hypotheses

Table 3.1 Options for Placing Theory in a Quantitative Study

Placement	Advantages	Disadvantages
In the introduction	As an approach often found in journal articles, it will be familiar to readers. It conveys a deductive approach.	It is difficult for a reader to isolate and separate theory base from other components of the research process (e.g., with the methods).
In the literature review	Theories are found in the literature, and their inclusion in a literature review is a logical extension or part of the literature.	It is difficult for a reader to see the theory in isolation from topics being reviewed in the literature.
After hypotheses or research questions as a rationale	The theory discussion is a logical extension of hypotheses or research questions because it explains how and why variables are related.	A writer may include a theoretical rationale after hypotheses and questions and leave out an extended discussion about the origin and rationale for the use of the theory.
In a separate section	This approach clearly separates the theory from other components of the research process, and it enables a reader to better identify and to understand the theory base for the study.	The theory discussion stands in isolation from other components of the research process (e.g., the questions or the methods) and, as such, a reader may not easily connect it with other components of the research process.

or research questions (as a rationale for the connections among the variables), or in a separate section of the study. Each placement has its advantages and disadvantages.

Here is a **research tip**: We write the theory into a separate section in a research proposal so that readers can clearly identify the theory from other components. Such a separate passage provides a complete explication of the theory section, its use, and how it relates to the study.

Writing a Quantitative Theoretical Perspective

Using these ideas, the following presents a model for writing a quantitative theoretical perspective section into a research plan. Assume that the task is to identify a theory that explains the relationship between independent and dependent variables.

1. Look in the discipline-based literature for a theory. If the unit of analysis for variables is an individual, look in the psychology literature; to study groups or organizations, look in the sociological literature. If the project examines individuals and groups, consider the social psychology literature. Of course, theories from other disciplines may be useful, too (e.g., to study an economic issue, the theory may be found in economics).

2. Examine also prior studies that address the topic or a closely related topic. What theories did the authors use? Limit the number of theories and try to identify *one overarching theory* that explains the central hypothesis or major research question.

3. As mentioned earlier, ask the rainbow question that bridges the independent and dependent variables: What explains why the independent variable(s) would influence the dependent variables?

4. Script out the theory section. Follow these lead sentences: "The theory that I will use is _____ (name the theory). It was developed by _____ (identify the origin, source, or developer of the theory), and it was used to study _____ (identify the topics where one finds the theory being applied). This theory indicates that _____ (identify the propositions or hypotheses in the theory). As applied to my study, this theory holds that I would expect my independent variable(s) _____ (state independent variables) to influence or explain the dependent variable(s) _____ (state dependent variables) because _____ (provide a rationale based on the logic of the theory)."

Thus, the topics to include in a quantitative theory discussion are the theory to be used, its central hypotheses or propositions, information about past use of the theory and its application, and statements that reflect how it relates to a proposed study. Example 3.1, which contains a passage by Crutchfield (1986) from her dissertation, illustrates the use of this model.

Example 3.1   A Quantitative Theory Section

Crutchfield (1986) wrote a doctoral dissertation titled *Locus of Control, Interpersonal Trust, and Scholarly Productivity*. Surveying nursing educators, her intent was to determine if locus of control and interpersonal trust affected the levels of publications of the faculty. Her dissertation included a separate section in the introductory chapter titled "Theoretical Perspective," which follows. It includes these points:

- The theory she planned to use

- The central hypotheses of the theory

- Information about who has used the theory and its applicability

- An adaptation of the theory to variables in her study using if-then logic

We have added annotations in italics to mark key passages.

Theoretical Perspective

In formulation of a theoretical perspective for studying the scholarly productivity of faculty, social learning theory provides a useful prototype. This conception of behavior attempts to achieve a balanced synthesis of cognitive psychology with the principles of behavior modification (Bower & Hilgard, 1981). Basically, this unified theoretical framework "approaches the explanation of human behavior in terms of a continuous (reciprocal) interaction between cognitive, behavioral, and environmental determinants" (Bandura, 1977, p. vii). *[Author identifies the theory for the study.]*

While social learning theory accepts the application of reinforcements such as shaping principles, it tends to see the role of rewards as both conveying information about the optimal response and providing incentive motivation for a given act because of the anticipated reward. In addition, the learning principles of this theory place special emphasis on the important roles played by vicarious, symbolic, and self-regulating processes (Bandura, 1971).

Social learning theory not only deals with learning, but also seeks to describe how a group of social and personal competencies (so called personality) could evolve out of social conditions within which the learning occurs. It also addresses techniques of personality assessment (Mischel, 1968), and behavior modification in clinical and educational settings (Bandura, 1977; Bower & Hilgard, 1981; Rotter, 1954). *[Author describes social learning theory.]*

Further, the principles of social learning theory have been applied to a wide range of social behavior such as competitiveness, aggressiveness, sex roles, deviance, and pathological behavior (Bandura & Walters, 1963; Bandura, 1977; Mischel, 1968; Miller & Dollard, 1941; Rotter, 1954; Staats, 1975). *[Author describes the use of the theory.]*

Explaining social learning theory, Rotter (1954) indicated that four classes of variables must be considered: behavior, expectancies, reinforcement, and psychological situations. A general formula for behavior was proposed which states: "the potential for a behavior to occur in any specific psychological situation is the function of the expectancy that the behavior will lead to a particular reinforcement in that situation and the value of that reinforcement" (Rotter, 1975, p. 57).

Expectancy within the formula refers to the perceived degree of certainty (or probability) that a causal relationship generally exists between behavior and rewards. This construct of generalized expectancy has been defined as internal locus of control when an individual believes that reinforcements are a function of specific behavior, or as external locus of control when the effects are attributed to luck, fate, or powerful others. The perceptions of causal relationships need not be absolute positions, but rather tend to vary in degree along a continuum depending upon previous experiences and situational complexities (Rotter, 1966). *[Author explains variables in the theory.]*

In the application of social learning theory to this study of scholarly productivity, the four classes of variables identified by Rotter (1954) will be defined in the following manner.

1. Scholarly productivity is the desired behavior or activity.

2. Locus of control is the generalized expectancy that rewards are or are not dependent upon specific behaviors.

3. Reinforcements are the rewards from scholarly work and the value attached to these rewards.

4. The educational institution is the psychological situation which furnishes many of the rewards for scholarly productivity.

With these specific variables, the formula for behavior which was developed by Rotter (1975) would be adapted to read: The potential for scholarly behavior to occur within an educational institution is a function of the expectancy that this activity will lead to specific rewards and of the value that the faculty member places on these rewards. In addition, the interaction of interpersonal trust with locus of control must be considered in relation to the expectancy of attaining rewards through behaviors (Rotter, 1967). Finally, certain characteristics, such as educational preparation, chronological age, post-doctoral fellowships, tenure, or full-time versus part-time employment may be associated with the scholarly productivity of nurse faculty in a manner similar to that seen within other disciplines. *[Author applied the concepts to her study.]*

The following statement represents the underlying logic for designing and conducting this study. If faculty believe that: (a) their efforts and actions in producing scholarly works will lead to rewards (locus of control), (b) others can be relied upon to follow through on their promises (interpersonal trust), (c) the rewards for scholarly activity are worthwhile (reward values), and (d) the rewards are available within their discipline or institution (institutional setting), then they will attain high levels of scholarly productivity (pp. 12–16). *[Author concluded with the if-then logic to relate the independent variables to the dependent variables.]*

Qualitative Theory Use

Variation in Theory Use in Qualitative Research

Qualitative inquirers use theory in their studies in several ways. First, much like in quantitative research, it is used as a broad explanation for behavior and attitudes, and it may be complete with variables, constructs, and hypotheses. For example, ethnographers employ cultural themes or aspects of culture to study in their qualitative projects, such as social control, language, stability and change, or social organization, such as kinship or families (see Wolcott's 2008 discussion about texts that address cultural topics in anthropology). Themes in this context provide a ready-made series of hypotheses to be tested from the literature. Although researchers might not refer to them as theories, they provide broad explanations that anthropologists use to study the culture-sharing behavior and attitudes of people. This approach is popular in qualitative health science research in which investigators begin with a theoretical or conceptual model, such as the adoption of health practices or a quality of life theoretical orientation.

Second, researchers increasingly use a **theoretical lens or perspective in qualitative research**, which provides an overall orienting lens for the study of questions of gender, class, and race (or other issues of marginalized groups). This lens becomes a transformative perspective that shapes the types of questions asked, informs how data are collected and analyzed, and provides a call for action or change. Qualitative research of the 1980s underwent a transformation to broaden its scope of inquiry to include these theoretical lenses. They guide the researchers as to what issues are important to examine (e.g., marginalization, empowerment, oppression, power) and the people who need to be studied (e.g., women, low economic social status, ethnic and racial groups, sexual orientation, disability). They also indicate how the researcher positions himself or herself in the qualitative study (e.g., up front or biased from personal, cultural, and historical contexts) and how the final written accounts need to be written (e.g., without further marginalizing individuals, by collaborating with participants), and recommendations for changes to improve lives and society. In critical ethnography studies, for example, researchers begin with a theory that informs their studies. This causal theory might be one of emancipation or repression (Thomas, 1993).

Some of these qualitative theoretical perspectives available to the researcher are as follows:

- *Feminist perspectives* view as problematic women's diverse situations and the institutions that frame those situations. Research topics may include policy issues related to realizing social justice for women in specific contexts or knowledge about oppressive situations for women (Olesen, 2000).

- *Racialized discourses* raise important questions about the control and production of knowledge, particularly about people and communities of color (Ladson-Billings, 2000).

- *Critical theory* perspectives are concerned with empowering human beings to transcend the constraints placed on them by race, class, and gender (Fay, 1987).

- *Queer theory*—a term used in this literature—focuses on individuals calling themselves lesbians, gays, bisexuals, or transgendered people. The research using this approach does not objectify individuals, is concerned with cultural and political means, and conveys the voices and experiences of individuals who have been suppressed (Gamson, 2000).

- *Disability inquiry* addresses understanding this population's sociocultural perspectives allowing them to take control over their lives rather than a biological understanding of disability (Mertens, 2009).

Rossman and Rallis (2012) captured the sense of theory as critical and postmodern perspectives in qualitative inquiry:

> As the 20th century draws to a close, traditional social science has come under increasing scrutiny and attack as those espousing critical and postmodern perspectives challenge objectivist assumptions and traditional norms for the conduct of research. The critical tradition is alive and well in the social sciences. Postmodernists reject the notion that knowledge is definite and univocal. Central to this attack are four interrelated assertions: (a) Research fundamentally involves issues of power; (b) the research report is not transparent but rather it is authored by a raced, gendered, classed, and politically oriented individual; (c) race, class, and gender (the canonical triumvirate to which we would add sexual orientation, able-bodiedness, and first language, among others) are crucial for understanding experience; and (d) historically, traditional research has silenced members of oppressed and marginalized groups. (p. 91)

Third, distinct from this theoretical orientation are qualitative studies in which theory (or some other broad explanation) becomes the *end point*. It is an inductive process of building from the data to broad themes to a generalized model or theory (see Punch, 2014). The logic of this inductive approach is shown in Figure 3.5.

The researcher begins by gathering detailed information from participants and then forms this information into categories or themes. These themes are developed into broad patterns, theories, or generalizations that are then compared with personal experiences or with existing literature on the topic.

The development of themes and categories into patterns, theories, or generalizations suggests varied end points for qualitative studies. For example, in case study research, Stake (1995) referred to an assertion as a *propositional generalization*—the researcher's summary of interpretations and claims—to which is added the researcher's own personal experiences, called "naturalistic generalizations" (p. 86). As another example, grounded theory provides a different end point. Inquirers hope to discover and advance a theory that is grounded in information from participants (Strauss & Corbin, 1998). Lincoln and Guba (1985) referred to "pattern theories" as explanations that develop during naturalistic or qualitative research. Rather than the deductive form found in quantitative studies, these pattern theories or generalizations represent interconnected thoughts or parts linked to a whole.

Fourth and finally, some qualitative studies *do not employ any explicit theory*. However, the case can be made that no qualitative study begins from pure observation and that prior conceptual structure composed of theory and method provides the starting point for all observations (Schwandt, 2014). Still, one sees qualitative studies that contain no *explicit* theoretical orientation, such as in phenomenology, in which inquirers attempt to build the essence of experience from participants (e.g., see Riemen, 1986). In these studies, the inquirer constructs a rich, detailed description of a central phenomenon.

Our **research tips** on theory use in a qualitative proposal are as follows:

- Decide if theory is to be used in the qualitative proposal.

- If it is used, then identify how the theory will be used in the study, such as an up-front explanation, as an end point, or as a transformative-advocacy lens.

- Locate the theory in the proposal early in the study or at the end.

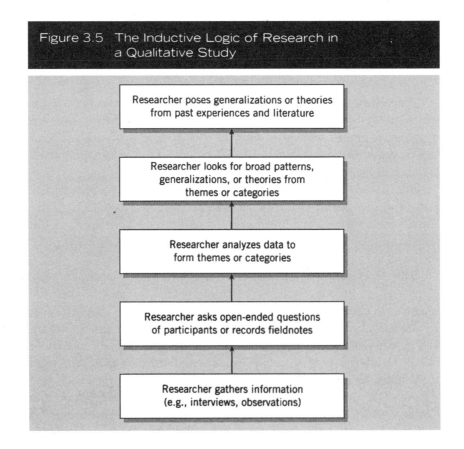

Figure 3.5   The Inductive Logic of Research in a Qualitative Study

Locating the Theory in Qualitative Research

How theory is used affects its placement in a qualitative study. In those studies with a cultural theme or a theoretical lens, the theory occurs in the opening passages of the study (see Example 3.2). Consistent with the emerging design of qualitative inquiry, the theory may appear at the beginning and be modified or adjusted based on participant views. Even in the most theory-oriented qualitative design, such as critical ethnography, Lather (1986) qualified the use of theory:

> Building empirically grounded theory requires a reciprocal relationship between data and theory. Data must be allowed to generate propositions in a dialectical manner that permits use of *a priori* theoretical frameworks, but which keeps a particular framework from becoming the container into which the data must be poured. (p. 267)

Example 3.2 A Theory Early in a Qualitative Study

Murguia, Padilla, and Pavel (1991) studied the integration of 24 Hispanic and Native American students into the social system of a college campus. They were curious about how ethnicity influenced social integration, and they began by relating the participants' experiences to a theoretical model, the Tinto model of social integration. They felt that the model had been "incompletely conceptualized and, as a consequence, only imprecisely understood and measured" (p. 433).

Thus, the model was not being tested, as one would find in a quantitative project, but modified. At the end of the study, the authors refined Tinto's model and advanced their modification that described how ethnicity functions. In contrast to this approach, in qualitative studies with an end point of a theory (e.g., a grounded theory), a pattern, or a generalization, the theory emerges at the end of the study. This theory might be presented as a logic diagram, a visual representation of relationships among concepts.

As Example 3.3 shows, we developed a visual model that interrelated variables, derived this model inductively from informant comments, and placed the model at the end of the study, where the central propositions in it could be contrasted with the existing theories and literature.

Mixed Methods Theory Use

Theory use in mixed methods studies may include using theory deductively, in quantitative theory testing and validity, or in using it inductively as in an emerging qualitative theory or pattern. In addition, there are several

Example 3.3 A Theory at the End of a Qualitative Study

Using a national database of 33 interviews with academic department chairpersons, we (Creswell & Brown, 1992) developed a grounded theory interrelating variables (or categories) of chair influence on scholarly performance of faculty. The theory section came into the article as the last section, where we presented a visual model of the theory developed inductively from categories of information supplied by interviewees. In addition, we also advanced directional hypotheses that logically followed from the model. Moreover, in the section on the model and the hypotheses, we compared the results from participants with results from other studies and the theoretical speculations in the literature. For example, we stated the following:

> This proposition and its sub-propositions represent unusual, even contrary evidence, to our expectations. Contrary to proposition 2.1, we expected that the career stages would be similar not in type of issue but in the range of issues. Instead we found that the issues for post-tenure faculty covered almost all the possible problems on the list. Why were the tenured faculty's needs more extensive than non-tenured faculty? The research productivity literature suggests that one's research performance does not decline with the award of tenure (Holley 1977). Perhaps diffuse career goals of post-tenure faculty expand the possibilities for "types" of issues. In any case, this sub-proposition focuses attention on the understudied career group that Furniss (1981) reminds us of needs to be examined in more detail (p. 58).

unique ways that theory is incorporated into a mixed methods study in which researchers collect, analyze, and integrate both quantitative and qualitative data using diverse mixed methods designs. This framework has taken two forms: (a) the use of a social science framework and (b) the use of a participatory–social justice framework. Both of these forms have emerged in the mixed methods literature over the past 5 to 10 years (see Creswell & Plano Clark, 2011).

Social Science Theory Use

A social science theory can become an overarching framework for mixed methods research. This social science theory may be drawn from diverse theories found in the social sciences, such as leadership, economics, political science, marketing, behavioral change, adoption or diffusion, or any number of social science theories. It may be presented as a literature review, as a conceptual model, or as a theory that helps to explain what the researcher seeks to find in a study.

The incorporation of a social science theory into mixed methods uses the procedures identified earlier in this chapter for inclusion of a quantitative theory-use in a study. The key points of this theory-use are as follows:

- Place the theory (model or conceptual framework) at the beginning of the article as an *a priori* framework to guide the questions/ hypotheses in the study.

- Write about the theory by first advancing the name of the theory to be used followed by a description of how it informs the quantitative and qualitative components of a mixed methods study. It should at least explain the major relationship of variables in the study. Discuss the studies that have used the theory, especially studies that relate to the topic being examined in the present study.

- Include a diagram of the theory that indicates the direction of the probable causal links in the theory and the major concepts or variables in the theory.

- Have the theory provide a framework for both the quantitative and the qualitative data collection efforts in the study.

- Return to the theory at the end of the study to review how it informed the findings and the results and compared with the use of the theory in other studies.

An example of a social science theory can be found in a mixed methods study about chronic pain and its management through learned resourcefulness by Kennett, O'Hagan, and Cezer (2008). These authors presented a mixed methods study to understand how learned resourcefulness empowers individuals. In this study, they gathered quantitative measures on Rosenbaum's Self-Control Schedule (SCS) and collected interviews with patients coping with chronic pain. In the opening paragraph of their study, they advanced the purpose:

> Taking a critical realist perspective informed by Rosenbaum's (1990, 2000) model of self-control, we combine a quantitative measure of learned resourcefulness with a qualitative text-based analysis to characterize the processes that come into play in the self-management of pain for high—and low—resourceful clients following a multimodel treatment-based pain program. (p. 318)

Following this passage, they then advanced the model of learned resourcefulness that guided their study. They introduced the major components of Rosenbaum's model. This was then followed by the research literature on resourcefulness as an important predictor of adopting healthy behavior and a discussion of one of Rosenbaum's experiments relating resourcefulness to coping with pain. The authors then discussed the factors of the model leading to self-control, such as factors related to process-regulating cognitions (e.g., supporting family and friends), coping strategies (e.g., ability to cope with pain such as diverting attention and reinterpreting pain), and staying in (or dropping out of) programs. The authors at this point might have drawn a diagram of the theory to be explicit about factors that influenced self-control. They provided next, however, a series of questions drawn from Rosenbaum's model and the literature that guided their study examining the impact of a cognitive-behavioral chronic pain management program on self-management and how resourcefulness and a sense of self-directedness influence self-management skills for chronic pain. Toward the end of the article, they revisited the factors leading to self-management and proposed a diagram of the most salient factors.

Participatory–Social Justice Theory Use

The use and acceptability of participatory–social justice theories in mixed methods research have been growing in the last decade. Undoubtedly, the impetus for this has been the work of Mertens (2003, 2009), who has not only conveyed the major purpose of this theory but also how it might be incorporated into the general research process and mixed methods. Both participatory and social justice frameworks have the effect of involving participants collaboratively in the research, bringing about change to address inequities, and helping underrepresented groups and populations. A number of empirical articles have appeared in the *Journal of Mixed Methods Research* advancing this theory-use in mixed methods, including a study of women's interest in science (Buck, Cook, Quigley, Eastwood, & Lucas, 2009) and a study of women's social capital (Hodgkin, 2008). A paper by Sweetman (2008) identified 34 mixed methods studies that utilized a transformative framework. Then in 2010, Sweetman, Badiee, and Creswell (2010) discussed transformative criteria—drawing on Mertens (2003, 2009)—that might be incorporated into mixed methods studies and surveyed 13 studies that included elements of the criteria.

The literature is growing on the use of this theoretical orientation framework and mixed methods research. It seems especially applicable to the study of community health issues and the study of marginalized groups, wherever they might appear in the world. Undergirding this theoretical orientation would be a broader philosophical stance, the transformative framework, as discussed in Chapter 1. In Chapter 1, we discussed the transformative worldview as one of the four primary worldviews that would inform quantitative, qualitative, and mixed methods research. Indeed, one could question whether the transformative framework lies at a broad, philosophical worldview level or at a narrower, more theoretical level informing what one might learn and explain in a study. Two issues have dominated the discussion of using a transformative framework in mixed methods: (a) What is a transformative framework? and (b) How would a mixed methods researcher incorporate it into a rigorous, sophisticated mixed methods study? Here we discuss it as a theoretical framework that can surround and inform a mixed methods project.

A transformative mixed methods framework (also called the transformative research paradigm; Mertens, 2009) is a set of assumptions and procedures used in research. Common themes are as follows:

- Underlying assumptions that rely on ethical stances of inclusion and challenging oppressive social structures.

- An entry process into the community that is designed to build trust and make goals and strategies transparent.

- Dissemination of findings in ways that encourage use of the results to enhance social justice and human rights. (p. 5)

Further, the transformative approach applies to people who experience discrimination and oppression, including (but not limited to) race/ethnicity, disability, immigrant status, political conflicts, sexual orientation, poverty, gender, and age (Mertens, 2010).

How this framework is integrated into a mixed methods study is still evolving, but Mertens (2003) identified several elements of the framework as they relate to the steps in the process of research. These elements are mentioned in Box 3.1. Reading through these questions, one gains a sense of the importance of studying issues of discrimination and oppression and of recognizing diversity among study participants. These questions also address treating individuals respectfully through gathering and communicating data collection and through reporting results that lead to changes in social processes and relationships.

These questions were further operationalized as a set of 10 criteria (and questions) that one might use to evaluate the inclusion of transformative theoretical thinking into a mixed methods study (Sweetman et al., 2010):

1. Did the authors openly reference a problem in a community of concern?

2. Did the authors openly declare a theoretical lens?

3. Were the research questions written with an advocacy lens?

4. Did the literature review include discussions of diversity and oppression?

5. Did authors discuss appropriate labeling of the participants?

6. Did the data collection and outcomes benefit the community?

7. Did the participants initiate the research, and/or were they actively engaged in the project?

8. Did the results elucidate power relationships?

9. Did the results facilitate social change?

10. Did the authors explicitly state use of a transformative framework?

Box 3.1

Transformative-Emancipatory Questions for Mixed Methods Researchers Throughout the Research Process

Defining the Problem and Searching the Literature

- Did you deliberately search the literature for concerns of diverse groups and issues of discrimination and oppression?

- Did the problem definition arise from the community of concern?

- Did your mixed methods approach arise from spending quality time with these communities (i.e., building trust? using an appropriate theoretical framework other than a deficit model? developing balanced—positive and negative— questions? developing questions that lead to transformative answers, such as questions focused on authority and relations of power in institutions and communities?)?

Identifying the Research Design

- Does your research design deny treatment to any groups and respect ethical considerations of participants?

Identifying Data Sources and Selecting Participants

- Are the participants of groups associated with discrimination and oppression?

- Are the participants appropriately labeled?

- Is there recognition of diversity within the target population?

- What can be done to improve the inclusiveness of the sample to increase the probability that traditionally marginalized groups are adequately and accurately represented?

Identifying or Constructing Data Collection Instruments and Methods

- Will the data collection process and outcomes benefit the community being studied?

- Will the research findings be credible to that community?

- Will communication with that community be effective?

- Will the data collection open up avenues for participation in the social change process?

Analyzing, Interpreting, and Reporting and Using Results

- Will the results raise new hypotheses?

- Will the research examine subgroups (i.e., multilevel analyses) to analyze the differential impact on diverse groups?

- Will the results help understand and elucidate power relationships?

- Will the results facilitate social change?

Source: Adapted from Mertens (2003). Reprinted with permission.

These are high standards for any publication, and the review of 13 studies by Sweetman and colleagues (2010) showed an uneven inclusion of the 10 criteria in mixed methods studies. Only 2 of the 13 studies explicitly referred to their framework as "transformative." More appropriate would be to consider these frameworks as theoretical lenses that might be applied within a mixed methods study. They can be incorporated by

- Indicating in the opening passages of a study that a framework (e.g., feminist, participatory) is being used.

- Mentioning this framework early in a study—that it relates to a marginalized or underrepresented community and specific issues faced by that community (e.g., oppression, power).

- Lodging this framework within a theoretical body of literature, such as feminist literature or racial literature.

- Involving the community of interest in the process of research (e.g., in the data collection).

- Taking a stand with the research question—advocating in its orientation (e.g., inequality does exist and the research will set out to substantiate it).

- Advancing in the design the collection, analysis, and integration of both quantitative and qualitative methods within the transformative framework.

- Talking about your experiences as a researcher and how your experiences and background shapes your understanding of the participants and issues under study.

- Ending the study by advocating for change to help the population under study and the issue.

One of the best ways to learn how to incorporate a transformative framework into a mixed methods study is to examine published journal articles and study how it is being incorporated into the process of research. Example 3.4 illustrates good use of the transformative framework.

Example 3.4 Theory in a Feminist Mixed Methods Study

An article published in the *Journal of Mixed Methods Research* by Hodgkin (2008) illustrates the use of a feminist emancipatory lens in a mixed methods study. Hodgkin examined if men and women have different social capital profiles and why women participated more in social and community activities than in civic activities in Australia. Her stated aim of the study was to "demonstrate the use of mixed methods in feminist research" (p. 296). Toward the beginning of her article, she discussed the feminist research component of

(Continued)

her study, such as drawing attention to the lack of gender focus in studies of social capital, using qualitative and quantitative research to give voice to women's experiences, and locating her study within the transformative paradigm. Through her quantitative results, she found a difference in social capital for men and women, and then she explored in a second phase the viewpoints of women, noting women's involvement in informal social participation and community participation. Participation in civic levels of involvement were low, and themes resulting from women were related to wanting to be a "good mother," wanting to avoid social isolation, and wanting to be an active citizen.

SUMMARY

Theory has a place in quantitative, qualitative, and mixed methods research. Researchers use theory in a quantitative study to provide an explanation or prediction about the relationship among variables in the study. Thus, it is essential to have grounding in the nature and use of variables as they form research questions and hypotheses. A theory explains how and why the variables are related, acting as a bridge between or among the variables. Theory may be broad or narrow in scope, and researchers state their theories in several ways, such as a series of hypotheses, if-then logic statements, or visual models. Using theories deductively, investigators advance them at the beginning of the study in the literature review. They also include them with the hypotheses or research questions or place them in a separate section. A script can help design the theory section for a research proposal.

In qualitative research, inquirers employ theory as a broad explanation, much like in quantitative research, such as in ethnographies. It may also be a theoretical lens or perspective that raises questions related to gender, class, race, or some combination of these. Theory also appears as an end point of a qualitative study, a generated theory, a pattern, or a generalization that emerges inductively from data collection and analysis. Grounded theorists, for example, generate a theory grounded in the views of participants and place it as the conclusion of their studies. Some qualitative studies do not include an explicit theory and present descriptive research of the central phenomenon.

Mixed methods researchers use theory as a framework informing many aspects of design as they collect, analyze, and interpret quantitative and qualitative data. This framework takes two forms: (a) a social science framework or (b) a participatory–social justice framework. A social science framework is placed at the beginning of studies, provides an explanation for the quantitative and (perhaps) qualitative components (e.g., data collection, analysis, interpretation) of a study, and informs the findings and results. A participatory–social justice theory in mixed methods is a framework that has emerged in recent years. It is a lens for looking at a problem recognizing the non-neutrality of knowledge, the pervasive influence of human interests, and issues such as power and social relationships. A mixed methods study helps to improve people and society. Groups often helped by this research are feminists; diverse ethnic/racial groups; people with disabilities; and lesbian, gay, bisexual, transgendered, and queer communities. Mixed methods researchers incorporate this framework into multiple stages of the research process, such as the introduction, the research questions, the data collection, and an interpretation that calls for change. Criteria have been developed for how to incorporate a participatory–social justice framework into a mixed methods study.

Writing Exercises

1. Write a theoretical perspective section for your research plan following the script for a quantitative theory discussion presented in this chapter.

2. For a quantitative proposal you are planning, draw a visual model of the variables in the theory using the procedures for causal model design advanced in this chapter.

3. Locate qualitative journal articles that (a) use an a priori theory that is modified during the process of research, (b) generate or develop a theory at the end of the study, and (c) represent descriptive research without the use of an explicit theoretical model.

4. Locate a mixed methods study that uses a theoretical lens, such as a feminist, ethnic/racial, or class perspective. Identify specifically how the lens shapes the steps taken in the research process, using Box 3.1 as a guide.

Additional Readings

Bachman, R. D., & Schutt, R. K. (2017). *Fundamentals of research in criminology and criminal justice* (4th ed.). Los Angeles, CA: Sage.

In their book, Ronet Bachman and Russell Schutt include an easy-to-understand chapter on causation and experimentation. They discuss the meaning of causation, the criteria for achieving it, and how to use this information to come to causal conclusions. Especially useful is their discussion of the conditions necessary for determining causality.

Blalock, H. (1991). Are there any constructive alternatives to causal modeling? *Sociological Methodology, 21*, 325–335.

For years we have used the ideas of Herbert Blalock to construct our meaning of causation in social research. In this thoughtful essay, Blalock stated that correlational methods do not equate to causation. He talked about the potential of "lagged" effects in understanding causation, variables that emerge over time and that can be difficult to specify. He also called for making assumptions explicit in causal mechanisms in experimental designs. With these points in mind, Blalock called for the use of more complex causal models to test important questions in social research.

Flinders, D. J., & Mills, G. E. (Eds.). (1993). *Theory and concepts in qualitative research: Perspectives from the field.* New York: Columbia University, Teachers College Press.

David Flinders and Geoffrey Mills have edited a book about perspectives from the field—"theory at work"—as described by different qualitative researchers. The chapters illustrate little consensus about defining theory and whether it is a vice or virtue. Further, theory operates at many levels in research, such as formal theories, epistemological theories, methodological theories, and meta-theories. Given this diversity, it is best to see actual theory at work in qualitative studies, and this volume illustrates practice from critical, personal, formal, and educational criticism.

Mertens, D. M. (2003). Mixed methods and the politics of human research: The transformative-emancipatory perspective. In A. Tashakkori & C. Teddlie (Eds.), *Handbook of mixed methods in social and behavioral research* (pp. 135–164). Thousand Oaks, CA: Sage.

Donna Mertens recognizes that historically, research methods have not concerned themselves with the issues of the politics of human research and social justice. Her chapter explores the transformative-emancipatory paradigm of research as a framework or lens for mixed methods research as it has emerged from scholars from diverse ethnic/racial groups, people with disabilities, and feminists. A unique aspect of her chapter is how she weaves together this paradigm of thinking and the steps in the process of conducting mixed methods research.

Thomas, G. (1997). What's the use of theory? *Harvard Educational Review, 67*(1), 75–104.

Gary Thomas presents a reasoned critique of the use of theory in educational inquiry. He notes the various definitions of theory and maps out four broad uses of theory: (a) as thinking and reflection, (b) as tighter or looser hypotheses, (c) as explanations for adding to knowledge in different fields, and (d) as formally expressed statements in science. Having noted these uses, he then embraces the thesis that theory unnecessarily structures and constrains thought. Instead, ideas should be in a constant flux and should be "ad hocery," as characterized by Toffler.

---

⑤SAGE edge™

https://edge.sagepub.com/creswellrd5e

Students and instructors, please visit the companion website for videos featuring John W. Creswell, full-text SAGE journal articles, quizzes and activities, plus additional tools for research design.

Writing Strategies and Ethical Considerations

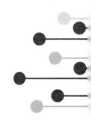

Before designing a proposal, it is important to have an idea of the general structure or outline of the topics and their order. The structure will differ depending on whether you write a quantitative, qualitative, or a mixed methods project. Another general consideration is to be aware of good writing practices that will help to ensure a consistent and highly readable proposal (or research project). Throughout the project, it is important to engage in ethical practices and to anticipate the ethical issues prior to the study that will likely arise. This chapter provides guidance for the overall structure of proposals or projects, writing practices that make projects easy to read, and ethical issues that need to be anticipated in research studies.

Writing the Proposal

Arguments Presented in a Proposal

It is helpful to consider early in planning the study the major points that need to be addressed in a proposal. These points—or topics—all need to be interconnected to provide a cohesive picture of the entire project. For us, these topics seem to span all proposals, whether the project is qualitative, quantitative, or mixed methods. We think that a good place to start is by examining Maxwell's (2013) list of the core arguments that need to be advanced in any proposal. We will summarize them in our own words:

1. What do readers need to better understand your topic?

2. What do readers need to know about your topic?

3. What do you propose to study?

4. What is the setting, and who are the people you will study?

5. What methods do you plan to use to collect data?

6. How will you analyze the data?

7. How will you validate your findings?

8. What ethical issues will your study present?

9. What do preliminary results show about the practicability and value of the proposed study?

These nine questions, if adequately addressed in one section for each question, constitute the foundation of good research, and they could provide the overall structure for a proposal. The inclusion of validating findings, ethical considerations (to be addressed shortly), the need for preliminary results, and early evidence of practical significance focus a reader's attention on key elements often overlooked in discussions about proposed projects.

Format for a Qualitative Proposal

Beyond these nine questions, it is also helpful to have an overall outline or general structure for topics that will be included in a proposal for a study. Unquestionably, in qualitative research, no one structure for a qualitative proposal prevails. We do think, however, that a couple of general outlines would be helpful, especially for the student who has never written a thesis or dissertation project. Here we propose two alternative models. Example 4.1 is drawn from a constructivist/interpretivist perspective whereas Example 4.2 is based more on a participatory–social justice model of qualitative research.

Example 4.1   A Qualitative Constructivist/Interpretivist Format

Introduction
    Statement of the problem (including existing literature about the problem, deficiencies in the literature, and relevance of study for audiences)
        Purpose of the study
        The research questions

Procedures
    Philosophical assumptions or worldview of qualitative research
    Qualitative design (e.g., ethnography, case study)
        Role of the researcher
        Data collection procedures

Data analysis procedures
Strategies for validating findings
Proposed narrative structure of the study
Anticipated ethical issues

Preliminary pilot findings (if available)

Expected impact and significance of study

References

Appendixes: Interview questions, observational forms, timeline, proposed budget, a summary of the proposed content of each chapter in the final study

In this example, the writer includes introduction, procedures, ethical issues, preliminary findings and expected impact of the study. A separate section reviewing the literature may be included, but it is optional, as discussed in Chapter 3. Several appendixes may seem unusual. Developing a timeline for the study and presenting a proposed budget provide useful information to committees, although these sections would be highly recommended, but optional in proposals. Also, because the number and type of chapters in qualitative research is highly variable, a summary of the proposed content of each chapter in the final study would be useful.

Example 4.2 A Qualitative Participatory–Social Justice Format

Introduction
   Statement of the problem (including power, oppression, discrimination, need to develop rapport with community, etc.; issue addressed; existing literature about the problem; deficiencies in the literature; and relevance of the study for audiences)
      Purpose of the study
      The research questions

Procedures
   Philosophical assumptions or worldview
   Qualitative research strategy
   Role of the researcher
   Data collection procedures (including the collaborative approaches used with participants)

Data analysis procedures
Strategies for validating findings
Proposed narrative structure
Anticipated ethical issues

Preliminary pilot findings (if available)

Significance of the study and transformative changes likely to occur

References

Appendixes: Interview questions, observational forms, timeline, proposed budget, and a summary of proposed chapters for the final study

This format is similar to the constructivist/interpretivist format except that the inquirer identifies a specific participatory–social justice issue being explored in the study (e.g., oppression, discrimination, community involvement), advances a collaborative form of data collection, and mentions the anticipated changes that the research study will likely bring.

Format for a Quantitative Proposal

For a quantitative study, the format conforms to sections typically found in quantitative studies reported in journal articles. The form generally follows the model of an introduction, a literature review, methods, results, and discussion. In planning a quantitative study and designing a dissertation proposal, consider the following format to sketch the overall plan (see Example 4.3).

Example 4.3   A Quantitative Format

Introduction
   Statement of the problem (issue, existing literature about problem, deficiencies in literature, relevance of study for audiences)
      Purpose of the study
      Research questions or hypotheses
      Theoretical perspective

Review of the literature (theory may be included in this section instead of the introduction)

Methods
   Type of research design (e.g., experimental, survey)
      Population, sample, and participants
      Data collection instruments, variables, and materials
      Data analysis procedures
      Anticipated ethical issues in the study

Preliminary studies or pilot tests

Appendixes: Instruments, timeline, and proposed budget

Example 4.3 is a standard format for a social science study (see Miller & Salkind, 2002), although the order of the sections, especially in the use of theory and the literature may vary from study to study (see, for example, Rudestam & Newton, 2014). This format, however, represents a typical order of topics for a quantitative proposal.

Format for a Mixed Methods Proposal

In a mixed methods design format, the researcher brings together approaches that are included in both the quantitative and qualitative formats. An example of such a format appears in Example 4.4 (adapted from Creswell & Plano Clark, 2011, 2018). Similar elements are found in a set of standards for publishing a mixed methods journal article being advanced by the American Psychological Association (Levitt et al., in press).

Example 4.4   A Mixed Methods Format

Introduction
   The research problem (existing research on the problem, deficiencies in the literature that point to the need for both quantitative and qualitative data, relevance of study for audiences)
      The purpose or study aim of the project and reasons or rationale for a mixed methods study
      The research questions and hypotheses (quantitative questions or hypotheses, qualitative questions, mixed methods questions)

Philosophical foundations for using mixed methods research (if needed)

Literature review (typically review quantitative, qualitative, and mixed methods studies)

Methods
    A definition of mixed methods research
    The type of design used and its definition
    Challenges (validity) in using this design and how they will be addressed; also validity approaches in both quantitative and qualitative research
    Examples of use of the type of design in your field of study
    A diagram of procedures
    Quantitative data collection (ordered to fit the mixed methods design steps)

Quantitative data analysis
Qualitative data collection
Qualitative data analysis
    Mixed methods or integration data analysis procedures

Researcher's resources and skills to conduct mixed methods research

Potential ethical issues

References

Appendixes: Instruments, protocols, diagrams, timeline, budget, summary of major content for each chapter

This format shows that the researcher poses both a purpose statement and research questions for quantitative and qualitative components, as well as mixed components. It is important to specify early in the proposal the reasons (rationale) for the mixed methods approach and to identify key elements of the design, such as the type of mixed methods study, a visual diagram of the procedures, and both the quantitative and qualitative data collection and analysis steps. All of these parts could make the mixed methods proposal lengthier than either the qualitative or quantitative proposal.

Designing the Sections of a Proposal

Here are several **research tips** that we give to students about designing the overall structure of a proposal:

- Specify the sections early in the design of a proposal. Work on one section will often prompt ideas for other sections. First develop an outline, and then write something for each section rapidly to get ideas down on paper. Then refine the sections as you consider in more detail the information that should go into each one.

- Find proposals that other students have authored under your adviser, and look at them closely. Ask your adviser for copies of proposals that he or she especially liked and felt were scholarly products to take to committees. Study the topics addressed and their order as well as the level of detail used in composing the proposal.

- Determine whether your program or institution offers a course on proposal development or some similar topic. Often such a class will be helpful as a support system for your project as well as providing individuals that can react to your proposal ideas as they develop.

- Sit down with your adviser, and go over his or her preferred format for a proposal. Ask this adviser for a copy of a proposal that might serve as a guide. Be cautious about using published journal articles as a model for the proposal: they may not provide the information desired by your adviser or graduate committee.

Writing Ideas

Over the years, John has collected books on how to write, and he typically is reading a new one during production of his research projects. In more recent years, he has bought fewer and fewer books about writing per se and instead has purchased good novels and nonfiction works from which to draw thoughts about writing tips. He routinely reads books on the *New York Times* top 10 list and popular books of fiction and nonfiction (for fiction, see Harding, 2009). He brings into his research methods classes segments from books to share to illustrate writing points. This is not to impress others with his literary acumen, but to encourage researchers, as writers, to reach out to their audience; to not wax eloquently in words, but to be concise, and to-the-point; and to practice writing rather than simply talk about it. This chapter, then, represents a collage of John's favorite books on writing and the tips both of us have found useful for our scholarship writing.

Writing as Thinking

One sign of inexperienced writers is that they prefer to discuss their proposed study rather than write about it. As Stephen King (2000) recommended, it is helpful to write it out quickly as rough as it may be in the first rendering. We recommend the following:

- *Early in the process of research, write ideas down rather than talk about them.* One author has talked directly about this concept of writing as thinking (Bailey, 1984). Zinsser (1983) also discussed the need to get words out of our heads and onto paper. Advisers react better when they read the ideas on paper than when they hear and discuss a research topic with a student or colleague. When a researcher renders ideas on paper, a reader can visualize the final product, actually see how it looks, and begin to clarify ideas. The concept of working ideas out on paper has served many experienced writers well. Before designing a proposal, draft a one- to two-page overview of your project and have your adviser approve the direction of your proposed study. This draft might contain the essential information: the research problem being addressed, the purpose of the study, the central questions being asked, the source of data, and the significance of the project for different audiences. It might also be useful to draft several one- to two-page statements on different topics and see which one your adviser likes best and feels would make the best contribution to your field.

- *Work through several drafts of a proposal rather than trying to polish the first draft.* It is illuminating to see how people think on paper. Zinsser (1983) identified two types of writers: (a) the "bricklayer," who makes every paragraph just right before going on to the next paragraph, and (b) the "let-it-all-hang-out-on-the-first-draft" writer, who writes an entire first draft not caring how sloppy it looks or how badly it is written. In between would be someone like Peter Elbow (1973), who recommended that one should go through the iterative process of writing, reviewing, and rewriting. He cited this exercise: With only 1 hour to write a passage, write four drafts (one every 15 minutes) rather than one draft (typically in the last 15 minutes) during the hour. Most experienced researchers write the first draft carefully but do not work for a polished draft; the polish comes relatively late in the writing process.

- *Do not edit your proposal at the early-draft stage.* Instead, consider Franklin's (1986) three-stage model, which we have found useful in developing proposals and in our scholarly writing:

1. First, develop an outline; it could be a sentence or word outline or a visual map.

2. Write out a draft and then shift and sort ideas, moving around entire paragraphs in the manuscript.

3. Finally, edit and polish each sentence.

The Habit of Writing

Establish the discipline or **habit of writing** in a regular and continuous way on your proposal. Although setting aside a completed draft of the proposal for a time may provide some perspective to review your work before final polishing. A start-and-stop process of writing often disrupts the flow of work. It may turn a well-meaning researcher into what we call a "weekend writer," an individual who has time for working on research only on weekends after all the *important* work of the week has been accomplished. Continual work on the proposal is writing something each day or at least being engaged daily in the processes of thinking, collecting information, and reviewing that goes into manuscript and proposal production. We do feel that some people have a stronger urge to write than others. Perhaps this comes from a need to express oneself or a comfort level with self-expression or simply with training.

Select a time of day to work that is best for you, and then discipline yourself to write at this time each day. Choose a place free of distractions. Boice (1990, pp. 77–78) offered ideas about establishing good writing habits:

- With the aid of the priority principle, make writing a daily activity, regardless of mood, regardless of readiness to write.

- If you feel you do not have time for regular writing, begin by charting your daily activities for a week or two in half-hour blocks. It is likely you'll find a time to write.

- Write while you are fresh.

- Avoid writing in binges.

- Write in small, regular amounts.

- Schedule writing tasks so that you plan to work on specific, manageable units of writing in each session.

- Keep daily charts. Graph at least three things: (a) time spent writing, (b) page equivalents finished, and (c) percentage of planned task completed.

- Plan beyond daily goals.

- Share your writing with supportive, constructive friends until you feel ready to go public.

- Try to work on two or three writing projects concurrently so that you do not become overloaded with any one project.

It is also important to acknowledge that writing moves along slowly and that a writer must ease into the process. Like the runner who stretches before a road race, the writer needs warm-up exercises for both the mind and the fingers. We are reminded of the piano player who engages in finger-stretching exercises before practicing a difficult piece that will put the hands into difficult positions. For your research, some leisurely writing activity, such as writing a letter to a friend, brainstorming on the computer, reading some good writing, or studying a favorite poem, can make the actual task of writing easier. We are reminded of John Steinbeck's (1969) "warm-up period" (p. 42) described in detail in *Journal of a Novel: The East of Eden Letters*. Steinbeck began each writing day by writing a letter to his editor and close friend, Pascal Covici, in a large notebook supplied by Covici.

Other exercises may prove useful as warm-ups. Carroll (1990) provided examples of exercises to improve a writer's control over descriptive and emotive passages:

- Describe an object by its parts and dimensions, without first telling the reader its name.

- Write a conversation between two people on any dramatic or intriguing subject.

- Write a set of directions for a complicated task.

- Take a subject and write about it three different ways. (pp. 113–116)

This last exercise seems appropriate for qualitative researchers who analyze their data for multiple codes and themes (see Chapter 9 for qualitative data analysis).

Consider also the writing implements and the physical location that aid the process of disciplined writing. The implements—an online dictionary and a thesaurus, a tablet for jotting down thoughts, a cup of coffee, and a handful of Triscuits (Wolcott, 2009)—offer the writer options for ways to be comfortable when writing. The physical setting can also help. Annie Dillard (1989), the Pulitzer Prize–winning novelist, avoided appealing workplaces:

> One wants a room with no view, so imagination can meet memory in the dark. When I furnished this study seven years ago, I pushed the long desk against a blank wall, so I could not see from either window. Once, fifteen years ago, I wrote in a cinder-block cell over a parking lot. It overlooked a tar-and-gravel roof. This pine shed under trees is not quite so good as the cinder-block study was, but it will do. (pp. 26–27)

Readability of the Manuscript

Before beginning the writing of a proposal, consider how you will enhance the readability of it for other people. The *Publication Manual of the American Psychological Association* (American Psychological Association [APA], 2010) discusses an orderly presentation by showing the relationships between ideas and through the use of transitional words. In addition, it is important to use consistent terms, a staging and foreshadowing of ideas, and coherence built into the plan.

- Use *consistent terms* throughout the proposal. Use the same term for each variable in a quantitative study and the same central phenomenon in a qualitative study. Refrain from using synonyms for these terms, a problem that causes the reader to work at understanding the meaning of ideas and to monitor subtle shifts in meaning. When terms shift, ever so slightly, it throws the reader off and causes them to question your ideas.

- Consider how narrative thoughts of different types guide a reader. Tarshis (1982) advanced the idea that writers should have in mind the purpose of different-sized narrative thoughts and purposes for segments of text. He said there were four types:

  1. Umbrella thoughts: the general or core ideas one is trying to get across

  2. **Big thoughts in writing**: specific ideas or images that fall within the realm of umbrella thoughts and serve to reinforce, clarify, or elaborate upon the umbrella thoughts

  3. Little thoughts: ideas or images whose chief function is to reinforce big thoughts

4. **Attention or interest thoughts**: ideas whose purposes are to keep the reader on track, organize ideas, and keep an individual's attention

Beginning researchers seem to struggle most with umbrella and attention thoughts. A proposal may include too many umbrella ideas—with the content not sufficiently detailed to support large ideas. This might occur in a literature review in which the researcher needs to provide fewer small sections and more larger sections that tie together large bodies of literature. A clear mark of this problem is a continual shift of ideas from one major idea to another in a manuscript. Often, one will see short paragraphs in introductions to proposals, like those written by journalists in newspaper articles. Thinking in terms of a detailed narrative to support umbrella ideas may help this problem.

Attention thoughts—those that provide organizational statements to guide the reader—are also needed. Readers need road signs to guide them from one major idea to the next (Chapters 6 and 7 of this book discuss major road signs in research, such as purpose statements and research questions and hypotheses). An organizing paragraph is often useful at the beginning and end of literature reviews. Readers need to see the overall organization of the ideas through introductory paragraphs and to be told the most salient points they should remember in a summary.

- Use *coherence* to add to the readability of the manuscript. **Coherence in writing** means that the ideas tie together and logically flow from one sentence to another and from one paragraph to another. For example, the repetition of the same variable names in the title, the purpose statement, the research questions, and the review of the literature headings in a quantitative project illustrate this thinking. This approach builds coherence into the study. Emphasizing a consistent order whenever independent and dependent variables are mentioned also reinforces this idea.

On a more detailed level, coherence builds through connecting sentences and paragraphs in the manuscript. Zinsser (1983) suggested that every sentence should be a logical sequel to the one that preceded it. The hook-and-eye exercise (Wilkinson, 1991) is useful for connecting thoughts from sentence to sentence and paragraph to paragraph. The basic idea here is that one sentence builds on the next and sentences in a paragraph build into the next paragraph. The way this occurs is by specific words that provide a linkage.

The passage in Example 4.5, from a draft of a student's proposal, shows a high level of coherence. It comes from the introductory section of a qualitative dissertation project about at-risk students. In this passage, we have taken the liberty of drawing hooks and eyes to connect the words from sentence to another sentence and from paragraph to paragraph. As mentioned, the objective of the hook-and-eye exercise (Wilkinson, 1991) is to connect major thoughts (and words) of each sentence and paragraph. If such a connection cannot easily be made, the written passage lacks coherence; the ideas and topics shift; and the reader needs to add transitional words, phrases, or sentences to establish a clear connection. The reader also does not get a sense of how the ideas build in a study.

In John's proposal development classes, he has provided a passage from an introduction to a proposal and asks students to connect the words and sentences using circles for key ideas and lines to connect these key words from sentence to sentence. It is important for a reader to find coherence in a proposal starting with the first page. He first gives his students an unmarked passage and then, after the exercise, provides a marked passage. Since the key idea of one sentence should connect to a key idea in the next sentence, they need to mark this relationship in the passage. If the sentences do not connect, then transition words are missing that need to be inserted. He also asks students to make sure that the paragraphs are connected with hooks and eyes as well as individual sentences.

Example 4.5 An Illustration of the Hook-and-Eye Technique

They sit in the back of the room not because they want to but because it was the place designated to them. Invisible barriers that exist in most classrooms divide the room and separate the students. At the front of the room are the "good" students who wait with their hands poised ready to fly into the air at a moment's notice. Slouched down like giant insects caught in educational traps, the athletes and their following occupy the center of the room. Those less sure of themselves and their position within the room sit in the back and around the edge of the student body.

The students seated in the outer circle make up a population whom for a variety of reasons are not succeeding in the American public education system. They have always been part of the student population. In the past they have been called disadvantaged, low achieving, retards, impoverished, laggards and a variety of other titles (Cuban, 1989; Presseisen, 1988). Today they are called students-at-risk. Their faces are changing and in urban settings their numbers are growing (Hodgkinson, 1985).

In the past eight years there has been an unprecedented amount of research on the need for excellence in education and the at-risk student. In 1983 the government released a document entitled A Nation At-Risk that identified problems within the American education system and called for major reform. Much of the early reform focused on more vigorous courses of study and higher standards of student achievement (Barber, 1987). In the midst of attention to excellence, it became apparent the needs of the marginal student were not being met. The question of what it would take to guarantee that all students have a fair chance at a quality education was receiving little attention (Hamilton, 1987; Toch, 1984). As the push for excellence in education increased, the needs of the at-risk student became more apparent.

(Continued)

(Continued)

Much of the early research focused on identifying characteristics of the at-risk student (OERI, 1987; Barber & McClellan, 1987; Hahn, 1987; Rumberger, 1987), while others in educational research called for reform and developed programs for at-risk students (Mann, 1987; Presseisen, 1988; Whelage, 1988; Whelege & Lipman, 1988; Stocklinski, 1991; and Levin, 1991). Studies and research on this topic have included experts within the field of education, business and industry as well as many government agencies.

Although progress has been made in identifying characteristics of the at-risk students and in developing programs to meet their needs, the essence of the at-risk issue continues to plague the American school system. Some educators feel that we do not need further research (DeBlois, 1989; Hahn, 1987). Others call for a stronger network between business and education (DeBlois, 1989; Mann, 1987; Whelege, 1988). Still others call for total restructuring of our education system (OERI, 1987; Gainer, 1987; Levin, 1988; McCune, 1988).

After all the research and studies by the experts, we still have students hanging on to the fringe of education. The uniqueness of this study will shift the focus from causes and curriculum to the student. It is time to question the students and to listen to their responses. This added dimension should bring further understanding to research already available and lead to further areas of reform. Dropouts and potential dropouts will be interviewed in depth to discover if there are common factors within the public school setting that interfere with their learning process. This information should be helpful to both the researcher who will continue to look for new approaches in education and the practitioner who works with these students every day.

Voice, Tense, and "Fat"

From working with broad thoughts and paragraphs, we recommend moving on to the level of writing sentences and words. Similar grammar and sentence construction issues are addressed in the APA *Publication Manual* (APA, 2010), but we include this section to highlight some common grammar issues that we have seen in student proposals and in my own writing.

Our thoughts are directed toward the "polish" level of writing, to use Franklin's (1986) term. It is a stage addressed late in the writing process. One can find an abundance of writing books about research writing and literary writing with rules and principles to follow concerning good sentence construction and word choice. Wolcott (2009), a qualitative ethnographer, for example, talks about honing editorial skills to eliminate unnecessary words (keeping the essential words); deleting the passive voice (using the active voice); scaling down qualifiers (keeping only one qualifier at best); eliminating overused phrases (completing striking these out); and reducing excessive quotations, use of italics, and parenthetical comments (all elements of good scholarly writing). The following additional ideas about active voice, verb tense, and reduced **fat** can strengthen and invigorate scholarly writing for dissertation and thesis proposals.

- Use the *active voice* as much as possible in scholarly writing (APA, 2010). According to the literary writer Ross-Larson (1982), "If the subject acts, the voice is active. If the subject is acted on, the voice is passive" (p. 29). In addition, a sign of passive construction is some variation of an auxiliary verb, such as *was*. Examples include *will be, have been*, and *is being*. Writers can use the passive construction when the person acting can logically be left out of the sentence and when what is acted on is the subject of the rest of the paragraph (Ross-Larson, 1982).

- Use *strong active verbs* appropriate for the passage. Lazy verbs are those that lack action, commonly called "to be" verbs, such as *is* or *was*, or verbs turned into adjectives or adverbs.

- Pay close attention to the *tense* of your verbs. A common practice exists in using the past tense to review the literature and report results of past studies. The past tense represents a commonly used form in quantitative research. The future tense appropriately indicates that the study will be conducted in the future, a key verb-use for proposals. Use the present tense to add vigor to a study, especially in the introduction, as this tense-form frequently occurs in qualitative studies. In mixed methods studies, researchers employ either the present or past tense and the appropriate tense often reflects whether the major orientation of the study will be quantitative or qualitative research (thus emphasizing one or the other in a study). The APA *Publication Manual* (APA, 2010) recommends the past tense (e.g., "Jones reported") or the present perfect tense (e.g., "Researchers have reported") for the literature review and procedures based on past events, the past tense to describe results (e.g., "stress lowered self-esteem"), and the present tense (e.g., "the qualitative findings show") to discuss the results and to present the conclusions. We see this not as a hard and fast rule but as a useful guideline.

- Expect to edit and revise drafts of a manuscript to trim the fat. Fat refers to additional words that are unnecessary to convey the meaning of ideas and need to be edited out. Writing multiple drafts of a manuscript is standard practice for most writers. The process typically consists of writing, reviewing, and editing. In the editing process, trim excess words from sentences, such as piled-up modifiers, excessive prepositions, and "the-of" constructions—for example, "the study of"—that add unnecessary verbiage (Ross-Larson, 1982). We were reminded of the unnecessary prose that comes into writing by the example mentioned by Bunge (1985):

> Nowadays you can almost see bright people struggling to reinvent the complex sentence before your eyes. A friend of mine who is a college administrator every now and then has to say a complex sentence, and he will get into one of those morasses that begins,

"I would hope that we would be able . . ." He never talked that way when I first met him, but even at his age, at his distance from the crisis in the lives of younger people, he's been to some extent alienated from easy speech. (p. 172)

Begin studying good writing about research using qualitative, quantitative, and mixed methods designs. In good writing, the eye does not pause and the mind does not stumble on a passage. In this present book, we have attempted to draw examples of good research from human and social science journals, such as *Administrative Science Quarterly*, *American Educational Research Journal*, *American Journal of Sociology*, *Image*, *Journal of Applied Psychology*, *Journal of Mixed Methods Research*, *Journal of Nursing Scholarship*, and *Sociology of Education*. In the qualitative area, good literature serves to illustrate clear prose and detailed passages. Individuals who teach qualitative research assign well-known books from literature, such as *Moby Dick*, *The Scarlet Letter*, and *The Bonfire of the Vanities*, as reading assignments (Webb & Glesne, 1992). *Journal of Contemporary Ethnography*, *Qualitative Family Research*, *Qualitative Health Research*, *Qualitative Inquiry*, and *Qualitative Research* represent good, scholarly journals in qualitative research to examine. When using mixed methods research, examine journals that report studies with combined qualitative and quantitative research and data, including many social science journals, such as the *Journal of Mixed Methods Research*, *The International Journal of Multiple Research Approaches*, *Field Methods*, *Quality and Quantity*, and the *International Journal of Social Research Methodology*. Examine the numerous articles cited in the *SAGE Handbook of Mixed Methods in Social and Behavioral Research* (Tashakkori & Teddlie, 2010) and in *The Mixed Methods Reader* (Plano Clark & Creswell, 2008).

Ethical Issues to Anticipate

In addition to conceptualizing the writing process for a proposal, researchers need to anticipate the ethical issues that may arise during their studies (Berg, 2001; Hesse-Biber & Leavy, 2011; Punch, 2005; Sieber, 1998). Research involves collecting data from people, about people (Punch, 2014). Writing about these anticipated ethical issues is required in making an argument for a study as well as being an important topic in the format for proposals. Researchers need to protect their research participants; develop a trust with them; promote the integrity of research; guard against misconduct and impropriety that might reflect on their organizations or institutions; and cope with new, challenging problems (Israel & Hay, 2006). Ethical questions are apparent today in such issues as personal disclosure, authenticity, and credibility of the research report; the role of researchers in cross-cultural contexts; and issues of personal privacy through forms of Internet data collection (Israel & Hay, 2006).

Table 4.1 Ethical Issues in Qualitative, Quantitative, and Mixed Methods Research

Where in the Process of Research the Ethical Issue Occurs	Type of Ethical Issue	How to Address the Issue
Prior to conducting the study	• Examine professional association standards. • Seek college/university approval on campus through an institutional review board (IRB). • Gain local permission from site and participants. • Select a site without a vested interest in outcome of study. • Negotiate authorship for publication.	• Consult the code of ethics for professional association in your area. • Submit proposal for IRB approval. • Identify and go through local approvals; find gatekeepers or key personnel to help. • Select sites that will not raise power issues with researchers. • Give credit for work done on the project; decide on author order in future publication.
Beginning the study	• Identify a research problem that will benefit participants. • Disclose purpose of the study. • Do not pressure participants into signing consent forms. • Respect norms and charters of indigenous societies. • Be sensitive to needs of vulnerable populations (e.g., children).	• Conduct a needs assessment or informal conversation with participants about their needs. • Contact participants, and inform them of the general purpose of the study. • Tell participants that they do not have to sign form. • Find out about cultural, religious, gender, and other differences that need to be respected. • Obtain appropriate consent (e.g., parents, as well as children).
Collecting data	• Respect the site, and disrupt as little as possible. • Make certain that all participants receive the same treatment. • Avoid deceiving participants. • Respect potential power imbalances and exploitation of participants (e.g., interviewing, observing). • Do not "use" participants by gathering data and leaving site. • Avoid collecting harmful information.	• Build trust, and convey extent of anticipated disruption in gaining access. • Put into place wait list provisions for treatment for controls. • Discuss purpose of the study and how data will be used. • Avoid leading questions. Withhold sharing personal impressions. Avoid disclosing sensitive information. Involve participants as collaborators. • Provide rewards for participating. • Stick to questions stated in an interview protocol.

(Continued)

Table 4.1   (Continued)

Where in the Process of Research the Ethical Issue Occurs	Type of Ethical Issue	How to Address the Issue
Analyzing data	• Avoid siding with participants (going native). • Avoid disclosing only positive results. • Respect the privacy and anonymity of participants.	• Report multiple perspectives. • Report contrary findings. • Assign fictitious names or aliases; develop composite profiles of participants.
Reporting, sharing, and storing data	• Avoid falsifying authorship, evidence, data, findings, and conclusions. • Do not plagiarize. • Avoid disclosing information that would harm participants. • Communicate in clear, straightforward, appropriate language. • Share data with others. • Keep raw data and other materials (e.g., details of procedures, instruments). • Do not duplicate or piecemeal publications. • Provide complete proof of compliance with ethical issues and lack of conflict of interest, if requested. • State who owns the data from a study.	• Report honestly. • See APA (2010) guidelines for permissions needed to reprint or adapt work of others. • Use composite stories so that individuals cannot be identified. • Use unbiased language appropriate for audiences of the research. • Provide copies of report to participants and stakeholders. Share results with other researchers. Consider website distribution. Consider publishing in different languages. • Store data and materials for 5 years (APA, 2010). • Refrain from using the same material for more than one publication. • Disclose funders for research. Disclose who will profit from the research. • Give credit for ownership to researcher, participants, and advisers.

Sources: Adapted from APA (2010); Creswell (2013); Lincoln (2009); Mertens and Ginsberg (2009); and Salmons (2010).

Ethical issues in research command increased attention today. The ethical considerations that need to be anticipated are extensive, and they are reflected through the research process. These issues apply to qualitative, quantitative, and mixed methods research and to all stages of research. Proposal writers need to anticipate them and actively address them in their research plans. Accordingly, it is helpful to address them as they relate to different phases of inquiry. As shown in Table 4.1, attention needs to be directed toward ethical issues prior to conducting the study; beginning a study; during data collection and data analysis; and in reporting, sharing, and storing the data.

Prior to Beginning the Study

- *Consider codes of ethics.* Consult early in the development of your proposal the **code of ethics** for your professional association. In the literature, ethical issues arise in discussions about codes of professional conduct for researchers and in commentaries about ethical dilemmas and their potential solutions (Punch, 2014). Many national professional associations have published standards or codes of ethics on their websites. For example, see the following websites:

   o   The American Psychological Association Ethical Principles of Psychologists and Code of Conduct, Including 2010 Amendments (www.apa.org/ethics/code/index.aspx)

   o   The American Sociological Association Code of Ethics, adopted in 1997 (www.asanet.org/membership/code-ethics)

   o   The American Anthropological Association's Code of Ethics, February 2009 (ethics.americananthro.org/category/statement/)

   o   The American Educational Research Association Ethical Standards of the American Educational Research Association, 2011 (www.aera.net/AboutAERA/AERA-Rules-Policies/Professional-Ethics)

   o   The American Nurses Association Code of Ethics for Nurses— Provisions, approved in June 2001 (www.nursingworld.org/codeofethics)

   o   The American Medical Association Code of Ethics (www.ama-assn.org/delivering-care/ama-code-medical ethics)

- *Apply to the institutional review board.* Researchers need to have their research plans reviewed by an **institutional review board (IRB)** on their college and university campuses. IRB committees exist on campuses because of federal regulations that provide protection against human rights violations. The IRB committee requires the researcher to assess the potential for risk to participants in a study, such as physical, psychological, social, economic, or legal harm (Sieber, 1998). Also, the researcher needs to consider the special needs of vulnerable populations, such as minors (under the age of 19), mentally incompetent participants, victims, persons with neurological impairments, pregnant women or fetuses, prisoners, and individuals with AIDS. As a researcher, you will need to file an application with the IRB that contains procedures and information about participants so that the committee can review the extent to which you place participants at risk in your study. In addition to this application, you need to have participants sign **informed consent forms** agreeing to the provisions of your study before they provide data. This form contains a standard set of elements that acknowledges protection of human rights. They include the following (Sarantakos, 2005):

- o Identification of the researcher

- o Identification of the sponsoring institution

- o Identification of the purpose of the study

- o Identification of the benefits for participating

- o Identification of the level and type of participant involvement

- o Notation of risks to the participant

- o Guarantee of confidentiality to the participant

- o Assurance that the participant can withdraw at any time

- o Provision of names of persons to contact if questions arise

- *Obtain necessary permissions.* Prior to the study, researchers need to obtain approval of individuals in authority (e.g., gatekeepers) to gain access to sites and to study participants. This often involves writing a letter that specifies the extent of time, the potential impact, and the outcomes of the research. Use of Internet responses gained through electronic interviews or surveys needs permission from participants. This can be obtained through first obtaining permission and then sending out the interview or survey.

- *Select a site without vested interests.* Selecting a site to study in which you have an interest in outcomes is not a good idea. It does not allow for the objectivity required for quantitative research or for the full expression of multiple perspectives needed in qualitative research. Select sites that will now raise these questions of power and influence in your study.

- *Negotiate authorship for publication.* If you plan to publish your study (often the case for a dissertation project), an important issue to negotiate before beginning the study is the question of authorship for individuals who contribute to the study. Order of authorship is important to state at the beginning so that individuals who contribute to a research study receive their due contribution. Israel and Hay (2006) discussed the unethical practice of so-called "gift authorship" to individuals who do not contribute to a manuscript and ghost authorship, in which junior staff who made significant contributions have been omitted from the list of authors. The inclusion of authors and the order of authorship may change during a study, but a preliminary understanding early in the project helps address this issue when publication is imminent.

Beginning the Study

- *Identify a beneficial research problem.* During the identification of the research problem, it is important to identify a problem that will benefit individuals being studied, one that will be meaningful for others besides the researcher (Punch, 2014). Hesse-Biber and Leavy (2011) asked, "How do ethical issues enter into your selection of a research problem?" (p. 86). To guard against this, proposal developers can conduct pilot projects, needs assessments, or hold informal conversations to establish trust and respect with the participants so that inquirers can detect any potential marginalization of participants as the study begins.

- *Disclose purpose of the study.* In developing the purpose statement or the central intent and questions for a study, proposal developers need to convey the purpose of the study that will be described to the participants (Sarantakos, 2005). Deception occurs when participants understand one purpose but the researcher has a different purpose in mind. It is also important for researchers to specify the sponsorship of their study. For example, in designing cover letters for survey research, sponsorship is an important element in establishing trust and credibility for a mailed survey instrument.

- *Do not pressure participants into signing consent forms.* When collecting consent for a study, the researcher should not force participants to sign the informed consent form. Participation in a study should be seen as voluntary, and the researcher should explain in the instructions for the consent form that participants can decide not to participate in the study.

- *Respect norms and charters of indigenous cultures.* The researcher needs to anticipate any cultural, religious, gender, or other differences in the participants and sites that need to be respected. Recent discussions about the norms and charters of indigenous populations, such as American Indian tribes, need to be observed (LaFrance & Crazy Bull, 2009). As American Indian tribes take over the delivery of services to members, they have reclaimed their right to determine what research will be done and how it will be reported in a sensitive way to tribal culture and charters.

Collecting the Data

- *Respect the site, and disrupt as little as possible.* Researchers need to respect research sites so that they are left undisturbed after a research study. This requires that inquirers, especially in qualitative studies involving prolonged observation or interviewing at a site, be cognizant of their impact and minimize their disruption of the physical setting. For example, they might time visits so that they intrude little on the flow of activities of participants. Also, organizations often have guidelines that provide guidance for conducting research without disturbing their settings.

- *Make sure that all participants receive the benefits.* In experimental studies, investigators need to collect data so that all participants, not only an experimental group, benefit from the treatments. This may require providing *some* treatment to all groups or staging the treatment so that ultimately all groups receive the beneficial treatment (e.g., a wait list). Further, both the researcher and the participants should benefit from the research. In some situations, power can easily be abused and participants can be coerced into a project. Involving individuals collaboratively in the research may provide reciprocity. Highly collaborative studies, popular in qualitative research, may engage participants as coresearchers throughout the research process, such as the design, data collection and analysis, report writing, and dissemination of the findings (Patton, 2002).

- *Avoid deceiving participants.* Participants need to know that they are actively participating in a research study. To counteract this problem, provide instructions that remind the participants about the purpose of the study.

- *Respect potential power imbalances.* Interviewing in qualitative research is increasingly being seen as a moral inquiry (Kvale, 2007). It could equally be seen as such for quantitative and mixed methods research. As such, interviewers need to consider how the interview will improve the human situation (as well as enhance scientific knowledge), how a sensitive interview interaction may be stressful for the participants, whether participants have a say in how their statements are interpreted, how critically the interviewees might be questioned, and what the consequences of the interview for the interviewees and the groups to which they belong might be. Interviews (and observations) should begin from the premise that a power imbalance exists between the data collector and the participants.

- *Avoid exploitation of participants.* There needs to be some reciprocity back to the participants for their involvement in your study. This might be a small reward for participating, sharing the final research report, or involving them as collaborators. Traditionally, some researchers have "used" the participants for data collection and then abruptly left the scene. This results in exploitation of the participants and rewards and appreciation can provide respect and reciprocity for those who provide value data in a study.

- *Avoid collecting harmful information.* Researchers also need to anticipate the possibility of harmful, intimate information being disclosed during the data collection process. It is difficult to anticipate and try to plan for the impact of this information during or after an interview (Patton, 2002). For example, a student may discuss parental abuse or prisoners may talk about an escape. Typically in these situations, the ethical code for researchers (which may be different for schools and prisons) is to protect the privacy of the participants and to convey this protection to all individuals involved in a study.

Analyzing the Data

- *Avoid going native.* It is easy to support and embrace the perspectives of participants in a study. In qualitative studies, this means "taking sides" and only discussing the results that place the participants in a favorable light. In quantitative research, it means disregarding data that proves or disproves personal hypotheses that the researcher may hold.

- *Avoid disclosing only positive results.* In research, it is academically dishonest to withhold important results or to cast the results in a favorable light to the participants' or researchers' inclinations. In qualitative research, this means that the inquirer needs to report the full range of findings, including findings that may be contrary to the themes. A hallmark of good qualitative research is the report of the diversity of perspectives about the topic. In quantitative research, the data analysis should reflect the statistical tests and not be underreported.

- *Respect the privacy of participants.* How will the study protect the anonymity of individuals, roles, and incidents in the project? For example, in survey research, investigators disassociate names from responses during the coding and recording process. In qualitative research, inquirers use aliases or pseudonyms for individuals and places, to protect the identities of participants.

Reporting, Sharing, and Storing Data

- *Falsifying authorship, evidence, data, findings, or conclusions.* In the interpretation of data, researchers need to provide an accurate account of the information. This accuracy may require debriefing between the researcher and participants in quantitative research (Berg, 2001). It may include, in qualitative research, using one or more of the strategies to check the accuracy of the data with participants or across different data sources, through strategies of validation. Other ethical issues in reporting the research will involve the potential of suppressing, falsifying, or inventing findings to meet a researcher's or an audience's needs. These fraudulent practices are not accepted in professional research communities, and they constitute scientific misconduct (Neuman, 2009). A proposal might contain a proactive stance by the researcher to not engage in these practices.

- *Do not plagiarize.* Copying extensive material from others is an ethical issue. Researchers should give credit for the work of others and quotation marks should indicate the exact words claimed from others. The key idea is to not present the work of another as your own (APA, 2010). Even when material is paraphrased, credit must be given to the original source. Journals typically have guidelines about how much material can be quoted from another source without the author having to pay a permission fee for the use of the material.

- *Avoid disclosing information that would harm participants.* One issue to anticipate about confidentiality is that some participants may not want to have their identity remain confidential. By permitting this, the researcher allows the participants to retain ownership of their voices and exert their independence in making decisions. They do, however, need to be well informed about the possible risks of non-confidentiality, such as the inclusion of data in the final report that they may not have expected, information that infringes on the rights of others that should remain concealed, and so forth (Giordano, O'Reilly, Taylor, & Dogra, 2007). In planning a study, it is important to anticipate the repercussions of conducting the research on certain audiences and not to misuse the results to the advantage of one group or another.

- *Communicate in clear straightforward, appropriate language.* Discuss how the research will not use language or words that are biased against persons because of gender, sexual orientation, racial or ethnic group, disability, or age. Review the three guidelines for biased language in the APA *Publication Manual* (APA, 2010). Present unbiased language at an appropriate level of specificity (e.g., rather than say, "The client's behavior was typically male," state, "The client's behavior was _____ [specify]"). Use language that is sensitive to labels (e.g., rather than "400 Hispanics," indicate "400 Mexicans, Spaniards, and Puerto Ricans"). Acknowledge participants in a study (e.g., rather than "subject," use the word *participant,* and rather than "woman doctor" use "doctor" or "physician").

- *Share data with others.* It is important to release the details of the research with the study design so that readers can determine for themselves the credibility of the study (Neuman, 2009). Detailed procedures for quantitative, qualitative, and mixed methods research will be emphasized in the chapters to follow. Some strategies for sharing include providing copies of reports to participants and stakeholders, making distributions of reports available on websites, and publishing studies in multiple languages when needed.

- *Keep raw data and other materials (e.g., details of procedures, instruments).* Data, once analyzed, need to be kept for a reasonable period of time (e.g., Sieber, 1998, recommends 5 to 10 years; the APA, 5 years). After this period, investigators should discard the data so that it does not fall into the hands of other researchers who might misappropriate it.

- *Do not duplicate or piecemeal publications.* Also, researchers should not engage in duplicate or redundant publication in which authors publish papers that present exactly the same data, discussions, and conclusions and do not offer new material. Some biomedical journals now require authors to declare whether they have published or are preparing to publish papers that are closely related to the manuscript that has been submitted (Israel & Hay, 2006).

- *Complete proof of compliance with ethical issues and a lack of conflict of interest.* Some academic campuses now require authors to file statements indicating that they do not have a conflict of interest in publishing the research. Such conflict might arise from payment for their research, a vested interest in the outcome of the data, or the intent to appropriate the use of the research for personal reasons. As a researcher, you need to comply with requests for disclosure about potential conflicts of interests that surround your research.

- *Understand who owns the data.* The question of who owns the data once it is collected and analyzed also can be an issue that splits research teams and divides individuals against each other. A proposal might mention this issue of ownership and discuss how it will be resolved, such as through the development of a clear understanding between the researcher, the participants, and possibly the faculty advisers (Punch, 2014). Berg (2001) recommended the use of personal agreements to designate ownership of research data.

SUMMARY

It is helpful to consider how to write a research proposal before actually engaging in the process. Consider the nine arguments advanced by Maxwell (2005) as the key elements to include, and then use one of the four topical outlines provided to craft a thorough qualitative, quantitative, or mixed methods proposal.

In proposal or project development, begin putting words down on paper early to think through ideas; establish the habit of writing on a regular basis; and use strategies such as

applying consistent terms, different levels of narrative thoughts, and coherence to strengthen writing. Writing in the active voice, using strong verbs, and revising and editing will help as well.

Before writing the proposal, it is useful to consider the ethical issues that can be anticipated and described in the proposal. These issues relate to all phases of the research process. With consideration for participants, research sites, and potential readers, studies can be designed that contain good ethical practices.

Writing Exercises

1. Develop a topical outline for a quantitative, qualitative, or mixed methods proposal. Include the major topics in the examples in this chapter.

2. Locate a journal article that reports qualitative, quantitative, or mixed methods research. Examine the introduction to the article and, using the hook-and-eye method illustrated in this chapter, identify the flow of ideas from sentence to sentence and from paragraph to paragraph and any deficiencies.

3. Consider one of the following ethical dilemmas that may face a researcher. Describe ways you might anticipate the

problem and actively address it in your research proposal.

a. A prisoner you are interviewing tells you about a potential breakout at the prison that night. What do you do?

b. A researcher on your team copies sentences from another study and incorporates them into the final written report for your project. What do you do?

c. A student collects data for a project from several individuals interviewed in families in your city. After the fourth interview the student tells you that approval has not been received for the project from the IRB. What will you do?

Additional Readings

American Psychological Association. (2010). *Publication Manual of the American Psychological Association* (6th ed.). Washington, DC: Author.

This style manual is an essential tool to have as a researcher. In terms of writing qualitative research, it reviews ethical issues and legal standards in publishing. It covers writing clearly and concisely, addressing such topics as continuity, tone, precision and clarity, and strategies to improve writing style. It gives ample illustrations about how to reduce bias in a scholarly research report. It includes sections on the mechanics of style, such as punctuation, spelling, capitalization, and abbreviations. These are a few of the tips for writing that scholars need.

Israel, M., & Hay, I. (2006). *Research ethics for social scientists: Between ethical conduct and regulatory compliance.* Thousand Oaks, CA: Sage.

Mark Israel and Iain Hay provide a thoughtful analysis of the practical value of thinking seriously and systematically about what constitutes ethical conduct in the social sciences. They review the different theories of ethics, such as the consequentialist and the nonconsequentialist approaches, virtue ethics, and normative and care-oriented approaches to ethical conduct. They also offer an international perspective, drawing on the history of ethical practices in countries around the world. Throughout the book, they offer practical case examples and ways researchers might treat the cases ethically. In the appendix, they provide three case examples and then call upon leading scholars to comment about how they would approach the ethical issue.

Maxwell, J. (2013). *Qualitative research design: An interactive approach* (3rd ed.). Thousand Oaks, CA: Sage.

Joe Maxwell provides a good overview of the proposal development process for qualitative research that is applicable in many ways to quantitative and mixed methods research as well. He states that a proposal is an argument to conduct a study and presents an example that describes nine necessary steps. Moreover, he includes a complete qualitative proposal and analyzes it as an illustration of a good model to follow.

Sieber, J. E. (1998). Planning ethically responsible research. In L. Bickman & D. J. Rog (Eds.), *Handbook of applied social research methods* (pp. 127–156). Thousand Oaks, CA: Sage.

Joan Sieber discusses the importance of ethical planning as integral to the process of research design. In this chapter, she provides a comprehensive review of many topics related to ethical issues, such as IRBs, informed consent, privacy, confidentiality, and anonymity, as well as elements of research risk and vulnerable populations. Her coverage is extensive, and her recommendations for strategies are numerous.

Wolcott, H. F. (2009). *Writing up qualitative research* (3rd ed.). Thousand Oaks, CA: Sage.

Harry Wolcott, a distinguished educational ethnographer, has compiled an excellent resource guide addressing numerous aspects of the writing process in qualitative research. He surveys techniques useful in getting started in writing; developing details; linking with the literature, theory, and method; tightening up with revising and editing; and finishing the process by attending to such aspects as the title and appendixes. For all aspiring writers, this is an essential book, regardless of whether a study is qualitative, quantitative, or mixed methods.

$\circledS$SAGE edge™

https://edge.sagepub.com/creswellrd5e

Students and instructors, please visit the companion website for videos featuring John W. Creswell, full-text SAGE journal articles, quizzes and activities, plus additional tools for research design.

Designing Research

This section relates the three approaches—(a) quantitative, (b) qualitative, and (c) mixed methods—to the steps in the process of research. Each chapter addresses a separate step in this process, beginning with introducing a study.

The Introduction

After having decided on a qualitative, quantitative, or mixed methods approach and after conducting a preliminary literature review and deciding on a format for a proposal, the next step in the process is to design or plan the study. A process of organizing and writing out ideas begins, starting with designing an introduction to a proposal. This chapter discusses the composition and writing of a scholarly introduction and examines the differences in writing an introduction for these three different types of designs. Then the discussion turns to the five components of writing a good introduction: (a) establishing the problem leading to the study, (b) reviewing the literature about the problem, (c) identifying deficiencies in the literature about the problem, (d) targeting an audience and noting the significance of the problem for this audience, and (e) identifying the purpose of the proposed study. These components comprise a *social science deficiency model* of writing an introduction, because a major component of the introduction is to set forth the deficiencies in past research. To illustrate this model, a complete introduction in a published research study is presented and analyzed.

The Importance of Introductions

An introduction is the first passage in a journal article, dissertation, or scholarly research study. It sets the stage for the entire project. Wilkinson (1991) mentioned the following:

> The introduction is the part of the paper that provides readers with the background information for the research reported in the paper. Its purpose is to establish a framework for the research, so that readers can understand how it is related to other research. (p. 96)

The introduction establishes the issue or concern leading to the research by conveying information about a problem. Because it is the initial passage in a study or proposal, special care must be given to writing it. The introduction needs to create reader interest in the topic, establish the problem that leads to the study, place the study within the larger context of the scholarly literature, and reach out to a specific audience. All of this is achieved in a concise section of a few pages. Because of the messages they must convey and the limited space allowed, introductions are challenging to write and understand.

A research problem is the problem or issue that leads to the need for a study. It can originate from many potential sources. It might spring from an experience researchers have had in their personal lives or workplaces. It may come from an extensive debate that has appeared in the literature. The literature may have a gap that needs to be addressed, alternative views that should be resolved, or a branch that needs to be studied. Further, the research problem might develop from policy debates in government or among top executives. The sources of research problems are often multiple. Identifying and stating the research problem that underlies a study is not easy. For example, to identify the issue of teenage pregnancy is to point to a problem for women and for society at large. Unfortunately, too many authors do not clearly identify the research problem, leaving readers to decide for themselves the importance of the issue. When the problem is not clear, it is difficult to understand all the other aspects of a research study, especially the significance of the research. Furthermore, the research problem is often confused with the research questions—those questions that the investigator would like answered in order to understand or explain the problem. To this complexity is added the need for introductions to carry the weight of encouraging the reader to read further and to see significance in the study.

Fortunately, there is a model for writing a good, scholarly social science introduction. Before introducing this model, it is necessary to briefly discuss the composition of a good abstract and then to distinguish subtle differences between introductions for qualitative, quantitative, and mixed methods studies.

An Abstract for a Study

An abstract is a brief summary of the contents of a study, and it allows readers to quickly survey the essential elements of a project. It is placed at the beginning of studies, and it is useful to have both for proposals for studies and for the final thesis or dissertation. The *Publication Manual of the American Psychological Association* (American Psychological Association [APA], 2010) indicates that the abstract can be the most important single paragraph in a study. It also needs to be accurate, non-evaluative (by adding comments beyond the scope of the research), coherent, readable, and concise. Its length varies, and some colleges and universities have requirements for an appropriate length (e.g., 250 words). The APA *Publication Manual* (APA, 2010) guidelines say that most abstracts are from 150 to 250 words.

There are the major components that we would include in an abstract. The content varies for abstracts for a report, a literature review, a theory-oriented paper, and for a methodological paper. We will focus here on the abstract for a proposal for an empirical article. We see several major components as part of the abstract, and these would be the same whether the proposal is quantitative, qualitative, or mixed methods. Also, we would order these components in the order in which they can be presented:

1. Start with the *issue* or *problem* leading to a need for the research. This issue might be related to a need for more literature, but we like to think about a real-life problem that needs to be addressed, such as

the spread of AIDS, teenage pregnancies, college students dropping out of school, or the lack of women in certain professions. These are all real-life problems that need to be addressed. The problem could also indicate a deficiency in the literature, such as a gap, a need to extend a topic, or to resolve differences among research studies. You could cite a reference or two about this "problem," but generally the abstract is too short to include many references.

2. Indicate the *purpose of the study*. Use the word *purpose* or the term *study aim* or *objective,* and talk about the central phenomenon being explored, the participants who will be studied, and the site where the research will take place.

3. Next state what *data will be collected* to address this purpose. You might indicate the type of data, the participants, and where the data will be collected.

4. After this, indicate qualitative *themes*, quantitative *statistical results,* or the mixed methods integrative findings that will likely arise in your study. At the early stages of planning a project, you will not know what these results will be, so you might have to guess as to what they might be. Indicate four to five themes, primary statistical results, or integrative mixed methods insights.

5. Finish the abstract by mentioning the *practical implications* of the study. State the specific audiences who will benefit from the project and why they will benefit.

Here is an example of a short abstract for a qualitative study that contains all five elements.

The issue that this study addresses is the lack of women in martial arts competitions. To address this problem, the purpose of this study will be exploring motivation of female athletes in Tae Kwon Do competitions. To gather data, interviews with 4 female Tae Kwon Do tournament competitors were conducted. The interviews were transcribed and analyzed. This data leads to the following 3 themes: social support, self-efficacy, and goal orientation. These themes will be useful for understanding the optimal way to increase motivation in female martial artists. (Witte, 2011, personal communication)

Qualitative, Quantitative, and Mixed Methods Introductions

A general review of all introductions shows that they follow a similar pattern: the author announces a problem and justifies why it needs to be studied. The type of problem presented in an introduction will vary depending on the approach (see Chapter 1). In a *qualitative* project, the author will describe a research problem that can best be understood by exploring a concept or phenomenon. We have suggested that qualitative research is exploratory and that researchers use it to probe a topic when the variables and theory base are unknown. For example, Morse (1991) said this:

> Characteristics of a qualitative research problem are: (a) the concept is "immature" due to a conspicuous lack of theory and previous research; (b) a notion that the available theory may be inaccurate, inappropriate, incorrect, or biased; (c) a need exists to explore and describe the phenomena and to develop theory; or (d) the nature of the phenomenon may not be suited to quantitative measures. (p. 120)

For example, urban sprawl (a problem) needs to be explored because it has not been examined in certain areas of a state. Alternatively, kids in elementary classrooms have anxiety that interferes with learning (a problem), and the best way to explore this problem is to go to schools and visit directly with teachers and students. Some qualitative researchers have a transformative lens through which the problem will be examined (e.g., the inequality of pay among women and men or the racial attitudes involved in profiling drivers on the highways). Thomas (1993) suggested that "critical researchers begin from the premise that all cultural life is in constant tension between control and resistance" (p. 9). This theoretical orientation shapes the structure of an introduction. Beisel (1990), for example, proposed to examine how the theory of class politics explained the lack of success of an anti-vice campaign in one of three American cities. Thus, within some qualitative studies, the approach in the introduction may be less inductive while still relying on the perspective of participants, like most qualitative studies. In addition, qualitative introductions may begin with a personal statement of experiences from the author, such as those found in phenomenological studies (Moustakas, 1994). They also may be written from a personal, first person, subjective point of view in which the researcher positions herself or himself in the narrative.

Less variation is seen in quantitative introductions. In a quantitative project, the problem is best addressed by understanding what factors or variables influence an outcome. For example, in response to worker cutbacks (a problem for all employees), an investigator may seek to discover what factors influence businesses to downsize. Another researcher may need to understand the high divorce rate among married couples (a problem) and examine whether financial issues contribute to divorce. In both of these situations, the research problem is one in which understanding the factors that explain or relate to an outcome helps the investigator best understand and explain the problem. In addition, in quantitative introductions, researchers sometimes advance a theory to test, and they will incorporate substantial reviews of the literature to identify research questions that need to be answered. A quantitative introduction may be written from the impersonal point of view and in the past tense, to convey objectivity.

A mixed methods study can employ either the qualitative or the quantitative approach (or some combination) to writing an introduction. In any given mixed methods study, the emphasis might tip in the direction of either quantitative or qualitative research, and the introduction will mirror that emphasis. For other mixed methods projects, the emphasis will be equal between qualitative and quantitative research. In this case, the problem may be one in which a need exists to both understand quantitatively the relationship among variables in a situation and explore qualitatively the topic in further depth. A mixed methods problem may also be that the existing research is primarily quantitative or qualitative in methodology, and a need exists to expand the approach to be more inclusive of diverse methodologies. A mixed methods project may initially seek to explain the relationship between smoking behavior and depression among adolescents, then explore the detailed views of these youth, and display different patterns of smoking and depression. With the first phase of this project as quantitative, the introduction may emphasize a quantitative approach with inclusion of a theory that predicts this relationship and a substantive review of the literature.

A Model for an Introduction

These differences among the various approaches are small, and they relate largely to the different types of problems addressed in qualitative, quantitative, and mixed methods studies. It should be helpful to illustrate an approach to designing and writing an introduction to a research study that researchers might use regardless of their approach.

The **deficiencies model of an introduction** is an approach to writing an introduction to a research study that builds on gaps existing in the literature. It includes the elements of stating the research problem, reviewing past studies about the problem, indicating deficiencies in these studies, and advancing the significance of the study. It is a general template for writing a good introduction. It is a popular approach used in the social sciences, and once its structure is elucidated, the reader will find it appearing repeatedly in many published research studies (not always in the order presented here). It consists of five parts, and a separate paragraph can be devoted to each part, for an introduction of about two pages in length:

1. State the research problem.

2. Review studies that have addressed the problem.

3. Indicate deficiencies in the studies.

4. Advance the **significance of the study** for particular audiences.

5. State the purpose statement.

An Illustration

Before a review of each part, here is an excellent example from a quantitative study published by Terenzini, Cabrera, Colbeck, Bjorklund, and Parente (2001) in *The Journal of Higher Education* and titled "Racial and Ethnic Diversity in the Classroom" (reprinted with permission). Following each major section in the introduction, we briefly highlight the component being addressed.

Since passage of the Civil Rights Act of 1964 and the Higher Education Act of 1965, America's colleges and universities have struggled to increase the racial and ethnic diversity of their students and faculty members, and "affirmative action" has become the policy-of-choice to achieve that heterogeneity. *[Authors state the narrative hook to create reader interest.]* These policies, however, are now at the center of an intense national debate. The current legal foundation for affirmative action policies rests on the 1978 *Regents of the University of California v. Bakke* case, in which Justice William Powell argued that race could be considered among the factors on which admissions decisions were based. More recently, however, the U.S. Court of Appeals for the Fifth Circuit, in the 1996 *Hopwood v. State of Texas* case, found Powell's argument wanting. Court decisions turning affirmative action policies aside have been accompanied by state referenda, legislation, and related actions banning or sharply reducing race-sensitive admissions or hiring in California, Florida, Louisiana, Maine, Massachusetts, Michigan, Mississippi, New Hampshire, Rhode Island, and Puerto Rico (Healy, 1998a, 1998b, 1999).

In response, educators and others have advanced educational arguments supporting affirmative action, claiming that a diverse student body is more educationally effective than a more homogeneous one. Harvard University President Neil Rudenstine claims that the "fundamental rationale for student diversity in higher education [is] its educational value" (Rudenstine, 1999, p. 1). Lee Bollinger, Rudenstine's counterpart at the University of Michigan, has asserted, "A classroom that does not have a significant representation from members of different races produces an impoverished discussion" (Schmidt, 1998, p. A32). These two presidents are not alone in their beliefs. A statement published by the Association of American Universities and endorsed by the presidents of 62 research universities stated: "We speak first and foremost as educators. We believe that our students benefit significantly from education that takes place within a diverse setting" ("On the Importance of Diversity in University Admissions," *The New York Times,* April 24, 1997, p. A27). *[Authors identify the research problem of the need for diversity.]*

Studies of the impact of diversity on student educational outcomes tend to approach the ways students encounter "diversity" in any of three ways. A small group of studies treat students' contacts with "diversity" largely as a function of the numerical or proportional racial/ethnic or gender mix of students on a campus (e.g., Chang, 1996, 1999a; Kanter, 1977; Sax, 1996). . . . A second considerably larger set of studies take some modicum of structural diversity as a given and operationalizes students' encounters with diversity using the frequency or nature of their reported interactions with peers who are racially/ethnically different from themselves. . . . A third set of studies examines institutionally structured and purposeful programmatic efforts to help students engage racial/ethnic and/or gender "diversity" in the form of both ideas and people.

These various approaches have been used to examine the effects of diversity on a broad array of student educational outcomes. The evidence is almost uniformly consistent in indicating that students in a racial/ethnically or gender-diverse community, or engaged in a diversity-related activity, reap a wide array of positive educational benefits. *[Authors mention studies that have addressed the problem.]*

Only a relative handful of studies (e.g., Chang, 1996, 1999a; Sax, 1996) have specifically examined whether *the racial/ethnic or gender composition* of the students on a campus, in an academic major, or in a classroom (i.e., structural diversity) has the educational benefits claimed. . . . Whether the degree of racial diversity of a campus or classroom has a *direct* effect on learning outcomes, however, remains an open question. *[Deficiencies or the limitations in existing studies are noted.]*

The scarcity of information on the educational benefits of the structural diversity on a campus or in its classrooms is regrettable because it is the sort of evidence the courts appear to be requiring if they are to support race-sensitive admissions policies. *[Importance of the study for campus audiences is mentioned.]*

This study attempted to contribute to the knowledge base by exploring the influence of structural diversity in the classroom on students' development of academic and intellectual skills. . . . This study examines both the direct effect of classroom diversity on academic/intellectual outcomes and whether any effects of classroom diversity may be moderated by the extent to which active and collaborative instructional approaches are used in the course. *[Purpose of the study is identified.]* (pp. 510–512, reprinted by permission of *The Journal of Higher Education*)

The Research Problem

In Terenzini and colleagues' (2001) article, the first sentence accomplishes both primary objectives for an introduction: (a) piquing interest in the study and (b) conveying a distinct research problem or issue. What effect did this sentence have? Would it entice a reader to read on? Was it pitched at a level so that a wide audience could understand it? These questions are important for opening sentences, and they are called a **narrative hook**, a term drawn from English composition, meaning words that serve to draw, engage, or hook the reader into the study. To learn how to write good narrative hooks, study first sentences in leading journals in different fields of study. Often, journalists provide good examples in the lead sentences of newspaper and magazine articles. Here, follow a few examples of lead sentences from social science journals:

- "The transsexual and ethno methodological celebrity Agnes changed her identity nearly three years before undergoing sex reassignment surgery." (Cahill, 1989, p. 281)

- "Who controls the process of chief executive succession?" (Boeker, 1992, p. 400)

- "There is a large body of literature that studies the cartographic line (a recent summary article is Butte in field, 1985), and generalization of cartographic lines (McMaster, 1987)." (Carstensen, 1989, p. 181)

All three of these examples present information easily understood by many readers. The first two—introductions in qualitative studies—demonstrate how reader interest can be created by reference to the single participant and by posing a question. The third example, a quantitative-experimental study, shows how one can begin with a literature perspective. All three examples demonstrate well how the lead sentence can be written so that the reader is not taken into a detailed morass of thought but lowered gently into the topic.

We use the metaphor of the writer lowering a barrel into a well. The *beginning* writer plunges the barrel (the reader) into the depths of the well (the article). The reader sees only unfamiliar material. The *experienced* writer lowers the barrel (the reader, again) slowly, allowing the reader to acclimate to the depths (of the study). This lowering of the barrel begins with *a narrative hook* of sufficient generality that the reader understands and can relate to the topic.

Beyond this first sentence, it is important to clearly identify the issue(s) or problem(s) that leads to a need for the study. Terenzini and colleagues (2001) discussed a distinct problem: the struggle to increase the racial and ethnic diversity on U.S. college and university campuses. They noted that policies to increase diversity are at "the center of an intense national debate" (p. 509).

In applied social science research, problems arise from issues, difficulties, and current practices in real-life situations. The research problem in a study begins to become clear when the researcher asks, "What is the need for this study?" or "What problem influenced the need to undertake this study?" For example, schools may not have implemented multicultural guidelines, the needs of faculty in colleges are such that they need to engage in professional development activities in their departments, minority students need better access to universities, or a community needs to better understand the contributions of its early female pioneers. These are all significant research problems that merit further study and establish a practical issue or concern that needs to be addressed. When designing the opening paragraphs of a proposal, which includes the research problem, keep in mind these **research tips**:

- Write an opening sentence that will stimulate reader interest as well as convey an issue to which a broad audience can relate.

- As a general rule, refrain from using quotations—especially long ones—in the lead sentence because it will be difficult for readers to grasp the key idea you would like for them to see. Quotations raise many possibilities for interpretation and thus create unclear beginnings. However, as is evident in some qualitative studies, quotations can create reader interest.

- Stay away from idiomatic expressions or trite phrases (e.g., "The lecture method remains a 'sacred cow' among most college and university instructors.").

- Consider numeric information for impact (e.g., "Every year, an estimated 5 million Americans experience the death of an immediate family member.").

- Clearly identify the research problem (i.e., dilemma, issue) leading to the study. Ask yourself, "Is there a specific sentence (or sentences) in which I convey the research problem?"

- Indicate why the problem is important by citing numerous references that justify the need to study the problem. In perhaps a less than joking manner, we say to our students that if they do not have a dozen references cited on the first page of their proposal, they do not have a scholarly study.

- Make sure that the problem is framed in a manner consistent with the approach to research in the study (e.g., exploratory in qualitative, examining relationships or predictors in quantitative, and either approach in mixed methods inquiry).

- Consider and write about whether there is a single problem involved in the proposed study or multiple problems that lead to a need for the study. Often, multiple research problems are addressed in research studies.

Studies Addressing the Problem

After establishing the research problem in the opening paragraphs, Terenzini and colleagues (2001) next justified its importance by **reviewing studies** that have examined the issue. We do not have in mind a complete literature review for the introduction passage. It is later, in the literature review section of a proposal, that students thoroughly review the literature. Instead, in the introduction, this literature review passage should summarize large groups of studies instead of individual ones. We tell students to reflect on their literature maps (described in Chapter 2) and look at and summarize the broad categories at the top into which they assigned their literature. These broad categories are what we mean by reviewing studies in an introduction to a proposal.

The purpose of reviewing studies in an introduction is to justify the importance of the study and to create distinctions between past studies and the proposed one. This component might be called "setting the research problem within the ongoing dialogue in the literature." Researchers do not want to conduct a study that replicates exactly what someone else has examined. New studies need to add to the literature or to extend or retest what others have investigated. The ability to frame the study in this way separates novices from more experienced researchers. The veteran has reviewed and understands what has been written about a topic or certain problem in the field. This knowledge comes from years of experience following the development of problems and their accompanying literature.

The question often arises as to what type of literature to review. Our best advice would be to review research studies in which authors advance research questions and report data to answer them (i.e., empirical articles). These studies might be quantitative, qualitative, or mixed methods studies. The important point is that the literature provides the research being addressed in the proposal. Beginning researchers often ask, "What do I do now? No research has been conducted on my topic." Of course, in some narrowly construed studies or in new, exploratory projects, no literature exists to document the research problem. Also, it makes sense that a topic is being proposed for study precisely because little research has been conducted on it. To counter this comment we suggest that an investigator think about the literature, using an inverted triangle as an image. At the bottom of the apex of the inverted triangle lies the scholarly study being proposed. This study is narrow and focused (and studies may not exist on it). If one broadens the review of the literature upward from the base of the inverted triangle, literature can be found, although it may be somewhat removed from the study at hand. For example, the narrow topic of at-risk African Americans in primary school may not have been researched; however, more broadly speaking, the topic of at-risk students generally in the primary school or at any level in education, may have been studied. The researcher would summarize the more general literature and end with statements about a need for studies that examine at-risk African American students at the primary school level.

To review the literature related to the research problem for an introduction to a proposal, consider these **research tips**:

- Refer to the literature by summarizing groups of studies, not individual ones (unlike the focus on single studies in the integrated review in Chapter 2). The intent should be to establish broad areas of research.

- To deemphasize single studies, place the in-text references at the end of a paragraph or at the end of a summary point about several studies.

- Review research studies that used quantitative, qualitative, or mixed methods approaches.

- Find recent literature to summarize, such as that published in the past 10 years. Cite older studies if they are valuable because they have been widely referenced by others.

Deficiencies in Past Literature

After advancing the problem and reviewing the literature about it, the researcher then identifies *deficiencies* found in this literature. Hence, we call this template for writing an introduction a *deficiencies model*. The nature of these deficiencies varies from study to study. **Deficiencies in past literature** may exist because topics have not been explored with a particular group, sample, or population; the literature may need to be replicated or repeated to see if the same findings hold because of mixed results given new samples of people or new sites for study; or the voices of underrepresented groups have not been heard in published literature. In any study, authors may mention one or more of these deficiencies. Deficiencies can often be found in the "suggestions for future research" sections of journal articles, and authors can reference these ideas and provide further justification for their proposed study.

Beyond mentioning the deficiencies, proposal writers need to tell how their planned study will remedy or address these deficiencies. For example, because past studies have overlooked an important variable, a study will include it and analyze its effect. For instance, because past studies have overlooked the examination of Native Americans as a cultural group, a study will include them as the participants in the project.

In Examples 5.1 and 5.2, the authors point out the gaps or shortcomings of the literature. Notice their use of key phrases to indicate the shortcomings: "what remains to be explored," "little empirical research," and "very few studies."

In summary, when identifying deficiencies in the past literature, proposal developers might use the following **research tips**:

- Cite several deficiencies to make the case even stronger for a study.

- Identify specifically the deficiencies of other studies (e.g., methodological flaws, variables overlooked).

- Write about areas overlooked by past studies, including topics, special statistical treatments, significant implications, and so forth.

- Discuss how a proposed study will remedy these deficiencies and provide a unique contribution to the scholarly literature.

These deficiencies might be mentioned using a series of short paragraphs that identify three or four shortcomings of the past research or focus on one major shortcoming, as illustrated in the Terenzini and colleagues' (2001) introduction.

Significance of a Study for Audiences

In dissertations, writers often include a specific section describing the significance of the study for select audiences in order to convey the importance of the problem for different groups that may profit from reading and using the study. By including this section, the writer creates a clear rationale for the importance of the study. The more audiences that can be mentioned, the greater the importance of the study and the more it will be seen by readers to have wide application. In designing this section, one might include the following:

- Three or four reasons that the study adds to the scholarly research and literature in the field

- Three or four reasons about how the study helps improve practice

- Three or four reasons as to why the study will improve policy or decision making

In Example 5.3, the author stated the significance of the study in the opening paragraphs of a journal article. This study by Mascarenhas (1989) examined ownership of industrial firms. He identified explicitly decision makers, organizational members, and researchers as the audience for the study.

Example 5.3 Significance of the Study Stated in an Introduction to a Quantitative Study

A study of an organization's ownership and its domain, defined here as markets served, product scope, customer orientation, and technology employed (Abell and Hammond, 1979; Abell, 1980; Perry and Rainey, 1988), is important for several reasons. First, understanding relationships among ownership and domain dimensions can help to reveal the underlying logic of organizations' activities and can help organization members evaluate strategies. . . . Second, a fundamental decision confronting all societies concerns the type of institutions to encourage or adopt for the conduct of activity. . . . Knowledge of the domain consequences of different ownership types can serve as input to that decision. . . . Third, researchers have often studied organizations reflecting one or two ownership types, but their findings may have been implicitly over generalized to all organizations.

(Mascarenhas, 1989, p. 582)

Terenzini and colleagues (2001) ended their introduction by mentioning how courts could use the information of the study to require colleges and universities to support "race-sensitive admissions policies" (p. 512). In addition, the authors might have mentioned the importance of this study for admissions offices and students seeking admission as well as the committees that review applications for admission.

Finally, good introductions to research studies end with a statement of the purpose or intent of the study. Terenzini and colleagues (2001) ended their introduction by conveying that they planned to examine the influence of structural diversity on student skills in the classroom. The purpose will be discussed in the next chapter: Chapter 6.

SUMMARY

This chapter provides advice about composing and writing an introduction to a scholarly study. The first element is to consider how the introduction incorporates the research problems associated with quantitative, qualitative, or mixed methods research. Then, a five-part introduction is suggested as a model or template to use. Called *the deficiencies model*, it is based on first identifying the research problem (and including a narrative hook). Then it includes briefly reviewing the literature that has addressed the problem, indicating one or more deficiencies in the past literature and suggesting how the study will remedy these deficiencies. Finally, the researcher addresses specific audiences that will profit from research on the problem, and the introduction ends with a purpose statement that sets forth the intent of the study (that will be addressed in the next chapter).

Writing Exercises

1. Draft several examples of narrative hooks for the introduction to a study, and share these with colleagues to determine if the hooks draw readers in, create interest in the study, and are presented at a level to which readers can relate.

2. Write the introduction to a proposed study. Include one paragraph each for the research problem, the related literature about this problem, the deficiencies in the literature, and the audiences who will potentially find the study of interest.

3. Locate several research studies published in scholarly journals in a particular field of study. Review the introductions, and locate the sentence or sentences in which the authors state the research problem or issue.

Additional Readings

Bem, D. J. (1987). Writing the empirical journal article. In M. P. Zanna & J. M. Darley (Eds.), *The compleat academic: A practical guide for the beginning social scientist* (pp. 171–201). New York: Random House.

Daryl Bem emphasizes the importance of the opening statement in published research. He provides a list of rules of thumb for opening statements, stressing the need for clear, readable prose and a structure that leads the reader step-by-step to the problem statement. Examples are provided of both satisfactory and unsatisfactory opening statements. Bem calls for opening statements that are accessible to the nonspecialist yet not boring to the technically sophisticated reader.

Creswell, J. W., & Gutterman, T. (in press). *Educational research: Designing, conducting, and evaluating qualitative and quantitative research* (6th ed.). Upper Saddle River, NJ: Pearson Education.

John Creswell and Tim Gutterman include a chapter on introducing an educational research study. They provide details about establishing the importance of a research problem and give an example of the deficiencies model for crafting a good introduction to a study.

Maxwell, J. A. (2005). *Qualitative research design: An interactive approach* (2nd ed.). Thousand Oaks, CA: Sage.

Joe Maxwell reflects on the purpose of a proposal for a qualitative dissertation. One of the fundamental aspects of a proposal is to justify the project—to help readers understand not only what you plan to do but also why. He mentions the importance of identifying the issues you plan to address and indicating why they are important to study. In an example of a graduate student dissertation proposal, he shares the major issues the student has addressed to create an effective argument for the study.

Wilkinson, A. M. (1991). *The scientist's handbook for writing papers and dissertations*. Englewood Cliffs, NJ: Prentice Hall.

Antoinette Wilkinson identifies the three parts of an introduction: (a) the derivation and statement of the problem and a discussion of its nature, (b) the discussion of the background of the problem, and (c) the statement of the research question. Her book offers numerous examples of these three parts—together with a discussion of how to write and structure an introduction. Emphasis is placed on ensuring that the introduction leads logically and inevitably to a statement of the research question.

$SAGE edge™

https://edge.sagepub.com/creswellrd5e

Students and instructors, please visit the companion website for videos featuring John W. Creswell, full-text SAGE journal articles, quizzes and activities, plus additional tools for research design.

The Purpose Statement

The last section of an introduction, as mentioned in Chapter 5, is to present a purpose statement that establishes the intent of the entire research study. It is the most important statement in the entire study, and it needs to be clear, specific, and informative. From it, all other aspects of the research follow, and readers will be lost unless it is carefully drafted. In journal articles, researchers write the purpose statement into introductions as the final statement; in theses and dissertations, it often stands as a separate section.

In this chapter devoted exclusively to the purpose statement, we address the reasons for developing it, key principles to use in its design, and examples of good models in crafting one for your proposal.

Significance and Meaning of a Purpose Statement

According to Locke, Spirduso, and Silverman (2013), the purpose statement indicates why you want to conduct the study and what you intend to accomplish. Unfortunately, proposal-writing texts give little attention to the purpose statement, and writers on method often incorporate it into discussions about other topics, such as specifying research questions or hypotheses. Wilkinson (1991), for example, refers to it within the context of the research question and objective. Other authors frame it as an aspect of the research problem (Castetter & Heisler, 1977). Closely examining their discussions, however, indicates that they both refer to the purpose statement as the central, controlling idea in a study.

This passage is called the purpose statement because it conveys the overall intent of a proposed study in a sentence or several sentences. It may also be called a study aim or the research objective of a project. In proposals, researchers need to distinguish clearly between the purpose statement, the research problem, and the research questions. The purpose statement sets forth the intent of the study, not the problem or issue leading to a need for the study (see Chapter 5). The purpose is also not the research questions—those questions that the data collection will attempt to answer (discussed in Chapter 7). Instead and again, the purpose statement sets the objectives, the intent, or the major idea of a proposal or a study. This idea builds on a need (the problem) and is refined into specific questions (the research questions).

Given the importance of the purpose statement, it is helpful to set it apart from other aspects of the proposal or study and to frame it as a single sentence or paragraph that readers can easily identify. Although qualitative, quantitative, and mixed methods purpose statements share similar topics, each is identified in the following paragraphs and illustrated with fill-in scripts for constructing a thorough but manageable purpose statement.

A Qualitative Purpose Statement

Good **qualitative purpose statements** contain information about the **central phenomenon** explored in the study, the participants in the study, and the research site. It also conveys an emerging design and uses research words drawn from the language of qualitative inquiry (Schwandt, 2014). Thus, one might consider several basic design features for writing this statement:

- Use words such as *purpose, intent, study aim,* or *objective* to signal attention to this statement as the central controlling idea. Set the statement off as a separate sentence or paragraph, and use the language of research, such as "The purpose (or intent or objective) of this study is (was) (will be) . . ." Researchers often use the present or past verb tense in journal articles and dissertations and the future tense in proposals because researchers are presenting a proposal for a study not yet undertaken.

- Focus on a single phenomenon (or concept or idea). Narrow the study to one idea to be explored or understood. This focus means that a purpose does not convey relating two or more variables or comparing two or more groups, as is typically found in quantitative research. Instead, advance a single phenomenon, recognizing that the study may evolve into an exploration of relationships or comparisons among ideas. None of these related explorations could be anticipated at the beginning. For example, a project might begin by exploring teacher identity and the marginalization of this identity in a particular school (Huber & Whelan, 1999), the meaning of baseball culture in a study of the work and talk of stadium employees (Trujillo, 1992), or how individuals cognitively represent AIDS (Anderson & Spencer, 2002). These examples illustrate a focus on a single idea.

- Use action verbs to convey how learning will take place. Action verbs and phrases, such as, *understand, develop, explore, examine the meaning of, generate,* or *discover,* keep the inquiry open and convey an emerging design.

- Use neutral words and phrases—nondirectional language—such as, exploring the "self-expression experiences of individuals" rather than the "*successful* self-expression of individuals." Other words and phrases that may be problematic include *useful, positive,* and *informing*—all words that suggest a directional outcome that may or may not occur. McCracken (1988) referred to the need in qualitative interviews to let the respondent describe his or her experience. Interviewers (or purpose statement writers) can easily violate the "law of nondirection" (McCracken, 1988, p. 21) in qualitative research by using words that suggest a directional orientation.

- Provide a general working definition of the central phenomenon or idea, especially if the phenomenon is a term that is not typically understood by a broad audience. Consistent with the rhetoric of qualitative research, this definition is not rigid and set but tentative and evolving throughout a study based on information from participants. Hence, a writer might say, "A tentative definition at this time for _____ (central phenomenon) is . . ." It should also be noted that this definition is not to be confused with the detailed definition of terms section as discussed in Chapter 2 on the review of the literature. The intent here is to convey to readers at an early stage in a proposal or research study a general sense of the central phenomenon so that they can better understand the types of questions and responses asked of participants and data sources.

- Include words denoting the strategy of inquiry to be used in data collection, analysis, and the process of research, such as whether the study will use an ethnographic, grounded theory, case study, phenomenological, narrative approach, or some other strategy.

- Mention the participants in the study, such as one or more individuals, a group of people, or an entire organization.

- Identify the site for the research, such as homes, classrooms, organizations, programs, or events. Describe this site in enough detail so that the reader knows exactly where a study will take place.

- As a final thought in the purpose statement, include some language that delimits the scope of participation or research sites in the study. For example, the study may be limited to women or Latinas only. The research site may be limited to one metropolitan city or to one small geographic area. The central phenomenon may be limited to individuals in business organizations who participate in creative teams. These delimitations help to further define the parameters of the research study.

Although considerable variation exists in the inclusion of these points in purpose statements, a good dissertation or thesis proposal should contain many of them.

To assist you, here is a **script** that should be helpful in drafting a complete statement. A script, as used in this book, contains the major words and ideas of a statement and provides space for the researcher to insert information.

> The purpose (or study aim) of this _____ (strategy of inquiry, such as ethnography, case study, or other type) study is (was? will be?) to _____ (understand? explore? develop? generate? discover?) the _____ (central phenomenon being studied) for _____ (the participants, such as the individual, groups, organization) at _____ (research site). At this stage in the research, the _____ (central phenomenon being studied) will be generally defined as _____ (provide a general definition).

Examples 6.1–6.4 may not illustrate perfectly all the elements of this script, but they represent adequate models to study and emulate.

Example 6.1 A Purpose Statement in a Qualitative Phenomenology Study

Lauterbach (1993) studied five women who had each lost a baby in late pregnancy and their memories and experiences of this loss. Her purpose statement was as follows:

> The phenomenological inquiry, as part of uncovering meaning, articulated "essences" of meaning in mothers' lived experiences when their wished-for babies died. Using the lens of the feminist perspective, the focus was on mothers' memories and their "living through" experience. This perspective facilitated breaking through the silence surrounding mothers' experiences; it assisted in articulating and amplifying mothers' memories and their stories of loss. Methods of inquiry included phenomenological reflection on data elicited by existential investigation of mothers' experiences, and investigation of the phenomenon in the creative arts. (p. 134)

We found Lauterbach's (1993) purpose statement in the opening section of the journal article under the heading "Aim of Study." Thus, the heading calls attention to this statement. "Mothers' lived experiences" would be the central phenomenon, the key being explored in a qualitative study, and the author uses the action word *portray* to discuss the *meaning* (a neutral word) of these experiences. The author further defined what experiences were examined when she identifies "memories" and "lived through" experiences. Throughout this passage, it is clear that Lauterbach

Example 6.2 A Purpose Statement in a Case Study

Kos (1991) conducted a multiple case study of perceptions of reading-disabled middle school students concerning factors that prevented these students from progressing in their reading development. Her purpose statement read as follows:

> The purpose of this study was to explore affective, social, and educational factors that may have contributed to the development of reading disabilities in four adolescents. The study also sought explanation as to why students' reading disabilities persisted despite years of instruction. This was not an intervention study and, although some students may have improved their reading, reading improvement was not the focus of the study. (pp. 876–877)

used the strategy of phenomenology. Also, the passage conveys that the participants were mothers, and later in the article, the reader learns that the author interviewed a convenience sample of five mothers, each of whom had experienced a perinatal death of a child in her home.

Notice Kos's (1991) disclaimer that this study was not a quantitative study measuring the magnitude of reading changes in the students. Instead, Kos clearly placed this study within the qualitative approach by using words such as *explore*. She focused attention on the central phenomenon of "factors" and provided a tentative definition by mentioning examples, such as "affective, social, and educational factors." She included this statement under a heading called "Purpose of the Study" to call attention to it, and she mentioned the participants. In the abstract and the methodology section, a reader finds out that the study used the inquiry strategy of case study research and that the study took place in a classroom.

Example 6.3 A Purpose Statement in an Ethnography

Rhoads (1997) conducted a 2-year ethnographic study exploring how the campus climate can be improved for gay and bisexual males at a large university. His purpose statement, included in the opening section, was as follows:

> The article contributes to the literature addressing the needs of gay and bisexual students by identifying several areas where progress can be made in improving the campus climate for them. This paper derives from a two-year ethnographic study of a student subculture composed of gay and bisexual males at a large research university; the focus on men reflects the fact that lesbian and bisexual women constitute a separate student subculture at the university under study. (p. 276)

With intent to improve the campus, this qualitative study falls into the genre of participatory–social justice research as mentioned in Chapter 3. Also, these sentences occur at the beginning of the article to signal the reader about the purpose of the study. The needs of these students become the central phenomenon under study, and the author seeks to identify areas that can improve the climate for gays and bisexual males. The author also mentioned that the strategy of inquiry is ethnographic and that the study will involve males (participants) at a large university (site). At this point, the author does not provide additional information about the exact nature of these needs or a working definition to begin the article. However, he does refer to identity and proffers a tentative meaning for that term in the next section of the study.

Example 6.4   A Purpose Statement in a Grounded Theory Study

Richie and colleagues (1997) conducted a qualitative study to develop a theory of the career development of 18 prominent, highly achieving African American Black and White women in the United States working in different occupational fields. In the second paragraph of this study, they stated the purpose:

> The present article describes a qualitative study of the career development of 18 prominent, highly achieving African-American Black and White women in the United States across eight occupational fields. Our overall aim in the study was to explore critical influences on the career development of these women, particularly those related to their attainment of professional success. (p. 133)

In this statement, the central phenomenon is career development, and the reader learns that the phenomenon is defined as critical influences in the professional success of the women. In this study, *success*, a directional word, serves to define the sample of individuals to be studied more than to limit the inquiry about the central phenomenon. The authors plan to explore this phenomenon, and the reader learns that the participants are all women, in different occupational groups. Grounded theory as a strategy of inquiry is mentioned in the abstract and later in the procedure discussion.

A Quantitative Purpose Statement

Quantitative purpose statements differ considerably from the qualitative models in terms of the language and a focus on relating or comparing variables or constructs. Recall from Chapter 3 the types of major variables: independent, mediating, moderating, and dependent.

The design of a quantitative purpose statement includes the variables in the study and their relationship, the participants, and the research site. It also includes language associated with quantitative research and the deductive testing of relationships or theories. A quantitative purpose statement begins with identifying the proposed major variables in a study (independent, intervening, dependent), accompanied by a visual model to clearly identify this sequence, and locating and specifying how the variables will be measured or observed. Finally, the intent of using the variables quantitatively will typically be either to relate variables, as one usually finds in a survey, or to compare samples or groups in terms of an outcome, as commonly found in experiments.

The major components of a good quantitative purpose statement include the following:

- Include words to signal the major intent of the study, such as *purpose, intent*, or *objective*. Start with "The purpose (or objective or intent) of this study is (was, will be) . . ."

- Identify the theory, model, or conceptual framework. At this point, one does not need to describe it in detail; in Chapter 3, we suggested the possibility of writing a separate "Theoretical Perspective" section for this purpose. Mentioning it in the purpose statement provides emphasis on the importance of the theory and foreshadows its use in the study.

- Identify the independent and dependent variables, as well as any mediating or moderating variables used in the study.

- Use words that connect the independent and dependent variables to indicate that they are related, such as "the relationship between" two or more variables or a "comparison of" two or more groups. Also, a purpose statement could be to "describe" variables. Most quantitative studies employ one or more of these three options for discussing variables in the purpose statement. A combination of comparing and relating might also exist—for example, a two-factor experiment in which the researcher has two or more treatment groups as well as a continuous independent variable. Although one typically finds studies about comparing two or more groups in experiments, it is also possible to compare groups in a survey study.

- Position or order the variables from left to right in the purpose statement—with the independent variable followed by the dependent variable. Place intervening variables between the independent and dependent variables. Many researchers also place the moderating variables as related to the independent variables. In experiments, the independent variable will always be the manipulated variable.

- Mention the specific type of strategy of inquiry (such as survey or experimental research) used in the study. By incorporating this information, the researcher anticipates the methods discussion and enables a reader to associate the relationship of variables to the inquiry approach.

- Make reference to the participants (or the unit of analysis) in the study, and mention the research site.

- Generally define each key variable, preferably using set and accepted established definitions found in the literature. General definitions are included at this point to help the reader best understand the purpose statement. They do not replace specific, operational definitions found later when a writer has a "Definition of Terms" section in a proposal (details about how variables will be measured). Also, delimitations that affect the scope of the study might be mentioned, such as the scope of the data collection or limited to certain individuals.

Based on these points, a quantitative purpose statement script can include these ideas:

The purpose of this _____ (experiment? survey?) study is (was? will be?) to test the theory of _____ that _____ (describes outcomes) or _____ (compares? relates?) the _____ (independent variable) to _____ (dependent variable), controlling for _____ (mediating or moderating variables) for _____ (participants) at _____ (the research site). The independent variable(s) _____ will be defined as _____ (provide a definition). The dependent variable(s) will be defined as _____ (provide a definition), and the intervening variable(s), _____, (identify the intervening variables) will be defined as _____ (provide a definition).

Examples 6.5–6.7 illustrate many of the elements in these scripts. The first two studies are surveys; the last one is an experiment.

Example 6.5 A Purpose Statement in a Published Survey Study

Kalof (2000) conducted a 2-year longitudinal study of 54 college women about their attitudes and experiences with sexual victimization. These women responded to two identical mail surveys administered 2 years apart. The author combined the purpose statement, introduced in the opening section, with the research questions.

This study is an attempt to elaborate on and clarify the link between women's sex role attitudes and experiences with sexual victimization. I used two years of data from 54 college women to answer these questions: (1) Do women's attitudes influence vulnerability to sexual coercion over a two-year period? (2) Are attitudes changed after experiences with sexual victimization? (3) Does prior victimization reduce or increase the risk of later victimization? (p. 48)

Although Kalof (2000) did not mention a theory that she sought to test, she identified both her independent variable (sex role attitudes) and the dependent variable (sexual victimization). She positioned these variables from independent to dependent. She also discussed linking rather than relating the variables to establish a connection between them (or describing them). This passage identified the participants (women) and the research site (a college setting). Later, in the method section, she mentioned that the study was a mailed survey. Although she did not define the major variables, she provided specific measures of the variables in the research questions.

Example 6.6 A Purpose Statement in a Dissertation Survey Study

DeGraw (1984) completed a doctoral dissertation in the field of education on the topic of educators working in adult correctional institutions. Under a section titled "Statement of the Problem," he advanced the purpose of the study:

> The purpose of this study was to examine the relationship between personal characteristics and the job motivation of certified educators who taught in selected state adult correctional institutions in the United States. Personal characteristics were divided into background information about the respondent (i.e., institutional information, education level, prior training, etc.) and information about the respondents' thoughts of changing jobs. The examination of background information was important to this study because it was hoped it would be possible to identify characteristics and factors contributing to significant differences in mobility and motivation. The second part of the study asked the respondents to identify those motivational factors of concern to them. Job motivation was defined by six general factors identified in the educational work components study (EWCS) questionnaire (Miskel & Heller, 1973). These six factors are: potential for personal challenge and development; competitiveness; desirability and reward of success; tolerance for work pressures; conservative security; and willingness to seek reward in spite of uncertainty vs. avoidance. (pp. 4–5)

This statement included several components of a good purpose statement. It was presented in a separate section, it used the word *relationship*, terms were defined, and the sample was specified. Further, from the order of the variables in the statement, one can clearly identify the independent variable and the dependent variable.

Example 6.7 A Purpose Statement in an Experimental Study

Booth-Kewley, Edwards, and Rosenfeld (1992) undertook a study comparing the social desirability of responding to a computer version of an attitude and personality questionnaire with completing a pencil-and-paper version. They replicated a study completed on college students that used an inventory, called Balanced Inventory of Desirable Responding (BIDR), composed of two scales: (a) impression management (IM) and (b) self-deception (SD). In the final paragraph of the introduction, they advanced the purpose of the study:

(Continued)

We designed the present study to compare the responses of Navy recruits on the IM and SD scales, collected under three conditions— with paper-and-pencil, on a computer with backtracking allowed, and on a computer with no back-tracking allowed. Approximately half of the recruits answered the questionnaire anonymously and the other half identified them-selves. (p. 563)

This statement also reflected many properties of a good purpose state-ment. The statement was separated from other ideas in the introduction as a separate paragraph; it mentioned that a comparison would be made, and it identified the participants in the experiment (i.e., the unit of analysis). In terms of the order of the variables, the authors advanced them with the dependent variable first, contrary to our suggestion (still, the groups are clearly identified). Although the theory base is not mentioned, the para-graphs preceding the purpose statement reviewed the findings of prior the-ory. The authors also did not tell us about the strategy of inquiry, but other passages, especially those related to procedures, identified the study as an experiment.

A Mixed Methods Purpose Statement

Mixed methods purpose statements contains the overall intent of the study, information about both the quantitative and qualitative strands of the study, and a rationale of incorporating both strands to study the research problem. These statements need to be identified early, in the introduction, and they provide major signposts for the reader to under-stand the quantitative and qualitative parts of a study. Several guidelines might direct the organization and presentation of the mixed methods pur-pose statement:

- Begin with words that signal intent, such as "The purpose of," "The study aim is," or "The intent of."

- Indicate the overall purpose of the study from a content perspective, such as "The intent is to learn about organizational effectiveness" or "The intent is to examine families with stepchildren." In this way, the reader has an anchor to use to understand the overall study before the researcher divides the project into quantitative and qualitative strands.

- Indicate the type of mixed methods design, such as a convergent design, an explanatory sequential design, an exploratory sequential design or a complex design (as discussed in Chapter 10).

- Discuss the reasons or justification for combining both quantitative and qualitative data. This reason could be one of the following (see Chapter 10 for more detail about these reasons):

  o To develop a complete understanding of a research problem by comparing quantitative and qualitative results from the two databases (a convergent design).

  o To understand the data at a more detailed level by using qualitative follow-up data collection to help explain quantitative results, such as a survey (see also O'Cathain, Murphy, & Nicholl, 2007) (an explanatory sequential design).

  o To develop a new measurement instrument that actually fits the culture of a sample by first exploring qualitatively (e.g., through interviews) and then testing the instrument with a large sample (an exploratory sequential design).

  o To incorporate these reasons (and designs) into a larger design, methodology, or theory such as an experimental design, a case study or evaluation methodology, or a theory of participatory–social justice research (see Chapter 10).

Based on these elements, three examples of mixed methods purpose statement scripts follow based on the convergent, explanatory sequential, and exploratory sequential designs (Creswell & Plano Clark, 2018). This first example of a mixed methods purpose statement is a script for a convergent mixed methods strategy in which quantitative and qualitative data are collected and analyzed separately and the two databases compared to best understand a research problem.

This mixed methods study will address _____ [overall content aim]. A convergent mixed methods design will be used, and it is a type of design in which qualitative and quantitative data are collected in parallel, analyzed separately, and then merged. In this study, _____ [quantitative data] will be used to test the theory of _____ [the theory] that predicts that _____ [independent variables] will _____ [positively, negatively] influence the _____ [dependent variables] for _____ [participants] at _____ [the site]. The _____ [type of qualitative data] will explore _____ [the central phenomenon] for _____ [participants] at _____ [the site]. The reason for collecting both quantitative and qualitative data is to _____ [the mixing reason].

This second script illustrates a mixed methods purpose statement for an explanatory sequential design in which the intent is to understand the quantitative database at a deeper level using follow-up qualitative data.

This study will address _____ [content aim]. An explanatory sequential mixed methods design will be used, and it will involve collecting quantitative data first and then explaining the quantitative results with in-depth qualitative data. In the first quantitative phase of the study, _____ [quantitative instrument] data will be collected from _____ [participants] at _____ [research site] to test _____ [name of theory] to assess whether _____ [independent variables] relate to _____ [dependent variables]. The second qualitative phase will be conducted as a follow up to the quantitative results to help explain the quantitative results. In this exploratory follow-up, the tentative plan is to explore _____ [the central phenomenon] with _____ [participants] at _____ [research site].

The final script is an illustration of the purpose statement that might be used for an exploratory sequential design in which the intent is to develop measures (or instruments) that work with a sample by first collecting qualitative data and then using it to design measures or the instrument that can be tested with a sample of a population.

This study addresses _____ [content aim]. The purpose of this exploratory sequential design will be to first qualitatively explore with a small sample, to design a feature (e.g., instrument, website, experimental intervention activities, new variables), and then to test this feature out with a large sample. The first phase of the study will be a qualitative exploration of _____ [the central phenomenon] in which _____ [types of data] will be collected from _____ [participants] at _____ [research site]. From this initial exploration, the qualitative findings will be used to develop a quantitative feature that can be tested with a large sample. In the tentatively planned quantitative phase, _____ [quantitative data] will be collected from _____ [participants] at _____ [research site].

Other examples are available that include embedding the core mixed methods designs (i.e., convergent, explanatory sequential, and exploratory sequential) into complex designs such as an intervention or experimental trial, a case study, a participatory–social justice framework, or an evaluation study can be found in Creswell and Plano Clark (2018).

It is helpful to look closely at several examples of purpose statements as found in recent published articles. Although these examples may not include all of the elements of the scripts, they do serve as examples of reasonably complete purpose statements that clearly convey the purpose of a mixed methods study. The discussion will be limited to the three core types of design: (a) a convergent design (Example 6.8), (b) an explanatory sequential design (Example 6.9), and (c) an exploratory sequential design (Example 6.10). Other designs that expand these possibilities will be detailed further in Chapter 10.

Example 6.8 A Convergent Mixed Methods Purpose Statement

Classen and colleagues (2007) developed a health promotion model for older driver safety. Conducting a large secondary analysis of a national database, they examined the risk and protective factors influencing driver injuries (the quantitative phase). They also conducted a qualitative meta-synthesis of six studies to determine narrative results pertaining to needs, factors influencing safety, and safety priorities of older driver stakeholders (the qualitative phase). They then compared the two databases to integrate the results from both sets of data. Their purpose statement was as follows:

This study provided an explicit socio-ecological view explaining the interrelation of possible causative factors, an integrated summary of these factors, and empirical guidelines for developing public health interventions to promote older driver safety. Using a mixed methods approach, we were able to compare and integrate main findings from a national crash dataset with perspectives of stakeholders. (p. 677)

This passage was written into the abstract and perhaps it would have been better inserted into the introduction. It indicated the use of both quantitative and qualitative data; although more detail might have been given to identify the theory (a model was advanced at the beginning of the study), the specific variables analyzed and the central phenomenon of the qualitative phase of the study.

Example 6.9 An Explanatory Sequential Mixed Methods Purpose Statement

Ivankova and Stick (2007) studied factors contributing to students' persistence in a distributed doctoral program (distance online learning). They first collected survey data to examine external and internal program factors that might predict student persistence, and then they followed up with qualitative

interviews of students that grouped into four categories of persistence. They ended by advancing case studies of four types of graduate persisters. The purpose statement was as follows:

The purpose of this mixed methods sequential explanatory study was

(Continued)

(Continued)

to identify factors contributing to students' persistence in the ELHE program by obtaining quantitative results from a survey of 278 current and former students and then following up with four purposefully selected individuals to explore those results in more depth through a qualitative case study analysis. In the first, quantitative, phase of the study, the research questions focused on how selected internal and external variables to the ELHE program (program-related, advisor- and faculty-related, institutional-related, student-related factors, and external factors) served as predictors to students' persistence in the program. In the second, qualitative, phase, four case studies from distinct participant groups explored in-depth the results from the statistical tests. In this phase, the research questions addressed seven internal and external factors, found to have differently contributed to the function discriminating the four groups: program, online learning environment, faculty, student support services, self motivation, virtual community, and academic advisor. (p. 95)

In this example, the purpose statement closely followed the script advanced earlier for an explanatory sequential design. It began with an overall intent statement, followed by the identification of the first quantitative phase (including the specific variables examined), and then the qualitative follow-up phase. It ended with the four case studies and the mixed methods rationale to use the case studies to further explore the results from the statistical tests.

Example 6.10 An Exploratory Sequential Mixed Methods Purpose Statement

Enosh and colleagues (2015) are researchers in the discipline of social work and human services. The topic of their 2015 exploratory sequential mixed methods study was to examine social workers' exposure to different forms of violence perpetrated by their clients. The overall purpose of their study was to explore social workers' experiences with client violence, develop an instrument for measuring client violence, and to obtain generalized information about client violence for social workers across different contexts. They stated their purpose statement as:

Therefore, the goal of this study was to develop a behavior-based instrument that could be used to compare between different types of workplaces, services (health, tourism), sectors (public, private), and occupations (social workers, nurses, bank workers, hotel personnel). In the current study, we have developed and validated the instrument for one specific population: social workers.

To accomplish the study's purpose, Enosh et al. (2015) reported that their exploratory sequential mixed methods study unfolded in "distinct stages of research" (p. 283). They began their study with a qualitative exploration of social workers' experiences with client violence. using qualitative interviews. In the second stage of the study, the researchers developed the Client Violence Questionnaire (CVQ). Once the instrument was developed, Enosh and colleagues initiated the final quantitative phase of the exploratory design. The authors implemented two different survey procedures to apply and test the developed instrument. Although the purpose was announced by the authors in several sections of the study, they included the overall intent, the collection of both quantitative and qualitative data, and the reason for collecting both forms of data.

SUMMARY

This chapter emphasizes the primary importance of a purpose statement. This statement advances the central idea in a study. In writing a qualitative purpose statement, a researcher needs to identify a single central phenomenon and to pose a tentative definition for it. Also, the researcher includes in this statement strong action words, such as *discover*, *develop*, or *understand*; uses nondirectional language; and mentions the strategy of inquiry, the participants, and the research site. In a quantitative purpose statement, the researcher states the theory being tested as well as the variables and their description, relationship, or comparison. It is important to position the independent variable first and the dependent variable second. The researcher conveys the strategy of inquiry as well as the participants and the research site for the investigation. In some purpose statements, the researcher also defines the key variables used in the study. In a mixed methods study, a purpose statement includes a statement of intent, the type of mixed methods design, the forms of qualitative and quantitative data collection and analysis, and the reason for collecting both forms of data.

Writing Exercises

1. Using the script for a qualitative purpose statement, write a statement by completing the blanks. Make this statement short; write no more than approximately three-quarters of a typed page.

2. Using the script for a quantitative purpose statement, write a statement. Also make this statement short, no longer than three-quarters of a typed page.

3. Using the script for a mixed methods purpose statement, write a purpose statement. Be sure to include the reason for mixing quantitative and qualitative data, and incorporate the elements of both a good qualitative and a good quantitative purpose statement.

Additional Readings

Creswell, J. W., & Plano Clark, V. L. (2018). *Designing and conducting mixed methods research* (3rd ed.). Thousand Oaks, CA: Sage.

John W. Creswell and Vicki L. Plano Clark have authored an overview and introduction to mixed methods research that covers the entire process of research from writing an introduction, collecting data, analyzing data, and interpreting and writing mixed methods studies. In their chapter on the introduction, they discuss qualitative, quantitative, and mixed methods purpose statements. They provide scripts and examples of mixed methods designs as well as overall guidelines for writing these statements.

Marshall, C., & Rossman, G. B. (2011). *Designing qualitative research* (5th ed.). Thousand Oaks, CA: Sage.

Catherine Marshall and Gretchen Rossman call attention to the major intent of the study: the purpose of the study. This section is generally embedded in the discussion of the topic, and it is mentioned in a sentence or two. It tells the reader what the results of the research are likely to accomplish. The authors characterize purposes as exploratory, explanatory, descriptive, and emancipatory. They also mention that the purpose statement includes the unit of analysis (e.g., individuals, dyads, or groups).

Wilkinson, A. M. (1991). *The scientist's handbook for writing papers and dissertations.* Englewood Cliffs, NJ: Prentice Hall.

Antoinette Wilkinson calls the purpose statement the "immediate objective" of the research study. She states that the purpose of the objective is to answer the research question. Further, the objective of the study needs to be presented in the introduction, although it may be implicitly stated as the subject of the research, the paper, or the method. If stated explicitly, the objective is found at the end of the argument in the introduction; it might also be found near the beginning or in the middle, depending on the structure of the introduction.

$SAGE edge™

https://edge.sagepub.com/creswellrd5e

Students and instructors, please visit the companion website for videos featuring John W. Creswell, full-text SAGE journal articles, quizzes and activities, plus additional tools for research design.

Research Questions and Hypotheses

Investigators place signposts to carry the reader through a plan for a study. The first signpost is the purpose statement, which establishes the central intent for the study. The next would be the research questions or hypotheses that narrow the purpose statement to predictions about what will be learned or questions to be answered in the study. This chapter begins by advancing several principles in designing qualitative research questions and helpful scripts for writing these questions. It then turns to the design of quantitative research questions and hypotheses and ways to write these elements into a study. Finally, it advances the use of research questions and hypotheses in mixed methods studies, and it suggests the development of a unique mixed methods question that ties together or integrates the quantitative and qualitative data in a study.

Qualitative Research Questions

In a qualitative study, inquirers state research questions, not objectives (i.e., specific goals for the research) or hypotheses (i.e., predictions that involve variables and statistical tests). These research questions assume two forms: (a) a central question and (b) associated subquestions.

- *Ask one or two central research questions.* The central question is a broad question that asks for an exploration of the central phenomenon or concept in a study. The inquirer poses this question, consistent with the emerging methodology of qualitative research, as a general issue so as to not limit the views of participants. To arrive at this question, *ask,* "What is the broadest question that I can ask in the study?" Beginning researchers trained in quantitative research might struggle with this approach because they are accustomed to reverse thinking. They narrow the quantitative study to specific, narrow questions or hypotheses based on a few variables. In qualitative research, the intent is to explore the general, complex set of factors surrounding the central phenomenon and present the broad, varied perspectives or meanings that participants hold. The following are guidelines for writing qualitative research questions:

- *Ask no more than five to seven subquestions in addition to your central questions.* Several subquestions follow each general central question; they narrow the focus of the study but leave open the questioning. This approach is well within the limits set by Miles and Huberman (1994), who recommended that researchers write no more than a dozen qualitative research questions in all (central and subquestions). The subquestions, in turn, become specific questions used during interviews (or in observing or when looking at documents). In developing an interview protocol or guide, the researcher might ask an icebreaker question at the beginning, for example, followed by five or so subquestions in the study (see Chapter 9). The interview would then end with an additional wrap-up or summary question or by asking, "Who should I turn to, to learn more about this topic?" (Asmussen & Creswell, 1995).

• *Relate the central question to the specific qualitative strategy of inquiry.* For example, the specificity of the questions in ethnography at this stage of the design differs from that in other qualitative strategies. In ethnographic research, Spradley (1980) advanced a taxonomy of ethnographic questions that included a mini-tour of the culture-sharing group, their experiences, use of native language, contrasts with other cultural groups, and questions to verify the accuracy of the data. In critical ethnography, the research questions may build on a body of existing literature. These questions become working guidelines rather than proven truths (Thomas, 1993, p. 35). Alternatively, in phenomenology, the questions might be broadly stated without specific reference to the existing literature or a typology of questions. Moustakas (1994) talked about asking what the participants experienced and what contexts or situations in which they experienced it. A phenomenological example is "What is it like for a mother to live with a teenage child who is dying of cancer?" (Nieswiadomy, 1993, p. 151). In grounded theory, the questions may be directed toward generating a theory of some process, such as the exploration of a process as to how caregivers and patients interact in a hospital setting. In a qualitative case study, the questions may address a description of the case and the themes that emerge from studying it.

• *Begin the research questions with the words* what *or how to convey an open and emerging design.* The word *why* often implies that the researcher is trying to explain why something occurs, and this suggests to us probable cause-and-effect thinking that we associate with *quantitative* research and that limits the explanations rather than opening them up for participant views.

• *Focus on a single phenomenon or concept.* As a study develops over time, factors will emerge that may influence this single phenomenon, but begin a study with a single focus to explore in great detail. We often ask, "What is the one, single concept that you want to explore?"

• *Use exploratory verbs that convey the language of emerging design.* These verbs tell the reader that the study will do the following:

○ Report (or reflect) the stories (e.g., narrative research)

○ Describe the essence of the experience (e.g., phenomenology)

○ Discover or generate (e.g., grounded theory)

○ Seek to understand (e.g., ethnography)

○ Explore a process (e.g., case study)

- *Use these more exploratory verbs as nondirectional rather than directional words of quantitative research, such as* affect, influence, impact, determine, cause, *and* relate.

- *Expect the research questions to evolve and change during the study in a manner consistent with the assumptions of an emerging design.* Often in qualitative studies, the questions are under continual review and reformulation (as in a grounded theory study). This approach may be problematic for individuals accustomed to quantitative designs in which the research questions remain fixed and never change throughout the study.

- *Use open-ended questions without reference to the literature or theory unless otherwise indicated by a qualitative strategy of inquiry.*

- *Specify the participants and the research site for the study if the information has not yet been given.*

Here is a typical script for a qualitative central question:

_____ (How or what?) is the _____ ("story for" for narrative research; "meaning of" the phenomenon for phenomenology; "theory that explains the process of" for grounded theory; "culture-sharing pattern" for ethnography; "issue" in the "case" for case study) of _____ (central phenomenon) for _____ (participants) at _____ (research site).

Examples 7.1 and 7.2 illustrate qualitative research questions drawn from several types of strategies.

Example 7.1   A Qualitative Central Question From an Ethnography

Mac an Ghaill and Haywood (2015) researched the changing cultural conditions inhabited by a group of British-born, working-class Pakistani and Bangladeshi young men over a 3-year period. They did not specifically construct a research question, but we would suggest it as follows:

> What are the core beliefs related to ethnicity, religion, and cultural belonging of the group of British-born, working-class Pakistani and Bangladeshi young men over a 3-year time period, and how do the young men construct and understand their geographically

specific experiences of family, schooling, and social life, as well as growing up and interacting within their local community in a rapidly changing Britain?

This question would have begun with "what," and it would single out the central phenomenon—core beliefs—for the young men. The young men are the participants in the study, and, as an ethnography, the study clearly attempts to examine the cultural beliefs of these young Pakistani and Bangladeshi young men. Further, from the question, we can see that the study is situated in Britain.

These three central questions all began with the word *how*; they included open-ended verbs, such as *describe,* and they focused on three aspects of the doctoral experience—returning to school, reentering, and changing. They also mentioned the participants as women in a doctoral program at a midwestern research university.

Quantitative Research Questions and Hypotheses

In quantitative studies, investigators use quantitative research questions and hypotheses, and sometimes objectives, to shape and specifically focus the purpose of the study. **Quantitative research questions** inquire about the relationships among variables that the investigator seeks to know. They are frequently used in social science research and especially in survey studies. **Quantitative hypotheses,** on the other hand, are predictions the researcher makes about the expected outcomes of relationships among variables. They are numeric estimates of population values based on data collected from samples. Testing of hypotheses employs statistical procedures in which the investigator draws inferences about the population from a study sample (see also Chapter 8). Hypotheses are used often in experiments or intervention trials in which investigators compare groups. Advisers sometimes recommend their use in a formal research project, such as a dissertation or thesis, as a means of stating the direction a study will take. Objectives, on the other hand, indicate the goals or objectives for a study. They often appear in proposals for funding, but tend to be used with less frequency in social and health science research. Because of this, the focus here will be on research questions and hypotheses.

Here is an example of a script for a quantitative research question describing outcomes of score for a variable:

What is the frequency and variation of scores on _____ (name the variable) for _____ (participants) in the study?

Here is an example of a script for a quantitative research question focused on examining the relationship among variables:

Does _____ (name the theory) explain the relationship between _____ (independent variable) and _____ (dependent variable), controlling for the effects of _____ (mediating variable)?

Alternatively, a script for a quantitative **null hypothesis** might be as follows:

There is no significant difference between _____ (the control and experimental groups on the independent variable) on _____ (dependent variable).

Guidelines for writing good quantitative research questions and hypotheses include the following.

• The use of variables in research questions or hypotheses is typically limited to three basic approaches. The researcher may *compare* groups on an independent variable to see its impact on a dependent variable (this would be an experiment or group comparisons). Alternatively, the investigator may *relate* one or more independent variables to one or more dependent variables (this would be a survey that correlates variables). Third, the researcher may *describe* responses to the independent, mediating, or dependent variables (this would be a descriptive study). Most quantitative research falls into one or more of these three categories.

• The most rigorous form of quantitative research follows from a test of a theory (see Chapter 3) and the specification of research questions or hypotheses that logically follow from the relationship among variables in the theory.

• The independent and dependent variables must be measured separately and not measured on the same concept. This procedure reinforces the cause-and-effect logic of quantitative research.

• To eliminate redundancy, write only research questions or hypotheses—not both—unless the hypotheses build on the research questions. Choose the form based on tradition, recommendations from an adviser or faculty committee, or whether past research indicates a prediction about outcomes.

• If hypotheses are used, there are two forms: (a) null and (b) alternative. A null hypothesis represents the traditional approach: It makes a prediction that in the general population, no relationship or no significant difference exists between groups on a variable. The wording is, "There is no difference (or relationship)" between the groups. Example 7.3 illustrates a null hypothesis.

Example 7.3 A Null Hypothesis

An investigator might examine three types of reinforcement for children with autism: (a) verbal cues, (b) a reward, and (c) no reinforcement. The investigator collects behavioral measures assessing social interaction of the children with their siblings. A null hypothesis might read as follows:

There is no significant difference between the effects of verbal cues, rewards, and no reinforcement in terms of social interaction for children with autism and their siblings.

• The second form, popular in journal articles, is the alternative or directional hypothesis. The investigator makes a prediction about the expected outcome, basing this prediction on prior literature and studies on the topic that suggest a potential outcome. For example, the researcher may predict that "scores will be higher for Group A than for Group B" on the dependent variable or that "Group A will change more than Group B" on the outcome. These examples illustrate a directional hypothesis because an expected prediction (e.g., higher, more change) is made. Example 7.4 illustrates a directional hypothesis.

Example 7.4 Directional Hypotheses

Mascarenhas (1989) studied the differences between types of ownership (state-owned, publicly traded, and private) of firms in the offshore drilling industry. Specifically, the study explored such differences as domestic market dominance, international presence, and customer orientation. The study was a controlled field study using quasi-experimental procedures.

Hypothesis 1: Publicly traded firms will have higher growth rates than privately held firms.

Hypothesis 2: Publicly traded enterprises will have a larger international scope than state-owned and privately held firms.

Hypothesis 3: State-owned firms will have a greater share of the domestic market than publicly traded or privately held firms.

Hypothesis 4: Publicly traded firms will have broader product lines than state-owned and privately held firms.

Hypothesis 5: State-owned firms are more likely to have state-owned enterprises as customers overseas.

Hypothesis 6: State-owned firms will have a higher customer-base stability than privately held firms.

Hypothesis 7: In less visible contexts, publicly traded firms will employ more advanced technology than state-owned and privately held firms. (pp. 585–588)

- Another type of alternative statement is the **nondirectional hypothesis**—a prediction is made, but the exact form of differences (e.g., higher, lower, more, less) is not specified because the researcher does not know what can be predicted from past literature. Thus, the investigator might write, "There is a difference" between the two groups. Example 7.5 incorporates both types of hypotheses.

Example 7.5 Nondirectional and Directional Hypotheses

Sometimes directional hypotheses are created to examine the relationship among variables rather than to compare groups because the researcher has some evidence from past studies of the potential outcome of the study. For example, Moore (2000) studied the meaning of gender identity for religious and secular Jewish and Arab women in Israeli society. In a national probability sample of Jewish and Arab women, the author identified three hypotheses for study. The first is nondirectional and the last two are directional.

H₁: Gender identity of religious and secular Arab and Jewish women are related to different sociopolitical social orders that reflect the different value systems they embrace.

H₂: Religious women with salient gender identity are less sociopolitically active than secular women with salient gender identities.

H₃: The relationships among gender identity, religiosity, and social actions are weaker among Arab women than among Jewish women.

- Unless the study intentionally employs demographic variables as predictors, use nondemographic variables (i.e., attitudes or behaviors) as **mediating variables.** These are variables that "stand between" the independent and dependent variables. Demographic variables are often used as **moderating variables** that affect the influence of the independent variable on the dependent variable. Because quantitative studies attempt to verify theories, demographic variables (e.g., age, income level, educational level) typically enter these studies as moderating variables instead of major independent variables.

- Use the same pattern of word order in the questions or hypotheses to enable a reader to easily identify the major variables. This calls for repeating key phrases and positioning the variables with the independent first and concluding with the dependent in left-to-right order (as discussed in Chapter 6 on good purpose statements). Example 7.6 illustrates word order with independent variables stated first in the phrase.

Example 7.6   Standard Use of Language in Hypotheses

1. There is no relationship between utilization of ancillary support services and academic persistence for nontraditional-aged women college students.

2. There is no relationship between family support systems and academic persistence for nontraditional-aged college women.

3. There is no relationship between ancillary support services and family support systems for non-traditional-aged college women.

A Model for Descriptive Questions and Hypotheses

Example 7.7 illustrates a model for writing questions or hypotheses based on writing descriptive questions (describing something) followed by inferential questions or hypotheses (drawing inferences from a sample to a population). These questions or hypotheses include both independent and dependent variables. In this model, the writer specifies descriptive questions for *each* independent and dependent variable and important intervening or moderating variables. Inferential questions (or hypotheses) that relate variables or compare groups follow these descriptive questions. A final set of questions may add inferential questions or hypotheses in which variables are controlled.

Example 7.7   Descriptive and Inferential Questions

To illustrate this approach, a researcher wants to examine the relationship of critical thinking skills (an independent variable measured on an instrument) to student achievement (a dependent variable measured by grades) in science classes for eighth-grade students in a large metropolitan school district. The researcher moderates the assessment of critical thinking using prior grades as indicators in science classes and controls for the mediating influence of parents' educational attainment. Following the proposed model, the research questions might be written as follows:

Descriptive Questions

1. How do the students rate on critical thinking skills? (A descriptive question focused on the independent variable)

2. What are the student's achievement levels (or grades) in science classes? (A descriptive question focused on the dependent variable)

3. What are the student's prior grades in science classes and their critical thinking skills? (A descriptive question focused on the moderating variable of prior grades)

4. What is the educational attainment of the parents of the eighth graders? (A descriptive question focused on a mediating variable, educational attainment of parents)

Inferential Questions

1. How does critical thinking ability relate to student achievement? (An inferential question relating the independent and the dependent variables)

2. How does critical thinking ability and prior grades influence student achievement? (An inferential question relating critical thinking times grades [moderating variable] and student achievement)

3. How does critical thinking ability (or critical thinking ability times grades) relate to student achievement, mediating for the effects of the educational attainment of the eighth-graders' parents? (An inferential question relating the independent and the dependent variables, controlling for the effects of the mediating variable)

This example illustrated how to organize all the research questions into descriptive and inferential questions. In another example, a researcher may want to compare groups, and the language may change to reflect this comparison in the inferential questions. In other studies, many more independent and dependent variables may be present in the model being tested, and a longer list of descriptive and inferential questions would result. We recommend this descriptive-inferential model. This example also illustrated the use of variables to describe as well as relate. It specified the independent variables in the first position in the questions, the dependent in the second, and the mediating variable in the third. It employed demographics (grades) as a moderating variable rather than as central variables in the questions, and a reader needed to assume that the questions flowed from a theoretical model.

Mixed Methods Research Questions and Hypotheses

In discussions about methods, researchers typically do not see specific questions or hypotheses especially tailored to mixed methods research. However, discussion now exists about the use of a new type of research question—a mixed methods question—in studies and commentary as to how to design them (see Creswell & Plano Clark, 2011, 2018 Tashakkori & Creswell, 2007). A strong mixed methods study should contain at least three research questions: the qualitative question, the quantitative question or hypothesis, and a mixed methods question. This mixed methods question represents what the researcher needs to know about the integration or combination of the quantitative and qualitative data. This configuration is necessary because mixed methods does not rely exclusively on either qualitative or quantitative research but on *both* forms of inquiry. Researchers should consider what types of questions should be presented and when and what information is most needed to convey the nature of the study:

- Both qualitative and quantitative research questions (or hypotheses) need to be advanced in a mixed methods study in order to narrow and focus the purpose statement. Before the two databases can be integrated or combined, they need to be analyzed separately in response to questions (or hypotheses). These questions or hypotheses can be advanced at the beginning or emerge during a later phase of the research. For example, if the study begins with a quantitative phase, the investigator might introduce hypotheses. Later in the study, when the qualitative phase is addressed, the qualitative research questions appear.

- When writing these questions or hypotheses, follow the guidelines in this chapter for scripting good questions or hypotheses.

- Some attention should be given to the order of the research questions and hypotheses. The order will reflect the type of mixed methods design being used, as will be discussed in Chapter 10. In a single-phase mixed methods project in which the quantitative and qualitative results are merged, either the quantitative or the qualitative questions can be posed first. In a two-phase project, the first-phase questions would come first, followed by the second-phase questions so that readers see them in the order in which they will be addressed in the proposed study. In a three-phase project, often the mixed methods question will reside in the middle in the order of questioning, and the first-phase question will be qualitative and the final-phase question will be quantitative. These different types of phased projects will be discussed later in Chapter 10 as specific types of mixed methods research designs.

- In addition to quantitative questions/hypotheses and qualitative questions, include a **mixed methods research question** that directly addresses the mixing or integration of the quantitative and qualitative strands of the research. This is the question that will be answered in the study based on the mixing (see Creswell & Plano Clark, 2018). This is an innovative form of a question in research methods, and Tashakkori and Creswell (2007, p. 208) call it a "hybrid" or "integrated" question.

- The mixed methods question can be written in different ways. This can assume one of three forms. The first is to write it in a way that conveys the methods or procedures in a study (e.g., Does the qualitative data help explain the results from the initial quantitative phase of the study?). The second form is to write it in a way that conveys the content of the study (e.g., Does the theme of social support help to explain why some students become bullies in schools?) (see Tashakkori & Creswell, 2007). The third approach is to combine the methods and content as a hybrid question (e.g., How does the qualitative interview data on student bullying further explain why social support, as measured quantitatively, tends to discourage bullying as measured on a bullying scale?).

- Consider how to present the quantitative, qualitative, and mixed methods questions in a mixed methods study. An ideal format would be to write the questions into separate sections, such as the quantitative questions or hypotheses, the qualitative questions, and the mixed methods question. This format highlights the importance of all three sets of questions and draws the readers' attention to the separate quantitative and qualitative strands coming together (or being integrated) in a mixed methods study. Often researchers position the mixed methods question (written in methods or content or some combination form) last because the study will build to this element of the design.

Example 7.8 is a good illustration of a mixed methods question focused on the intent of mixing, to integrate the qualitative interviews and the quantitative data, the relationship of scores and student performance. This question emphasized what the integration was attempting to accomplish—a comprehensive and nuanced understanding—and at the end of the article, the authors presented evidence answering this question.

Example 7.8 Hypotheses and Research Questions in a Mixed Methods Study

Houtz (1995) provided an example of a two-phase study with the separate quantitative and qualitative research hypotheses and questions stated in sections introducing each phase. She did not use a separate, distinct mixed methods research question because such a question had not been developed at the time of her project. Nevertheless, her study was a rigorous mixed methods investigation. She studied the differences between middle school (nontraditional) and junior high (traditional) instructional strategies for seventh-grade and eighth-grade students and their attitudes toward science and science achievement. Her study was conducted at a point when many schools were moving away from the 2-year junior high concept to the 3-year middle school (including sixth grade) approach to education. In this two-phase study, the first phase involved assessing pretest and posttest attitudes and achievement using scales and examination scores. Houtz then followed the quantitative results with qualitative interviews with science teachers, the school principal, and consultants. This second phase helped to explain differences and similarities in the two instructional approaches obtained in the first phase.

With a first-phase quantitative study, Houtz (1995) mentioned the hypotheses guiding her research:

(Continued)

(Continued)

It was hypothesized that there would be no significant difference between students in the middle school and those in the junior high in attitude toward science as a school subject. It was also hypothesized that there would be no significant difference between students in the middle school and those in the junior high in achievement in science (p. 630)

These hypotheses appeared at the beginning of the study as an introduction to the quantitative phase. Prior to the qualitative phase, Houtz (1995) raised questions to explore the quantitative results in more depth. Focusing in on the achievement test results, she interviewed science teachers, the principal, and the university consultants and asked three questions:

What differences currently exist between the middle school instructional strategy and the junior high instructional strategy at this school in transition? How has this transition period impacted science attitude and achievement of your students? How do teachers feel about this change process? (p. 649)

Examining this mixed methods study closely shows that the author included both quantitative and qualitative questions, specified them at the beginning of each phase of her study, and used good elements for writing both quantitative hypotheses and qualitative research questions. Had Houtz (1995) developed a mixed methods question, it might have been stated from a procedural perspective:

How do the interviews with teachers, the principal, and university consultants help to explain any quantitative differences in achievement for middle school and junior high students? (methods orientation)

Alternatively, the mixed methods question might have been written from a content orientation, such as the following:

How do the themes mentioned by the teachers help to explain why middle-school children score lower than the junior high students? (content orientation)

Example 7.9 illustrates another mixed methods question that employs both methods and content language.

Example 7.9 A Mixed Methods Question Written Using Methods and Content Language

To what extent and in what ways do qualitative interviews with students and faculty members serve to contribute to a more comprehensive and nuanced understanding of this predicting relationship between CEEPT scores and student academic performance, via integrative mixed methods analysis? (Lee & Greene, 2007, p. 369)

SUMMARY

Research questions and hypotheses narrow the purpose statement and become major signposts for readers. Qualitative researchers ask at least one central question and several subquestions. They begin the questions with words such as *how* or *what* and use exploratory verbs, such as *explore, understand,* or *discover.* They pose broad, general questions to allow the participants to explain their ideas. They also focus initially on one central phenomenon of interest. The questions may also mention the participants and the site for the research.

Quantitative researchers write either research questions or hypotheses. Both forms include variables that are described, related, or compared with the independent and dependent variables measured separately. In many quantitative proposals, writers use research questions; however, a more formal statement of research employs hypotheses. These hypotheses are predictions about the outcomes of the results, and they may be written as alternative hypotheses specifying the results to be expected (more or less, higher or lower of something). They also may be stated in the null form, indicating no expected difference or no relationship between groups on a dependent variable. Typically, the researcher writes the independent variable(s) first, followed by the dependent variable(s). One model for ordering the questions in a quantitative proposal is to begin with descriptive questions followed by the inferential questions that relate variables or compare groups.

We encourage mixed methods researchers to write quantitative, qualitative, *and* a mixed methods question into their studies. The mixed methods question might be written to emphasize the methods or the content of the study, or both, and these questions might be placed at different points in a study. By adding a mixed methods question, the researcher conveys the importance of integrating or combining the quantitative and qualitative elements. An ideal format would be to write the three types of questions into separate sections, such as the quantitative questions or hypotheses, the qualitative questions, and the mixed methods question into a study.

Writing Exercises

1. For a qualitative study, write one or two central questions followed by five to seven subquestions.

2. For a quantitative study, write two sets of questions. The first set should be descriptive questions about the independent and dependent variables in the study. The second set should pose questions that describe and relate (or compare) the independent variable(s) with the dependent variable(s). This follows the model presented in this chapter for combining descriptive and inferential questions.

3. Write a mixed methods research question. Write the question to include *both* the methods of a study as well as the content.

Additional Readings

Creswell, J. W. (2015). *Educational research: Planning, conducting, and evaluating quantitative and qualitative research* (5th ed.). Upper Saddle River, NJ: Pearson Education.

Creswell provides an introduction to writing quantitative hypotheses and research questions and qualitative research questions in his introductory text on educational research. He distinguishes among purpose statements, research questions, hypotheses, and objectives. He reviews why these statements are important, and then conveys the writing structure for questions and hypotheses using many examples from the literature.

Morse, J. M. (1994). Designing funded qualitative research. In N. K. Denzin & Y. S. Lincoln (Eds.), *Handbook of qualitative research* (pp. 220–235). Thousand Oaks, CA: Sage.

Janice Morse, a nursing researcher, identifies and describes the major design issues involved in planning a qualitative project. She compares several strategies of inquiry and maps the type of research questions used in each strategy. For phenomenology and ethnography, the research calls for meaning and descriptive questions. For grounded theory, the questions need to address process whereas in ethnomethodology and discourse analysis, the questions relate to verbal interaction and dialogue. She indicates that the wording of the research question determines the focus and scope of the study.

Tashakkori, A., & Creswell, J. W. (2007). Exploring the nature of research questions in mixed methods research [Editorial]. *Journal of Mixed Methods Research, 1*(3), 207–211.

This editorial addresses the use and nature of research questions in mixed methods research. It highlights the importance of research questions in the process of research and discusses the need for a better understanding of the use of mixed methods questions. It asks, "How does one frame a research question in a mixed methods study?" (p. 207). Three models are presented: (a) writing separate quantitative and qualitative questions, (b) writing an overarching mixed methods question, or (c) writing research questions for each phase of a study as the research evolves.

$SAGE edge™

Quantitative Methods

We turn now from the introduction, the purpose, and the questions and hypotheses to the method section of a proposal. This chapter presents essential steps in designing quantitative methods for a research proposal or study, with specific focus on survey and experimental designs. These designs reflect postpositivist philosophical assumptions, as discussed in Chapter 1. For example, determinism suggests that examining the relationships between and among variables is central to answering questions and hypotheses through surveys and experiments. In one case, a researcher might be interested in evaluating whether playing violent video games *is associated with* higher rates of playground aggression in kids, which is a correlational hypothesis that could be evaluated in a survey design. In another case, a researcher might be interested in evaluating whether violent video game playing *causes* aggressive behavior, which is a causal hypothesis that is best evaluated by a true experiment. In each case, these quantitative approaches focus on carefully measuring (or experimentally manipulating) a parsimonious set of variables to answer theory-guided research questions and hypotheses. In this chapter, the focus is on the essential components of a method section in proposals for a survey or experimental study.

Defining Surveys and Experiments

A **survey design** provides a quantitative description of trends, attitudes, and opinions of a population, or tests for associations among variables of a population, by studying a sample of that population. Survey designs help researchers answer three types of questions: (a) descriptive questions (e.g., What percentage of practicing nurses support the provision of hospital abortion services?); (b) questions about the relationships between variables (e.g., Is there a positive association between endorsement of hospital abortion services and support for implementing hospice care among nurses?); or in cases where a survey design is repeated over time in a longitudinal study; (c) questions about predictive relationships between variables over time (e.g., Does Time 1 endorsement of support for hospital abortion services predict greater Time 2 burnout in nurses?).

An **experimental design** systematically manipulates one or more variables in order to evaluate how this manipulation impacts an outcome (or outcomes) of interest. Importantly, an experiment isolates the effects of this manipulation by holding all other variables constant. When one group receives a treatment and the other group does not (which is a manipulated variable of interest), the experimenter can isolate whether the treatment and *not* other factors influence the outcome. For example, a sample of nurses could be randomly assigned to a 3-week expressive writing program (where they write about their deepest thoughts and feelings) or a matched 3-week control writing program (writing about the facts of their daily morning routine) to evaluate whether this expressive writing manipulation reduces job burnout in the months following the program (i.e., the writing condition is the manipulated variable of interest, and job burnout is the outcome of interest). Whether a quantitative study employs a survey or experimental design, both approaches share a common goal of helping the researcher make inferences about relationships among variables, and how the sample results may generalize to a broader population of interest (e.g., all nurses in the community).

Components of a Survey Study Method Plan

The design of a survey method plan follows a standard format. Numerous examples of this format appear in scholarly journals, and these examples provide useful models. The following sections detail typical components. In preparing to design these components into a proposal, consider the questions on the checklist shown in Table 8.1 as a general guide.

Table 8.1 A Checklist of Questions for Designing a Survey Study Plan	
_____	Is the purpose of a survey design stated?
_____	What type of design will be used and what are the reasons for choosing the design mentioned?
_____	Is the nature of the survey (cross-sectional vs. longitudinal) identified?
_____	Is the population and its size mentioned?
_____	Will the population be stratified? If so, how?
_____	How many people will be in the sample? On what basis was this size chosen?
_____	What will be the procedure for sampling these individuals (e.g., random, nonrandom)?
_____	What instrument will be used in the survey? For each instrument, who developed it, how many items does it contain, does it have acceptable reliability and validity, and what are the scale anchors?
_____	What procedure will be used to pilot or field-test the survey?
_____	What is the timeline for administering the survey?
_____	How will the measures be scored and converted into variables?
_____	How will the variables be used to test your research questions?

	What specific steps will be taken in data analysis to do the following:
(a) _____	Analyze returns?
(b) _____	Check for response bias?
(c) _____	Conduct a descriptive analysis?
(d) _____	Combine items into scales?
(e) _____	Check for reliability of scales?
(f) _____	Run inferential statistics to answer the research questions or assess practical implications of the results?
_____	How will the results be interpreted?

The Survey Design

The first parts of the survey method plan section can introduce readers to the basic purpose and rationale for survey research. Begin the section by describing the rationale for the design. Specifically:

- Identify the purpose of survey research. The primary purpose is to answer a question (or questions) about variables of interest to you. A sample purpose statement could read: "The primary purpose of this study is to empirically evaluate whether the number of overtime hours worked predicts subsequent burnout symptoms in a sample of emergency room nurses."

- Indicate why a survey method is the preferred type of approach for this study. In this rationale, it can be beneficial to acknowledge the advantages of survey designs, such as the economy of the design, rapid turnaround in data collection, and constraints that preclude you from pursuing other designs (e.g., "An experimental design was not adopted to look at the relationship between overtime hours worked and burnout symptoms because it would be prohibitively difficult, and potentially unethical, to randomly assign nurses to work different amounts of overtime hours.").

- Indicate whether the survey will be cross-sectional—with the data collected at one point in time—or whether it will be longitudinal—with data collected over time.

- Specify the form of data collection. Fowler (2014) identified the following types: mail, telephone, the Internet, personal interviews, or group administration (see also Fink, 2016; Krueger & Casey, 2014). Using an Internet survey and administering it online has been discussed extensively in the literature (Nesbary, 2000; Sue & Ritter, 2012). Regardless of the form of data collection, provide a rationale for the procedure, using arguments based on its strengths and weaknesses, costs, data availability, and convenience.

The Population and Sample

In the method section, follow the type of design with characteristics of the population and the sampling procedure. Methodologists have written excellent discussions about the underlying logic of sampling theory (e.g., Babbie, 2015; Fowler, 2014). Here are essential aspects of the population and sample to describe in a research plan:

- *The population.* Identify the population in the study. Also state the size of this population, if size can be determined, and the means of identifying individuals in the population. Questions of access arise here, and the researcher might refer to availability of sampling frames—mail or published lists—of potential respondents in the population.

- *Sampling design.* Identify whether the sampling design for this population is single stage or multistage (called clustering). Cluster sampling is ideal when it is impossible or impractical to compile a list of the elements composing the population (Babbie, 2015). A single-stage sampling procedure is one in which the researcher has access to names in the population and can sample the people (or other elements) directly. In a multistage or clustering procedure, the researcher first identifies clusters (groups or organizations), obtains names of individuals within those clusters, and then samples within them.

- *Type of sampling.* Identify and discuss the selection process for participants in your sample. Ideally you aim to draw a *random sample,* in which each individual in the population has an equal probability of being selected (a systematic or probabilistic sample). But in many cases it may be quite difficult (or impossible) to get a random sample of participants. Alternatively, a *systematic sample* can have precision-equivalent **random sampling** (Fowler, 2014). In this approach, you choose a random start on a list and select every *X* numbered person on the list. The *X* number is based on a fraction determined by the number of people on the list and the number that are to be selected on the list (e.g., 1 out of every 80th person). Finally, less desirable, but often used, is a nonprobability sample (or *convenience sample*), in which respondents are chosen based on their convenience and availability.

- *Stratification.* Identify whether the study will involve *stratification* of the population before selecting the sample. This requires that characteristics of the population members be known so that the population can be stratified first before selecting the sample (Fowler, 2014). Stratification means that specific characteristics of individuals (e.g., gender—females and males) are represented in the sample and the sample reflects the true proportion in the population of individuals with certain characteristics. When randomly selecting people from a population, these characteristics may or may not be present in the sample in the same proportions as in the population; stratification ensures their representation. Also identify the characteristics used in stratifying the population (e.g., gender, income levels, education). Within each stratum, identify whether the sample contains individuals with the characteristic in the same proportion as the characteristic appears in the entire population.

- *Sample size determination.* Indicate the number of people in the sample and the procedures used to compute this number. Sample size determination is at its core a tradeoff: A larger sample will provide more accuracy in the inferences made, but recruiting more participants is time consuming and costly. In survey research, investigators sometimes choose a sample size based on selecting a fraction of the population (say, 10%) or selecting a sample size that is typical based on past studies. These approaches are not optimal; instead sample size determination should be based on your analysis plans (Fowler, 2014).

- *Power analysis.* If your analysis plan consists of detecting a significant association between variables of interest, a power analysis can help you estimate a target sample size. Many free online and commercially available power analysis calculators are available (e.g., G*Power; Faul, Erdfelder, Lang, & Buchner, 2007; Faul, Erdfelder, Buchner, & Lang 2009). The input values for a formal power analysis will depend on the questions you aim to address in your survey design study (for a helpful resource, see Kraemer & Blasey, 2016). As one example, if you aim to conduct a cross-sectional study measuring the correlation between the number of overtime hours worked and burnout symptoms in a sample of emergency room nurses, you can estimate the sample size required to determine whether your correlation significantly differs from zero (e.g., one possible hypothesis is that there will be a significant positive association between number of hours worked and emotional exhaustion burnout symptoms). This power analysis requires just three pieces of information:

1. An estimate of the size of correlation (r). A common approach for generating this estimate is to find similar studies that have reported the size of the correlation between hours worked and burnout symptoms. This simple task can often be difficult, either because there are no published studies looking at this association or because suitable published studies do not report a correlation coefficient. One tip: In cases where a published report measures variables of interest to you, one option is to contact the study authors asking them to kindly provide the correlation analysis result from their dataset, for your power analysis.

2. A two-tailed alpha value (α). This value is called the Type I error rate and refers to the risk we want to take in saying we have a real non-zero correlation when in fact this effect is not real (and determined by chance), that is, a false positive effect. A commonly accepted alpha value is .05, which refers to a 5% probability (5/100) that we are comfortable making a Type I error, such that 5% of the time we will say that there's a significant (non-zero) relationship between number of hours worked and burnout symptoms when in fact this effect occurred by chance and is not real.

3. A beta value (β). This value is called the Type II error rate and refers to the risk we want to take in saying we do not have a significant effect when in fact there is a significant association, that is, a false negative effect. Researchers commonly try to balance the risks of making Type I versus Type II errors, with a commonly accepted beta value being .20. Power analysis calculators will commonly ask for estimated power, which refers to 1 − beta (1 − .20 = .80).

- You can then plug these numbers into a power analysis calculator to determine the sample size needed. If you assume that the estimated association is $r = .25$, with a two-tailed alpha value of .05 and a beta value of .20, the power analysis calculation indicates that you need at least 123 participants in the study you aim to conduct.

- To get some practice, try conducting this sample size determination power analysis. We used the G*Power software program (Faul et al., 2007; Faul et al., 2009), with the following input parameters:

  o Test family: Exact

  o Statistical test: Correlation: Bivariate normal model

  o Type of power analysis: A priori: Compute required sample size

  o Tails: Two

  o Correlation ρ H1: .25

  o α err prob: .05

  o Power (1 − β err prob): .8

  o Correlation ρ H0: 0

- This power analysis for sample size determination should be done during study planning prior to enrolling any participants. Many scientific journals now require researchers to report a power analysis for sample size determination in the Method section.

Instrumentation

As part of rigorous data collection, the proposal developer also provides detailed information about the actual survey instruments to be used in the study. Consider the following:

- *Name the survey instruments used to collect data.* Discuss whether you used an instrument designed for this research, a modified instrument, or an instrument developed by someone else. For example, if you aim to measure perceptions of stress over the last month, you could use the 10-item Perceived Stress Scale (PSS) (Cohen, Kamarck, & Mermelstein, 1983) as your stress perceptions instrument in your survey design. Many survey instruments, including the PSS, can be acquired and used for free as long as you cite the original source of the instrument. But in some cases, researchers have made the use of their instruments proprietary, requiring a fee for use. Instruments are increasingly being delivered through a multitude of online survey products now available (e.g., Qualtrics, Survey Monkey). Although these products can be costly, they also can be quite helpful for accelerating and improving the survey research process. For example, researchers can create their own surveys quickly using custom templates and post them on websites or e-mail them to participants to complete. These software programs facilitate data collection into organized spreadsheets for data analysis, reducing data entry errors and accelerating hypothesis testing.

- *Validity of scores using the instrument.* To use an existing instrument, describe the established validity of scores obtained from past use of the instrument. This means reporting efforts by authors to establish **validity in quantitative research**—whether you can draw meaningful and useful inferences from scores on the instruments. The three traditional forms of validity to look for are (a) content validity (Do the items measure the content they were intended to measure?), (b) predictive or concurrent validity (Do scores predict a criterion measure? Do results correlate with other results?), and (c) **construct validity** (Do items measure hypothetical constructs or concepts?). In more recent studies, construct validity has become the overriding objective in validity, and it has focused on whether the scores serve a useful purpose and have positive consequences when they are used in practice (Humbley & Zumbo, 1996). Establishing the validity of the scores in a survey helps researchers to identify whether an instrument might be a good one to use in survey research. This form of validity is different from identifying the threats to validity in experimental research, as discussed later in this chapter.

- *Reliability of scores on the instrument.* Also mention whether scores resulting from past use of the instrument demonstrate acceptable

reliability. Reliability in this context refers to the consistency or repeatability of an instrument. The most important form of reliability for multi-item instruments is the instrument's **internal consistency**—which is the degree to which sets of items on an instrument behave in the same way. This is important because your instrument scale items should be assessing the same underlying construct, so these items should have suitable intercorrelations. A scale's internal consistency is quantified by a Cronbach's alpha (α) value that ranges between 0 and 1, with optimal values ranging between .7 and .9. For example, the 10-item PSS has excellent internal consistency across many published reports, with the original source publication reporting internal consistency values of $\alpha = .84-.86$ in three studies (Cohen, Kamarck, and Mermelstein, 1983). It can also be helpful to evaluate a second form of instrument reliability, its test-retest reliability. This form of reliability concerns whether the scale is reasonably stable over time with repeated administrations. When you modify an instrument or combine instruments in a study, the original validity and reliability may not hold for the new instrument, and it becomes important to establish validity and reliability during data analysis.

- *Sample items*. Include sample items from the instrument so that readers can see the actual items used. In an appendix to the proposal, attach sample items or the entire instrument (or instruments) used.

- *Content of instrument*. Indicate the major content sections in the instrument, such as the cover letter (Dillman, 2007, provides a useful list of items to include in cover letters), the items (e.g., demographics, attitudinal items, behavioral items, factual items), and the closing instructions. Also mention the type of scales used to measure the items on the instrument, such as continuous scales (e.g., *strongly agree* to *strongly disagree*) and categorical scales (e.g., yes/no, rank from highest to lowest importance).

- *Pilot testing*. Discuss plans for pilot testing or field-testing the survey and provide a rationale for these plans. This testing is important to establish the content validity of scores on an instrument; to provide an initial evaluation of the internal consistency of the items; and to improve questions, format, and instructions. Pilot testing all study materials also provides an opportunity to assess how long the study will take (and to identify potential concerns with participant fatigue). Indicate the number of people who will test the instrument and the plans to incorporate their comments into final instrument revisions.

- *Administering the survey*. For a mailed survey, identify steps for administering the survey and for following up to ensure a high response rate. Salant and Dillman (1994) suggested a four-phase administration process (see Dillman, 2007, for a similar three-phase process). The first mail-out is a short advance-notice letter to all members of the sample, and the second mail-out is the actual mail survey, distributed about 1 week after the advance-notice letter. The third mail-out consists of a postcard follow-up sent to all members of the sample 4 to 8 days after the initial questionnaire. The fourth mail-out, sent to all nonrespondents, consists of a personalized cover letter with a handwritten signature, the questionnaire, and a preaddressed return envelope with postage. Researchers send this fourth mail-out 3 weeks after the second mail-out. Thus, in total, the researcher concludes the administration period 4 weeks after its start, providing the returns meet project objectives.

Variables in the Study

Although readers of a proposal learn about the variables in purpose statements and research questions/hypotheses sections, it is useful in the method section to relate the variables to the specific questions or hypotheses on the instrument. One technique is to relate the variables, the research questions or hypotheses, and sample items on the survey instrument so that a reader can easily determine how the data collection connects to the variables and questions/hypotheses. Plan to include a table and a discussion that cross-reference the variables, the questions or hypotheses, and specific survey

Table 8.2 Variables, Research Questions, and Items on a Survey

Variable Name	Research Question	Item on Survey
Independent Variable 1: Prior publications	Descriptive research Question 1: How many publications did the faculty member produce prior to receipt of the doctorate?	See Questions 11, 12, 13, 14, and 15: publication counts for journal articles, books, conference papers, book chapters published before receiving the doctorate
Dependent Variable 1: Grants funded	Descriptive research Question 2: How many grants has the faculty member received in the past 3 years?	See Questions 16, 17, and 18: grants from foundations, federal grants, state grants
Control Variable 1: Tenure status	Descriptive research Question 3: Is the faculty member tenured?	See Question 19: tenured (yes/no)
Relating the Independent Variable 1: Prior publications to the Dependent Variable: Grants funded	Inferential Question 4: Does prior productivity influence the number of grants received?	See Questions 11,12,13,14,15 to Questions 16, 17, 18

items. This procedure is especially helpful in dissertations in which investigators test large-scale models or multiple hypotheses. Table 8.2 illustrates such a table using hypothetical data.

Data Analysis

In the proposal, present information about the computer programs used and the steps involved in analyzing the data. Websites contain detailed information about the various statistical analysis computer programs available. Some of the more frequently used programs are the following:

- *IBM SPSS Statistics 24 for Windows and Mac (www.spss.com)*. The SPSS Grad Pack is an affordable, professional analysis program for students based on the professional version of the program, available from IBM.

- *JMP (www.jmp.com)*. This is a popular software program available from SAS.

- *Minitab Statistical Software 17 (minitab.com)*. This is an interactive software statistical package available from Minitab Inc.

- *SYSTAT 13 (systatsoftware.com)*. This is a comprehensive interactive statistical package available from Systat Software, Inc.

- *SAS/STAT (sas.com)*. This is a statistical program with tools as an integral component of the SAS system of products available from SAS Institute, Inc.

- *Stata, release 14 (stata.com)*. This is a data analysis and statistics program available from StataCorp.

Online programs useful in simulating statistical concepts for statistical instruction can also be used, such as the Rice Virtual Lab in Statistics found at http://onlinestatbook.com/rvls.html, or SAS Simulation Studio for JMP (www.jmp.com), which harnesses the power of simulation to model and analyze critical operational systems in such areas as health care, manufacturing, and transportation. The graphical user interface in SAS Simulation Studio for JMP requires no programming and provides a full set of tools for building, executing, and analyzing results of simulation models (Creswell & Guetterman, in press).

We recommend the following **research tip**—presenting data analysis plans as a series of steps so that a reader can see how one step leads to another:

Step 1. Report information about the number of participants in the sample who did and did not return the survey. A table with numbers and percentages describing respondents and nonrespondents is a useful tool to present this information.

Step 2. Discuss the method by which **response bias** will be determined. Response bias is the effect of nonresponses on survey estimates (Fowler, 2014). *Bias* means that if nonrespondents had responded, their responses would have substantially changed the overall results. Mention the procedures used to check for response bias, such as wave analysis or a respondent/nonrespondent analysis. In wave analysis, the researcher examines returns on select items week by week to determine if average responses change (Leslie, 1972). Based on the assumption that those who return surveys in the final weeks of the response period are nearly all nonrespondents, if the responses begin to change, a potential exists for response bias. An alternative check for response bias is to contact a few nonrespondents by phone and determine if their responses differ substantially from respondents. This constitutes a respondent-nonrespondent check for response bias.

Step 3. Discuss a plan to provide a **descriptive analysis** of data for all independent and dependent variables in the study. This analysis should indicate the means, standard deviations, and range of scores for these variables. Identify whether there is missing data (e.g., some participants may not provide responses to some items or whole scales), and develop plans to report how much missing data is present and whether a strategy will be implemented to replace missing data (for a review, see Schafer & Graham, 2002).

Step 4. If the proposal contains an instrument with multi-item scales or a plan to develop scales, first evaluate whether it will be necessary to reverse-score items, and then how total scale scores will be calculated. Also mention reliability checks for the internal consistency of the scales (i.e., the Cronbach alpha statistic).

Step 5. Identify the statistics and the statistical computer program for testing the major inferential research questions or hypotheses in the proposed study. The **inferential questions or hypotheses** relate variables or compare groups in terms of variables so that inferences can be drawn from the sample to a population. Provide a rationale for the choice of statistical test and mention the assumptions associated with the statistic. As shown in Table 8.3, base this choice on the nature of the research question (e.g., relating variables or comparing groups as the most popular), the number of independent and dependent variables, and the variables used as covariates (e.g., see Rudestam & Newton, 2014). Further, consider whether the variables will be measured on an instrument as a continuous score (e.g., age from 18 to 36) or as a categorical score (e.g., women = 1, men = 2). Finally, consider whether the scores from the sample might be normally distributed in a bell-shaped curve if plotted out on a graph or non-normally distributed. There are additional ways to determine if the scores are normally distributed (see Creswell, 2012). These factors, in combination, enable a researcher to determine what statistical test will be suited for answering the research question or hypothesis. In Table 8.3, we show how the factors, in combination, lead to the selection of a number of common statistical tests. For additional types of statistical tests, readers are referred to statistics methods books, such as Gravetter and Wallnau (2012).

Step 6. A final step in the data analysis is to present the results in tables or figures and interpret the results from the statistical test, discussed in the next section.

Interpreting Results and Writing a Discussion Section

An **interpretation in quantitative research** means that the researcher draws conclusions from the results for the research questions, hypotheses, and the larger meaning of the results. This interpretation involves several steps:

- Report how the results addressed the research question or hypothesis. The *Publication Manual of the American Psychological Association* (American Psychological Association [APA], 2010) suggests that the most complete meaning of the results come from reporting extensive description, **statistical significance testing**, confidence intervals, and effect sizes. Thus, it is important to clarify the meaning of these last three reports of the results. The statistical significance testing reports an assessment as to whether the observed scores reflect a pattern other than chance. A statistical test is considered to be significant if the results are unlikely by chance to have occurred, and the null hypothesis of "no effect" can be rejected. The researcher sets a rejection level of "no effect," such as $p = 0.001$, and then assesses whether the test statistic falls into this level of rejection. Typically results will be summarized as "the analysis of variance revealed a statistically significant difference between men and women in terms of attitudes toward banning smoking in restaurants $F (2, 6) = 8.55, p = 0.001$."

- Two forms of *practical evidence* of the results should also be reported: (a) the effect size and (b) the confidence interval. A **confidence interval** is a range of values (an interval) that describes a level of uncertainty around an estimated observed score. A confidence interval shows how good an estimated score might be. A confidence interval of 95%, for example, indicates that 95 out of 100 times the observed score will fall in the range of values. An **effect size** identifies the strength of the conclusions about group differences or the relationships among variables in quantitative studies. It is a descriptive statistic that is not dependent on whether the relationship in the data represents the true population. The calculation of effect size varies for different statistical tests: it can be used to explain the variance between two or more variables or the differences among means for groups. It shows the practical significance of the results apart from inferences being applied to the population.

Table 8.3 Criteria for Choosing Select Statistical Tests

Nature of Question	Number of Independent Variables	Number of Dependent Variables	Number of Control Variables (covariates)	Type of Score Independent/ Dependent Variables	Distribution of Scores	Statistical Test	What the Test Yields
Group comparison	1	1	0	Categorical/ continuous	Normal	t test	A comparison of two groups in terms of outcomes
Group comparison	1 or more	1	0	Categorical/ continuous	Normal	Analysis of variance	A comparison of more than two groups in terms of outcomes
Group comparison	1 or more	1	1	Categorical/ continuous	Normal	Analysis of covariance (ANCOVA)	A comparison of more than two groups in terms of outcomes, controlling for covariates
Association between groups	1	1	0	Categorical/ categorical	Non-normal	Chi-square	An association between two variables measured by categories
Relate variables	1	1	0	Continuous/ continuous	Normal	Pearson product moment correlation	Tells you the magnitude and direction of association between two variables measured on an interval (or ratio) scale
Relate variables	2 or more	1	0	Continuous/ continuous	Normal	Multiple regression	Learn about the relationship between several predictor or independent variables and an outcome variable. It provides the relative prediction of one variable among many in terms of the outcome

- The final step is to draft a discussion section where you discuss the implications of the results in terms of how they are consistent with, refute, or extend previous related studies in the scientific literature. How do your research findings address gaps in our knowledge base on the topic? It is also important to acknowledge the implications of the findings for practice and for future research in the area. It may also involve discussing theoretical and practical consequences of the results. It is also helpful to briefly acknowledge potential limitations of the study, and potential alternative explanations for the study findings.

Example 8.1 is a survey method plan section that illustrates many of the steps just mentioned. This excerpt (used with permission) comes from a journal article reporting a study of factors affecting student attrition in one small liberal arts college (Bean & Creswell, 1980, pp. 321–322).

Example 8.1 A Survey Method Plan

Methodology

The site of this study was a small (enrollment 1,000), religious, coeducational, liberal arts college in a Midwestern city with a population of 175,000 people. *[Authors identified the research site and population.]*

The dropout rate the previous year was 25%. Dropout rates tend to be highest among freshmen and sophomores, so an attempt was made to reach as many freshmen and sophomores as possible by distribution of the questionnaire through classes. Research on attrition indicates that males and females drop out of college for different reasons (Bean, 1978, in press; Spady, 1971). Therefore, only women were analyzed in this study.

During April 1979, 169 women returned questionnaires. A homogeneous sample of 135 women who were 25 years old or younger, unmarried, full-time U.S. citizens, and Caucasian was selected for this analysis to exclude some possible confounding variables (Kerlinger, 1973).

Of these women, 71 were freshmen, 55 were sophomores, and 9 were juniors. Of the students, 95% were between the ages of 18 and 21. This sample is biased toward higher-ability students as indicated by scores on the ACT test. *[Authors presented descriptive information about the sample.]*

Data were collected by means of a questionnaire containing 116 items. The majority of these were Likert-like items based on a scale from "a very small extent" to "a very great extent." Other questions asked for factual information, such as ACT scores, high school grades, and parents' educational level. All information used in this analysis was derived from questionnaire data. This questionnaire had been developed and tested at three other institutions before its use at this college. [*Authors discussed the instrument.*]

Concurrent and convergent validity (Campbell & Fiske, 1959) of these measures was established through factor analysis, and was found to be at an adequate level. Reliability of the factors was established through the coefficient alpha. The constructs were represented by 25 measures—multiple items combined on the basis of factor analysis to make indices—and 27 measures were single item indicators. [*Validity and reliability were addressed.*]

Multiple regression and path analysis (Heise, 1969; Kerlinger & Pedhazur, 1973) were used to analyze the data. In the causal model . . . , intent to leave was regressed on all variables which preceded it in the causal sequence. Intervening variables significantly related to intent to leave were then regressed on organizational variables, personal variables, environmental variables, and background variables. [*Data analysis steps were presented.*]

Components of an Experimental Study Method Plan

An experimental method plan follows a standard form: (a) participants and design, (b) procedure, and (c) measures. These three sequential sections generally are sufficient (often in studies with a few measures, the procedure and measures sections are combined into a single procedure section). In this section of the chapter, we review these components as well as information regarding key features of experimental design and corresponding statistical analyses. As with the section on survey design, the intent here is to highlight key topics to be addressed in an experimental method plan. An overall guide to these topics is found by answering the questions on the checklist shown in Table 8.4.

Participants

Readers need to know about the selection, assignment, and number of participants who will take part in the experiment. Consider the following suggestions when writing the method section plan for an experiment:

- Describe the procedures for recruiting participants to be in the study, and any selection processes used. Often investigators aim to recruit a study sample that shares certain characteristics by formally stating specific inclusion and exclusion study criteria when designing their study (e.g., inclusion criterion: participants must be English language speaking; exclusion criterion: participants must not be children under the age of 18). Recruitment approaches are

_____	Who are the participants in the study?
_____	How were the participants selected? Name specific study inclusion and exclusion criteria.
_____	How and when will the participants be randomly assigned?
_____	How many participants will be in the study?
	What experimental research design will be used? What would a visual model of this design look like?
_____	What are the independent variables and how are they operationalized?
_____	What are the dependent variables (i.e., outcome variables) in the study? How will they be measured?
_____	Will variables be included as manipulation checks or covariates in the experiment? How and when will they be measured?
_____	What instruments will be used to measure the dependent variables (outcomes) in the study? Why were they chosen? Who developed these measures? Do they have established validity and reliability?
_____	What are the sequential steps in the procedure for administering the experimental study to participants?
_____	What are potential threats to internal and external validity for the experimental design and procedure? How will they be addressed?
_____	How will pilot testing of materials and procedures be conducted prior to formal data collection?
_____	What statistics will be used to analyze the data (e.g., descriptive and inferential)?
_____	How will the results be interpreted?

wide-ranging, and can include random digit dialing of households in a community, posting study recruitment flyers or e-mails to targeted communities, or newspaper advertisements. Describe the recruitment approaches that will be used and the study compensation provided for participating.

- One of the principal features distinguishing an experiment from a survey study design is the use of random assignment. Random assignment is a technique for placing participants into study conditions of a manipulated variable of interest. When individuals are randomly assigned to groups, the procedure is called a **true experiment**. If random assignment is used, discuss how and when the study will _randomly assign_ individuals to treatment groups, which in experimental studies are referred to as levels of an independent variable. This means that of the pool of participants, Individual 1 goes to Group 1, Individual 2 to Group 2, and so forth so that there is no systematic bias in assigning the individuals. This procedure eliminates the possibility of systematic differences among characteristics of the participants that could affect the outcomes so that any differences in outcomes can be attributed to the study's manipulated variable (or variables) of interest (Keppel & Wickens, 2003). Often experimental studies may be interested in both randomly assigning participants to levels of a *manipulated* variable of interest (e.g., a new treatment approach for teaching fractions to children versus the traditional approach) while also *measuring* a second predictor variable of interest that cannot utilize random assignment (e.g., measuring whether the treatment benefits are larger among female compared to male children; it is impossible to randomly assign children to be male or female). Designs in which a researcher has only partial (or no) control over randomly assigning participants to levels of a manipulated variable of interest are called **quasi-experiments**.

- Conduct and report a power analysis for sample size determination (for a helpful resource, see Kraemer & Blasey, 2016). The procedures for a sample size power analysis mimic those for a survey design, although the focus shifts to estimating the number of participants needed in each condition of the experiment to detect significant group differences. In this case, the input parameters shift to include an estimate of the effect size referencing the estimated differences between the groups of your manipulated variable(s) of interest and the number of groups in your experiment. Readers are encouraged to review the power analysis section earlier in the survey design portion of this chapter and then consider the following example:

  o Previously we introduced a cross-sectional survey design assessing the relationship between number of overtime hours worked and burnout symptoms among nurses. We might decide to conduct an experiment to test a related question: Do nurses working full time have higher burnout symptoms compared to nurses working part time? In this case, we might conduct an experiment in which nurses are randomly assigned to work either full time (group 1) or part time (group 2) for 2 months, at which time we could measure burnout symptoms. We could conduct a power analysis to evaluate the sample size needed to detect a significant difference in burnout symptoms between these two groups. Previous literature might indicate an effect size difference between these two groups at $d = .5$, and as with our survey study design, we can assume a two-tailed alpha = .05 and beta = .20. We ran the calculation again using the G*Power software program (Faul et al., 2007; Faul et al., 2009) to estimate the sample size needed to detect a significant difference between groups:

Test family: *t* tests

Statistical test: Means: difference between two independent means (two groups)

Type of power analysis: A priori: Compute required sample size

Tails: Two

Effect size *d*: .5

α err prob: .05

Power (1 − β err prob): .8

Allocation ratio N2/N1: 1

- o With these input parameters, the power analysis indicates a total sample size of 128 participants (64 in each group) is needed in order to detect a significant difference between groups in burnout symptoms.

- At the end of the participants section, it is helpful to provide a formal experimental design statement that specifies the independent variables and their corresponding levels. For example, a formal design statement might read, "The experiment consisted of a one-way two-groups design comparing burnout symptoms between full-time and part-time nurses."

Variables

The variables need to be specified in the formal design statement and described (in detail) in the procedure section of the experimental method plan. Here are some suggestions for developing ideas about variables in a proposal:

- Clearly identify the independent variables in the experiment (recall the discussion of variables in Chapter 3) and how they will be manipulated in the study. One common approach is to conduct a 2 × 2 between-subjects factorial design in which two independent variables are manipulated in a single experiment. If this is the case, it is important to clarify how and when each independent variable is manipulated.

- Include a manipulation check measure that evaluates whether your study successfully manipulated the independent variable(s) of interest. A **manipulation check measure** is defined as a measure of the intended manipulated variable of interest. For example, if a study aims to manipulate self-esteem by offering positive test feedback (high self-esteem condition) or negative test feedback (low self-esteem condition) using a performance task, it would be helpful to quantitatively evaluate whether there are indeed self-esteem differences between these two conditions with a manipulation check measure. After this self-esteem study manipulation, a researcher may include a brief measure of state self-esteem as a manipulation check measure prior to administering the primary outcome measures of interest.

- Identify the dependent variable or variables (i.e., the outcomes) in the experiment. The dependent variable is the response or the criterion variable presumed to be caused by or influenced by the independent treatment conditions. One consideration in the experimental method plan is whether there are multiple ways to measure outcome(s) of interest. For example, if the primary outcome is aggression, it may be possible to collect multiple measures of aggression in your experiment (e.g., a behavioral measure of aggression in response to a provocation, self-reported perceptions of aggression).

- Identify other variables to be measured in the study. Three categories of variables are worth mentioning. First, include measures of participant demographic characteristics (e.g., age, gender, ethnicity). Second, measure variables that may contribute noise to the study design. For example, self-esteem levels may fluctuate during the day (and relate to the study outcome variables of interest) and so it may be beneficial to measure and record time of day in the study (and then use it as a covariate in study statistical analyses). Third, measure variables that may be potential confounding variables. For example, a critic of the self-esteem manipulation may say that the positive/negative performance feedback study manipulation also unintentionally manipulated rumination, and it was this rumination that is a better explanation for study results on the outcomes of interest. By measuring rumination as a potential confounding variable of interest, the researcher can quantitatively evaluate this critic's claim.

Instrumentation and Materials

Just like in a survey method plan, a sound experimental study plan calls for a thorough discussion about the instruments used—their development, their items, their scales, and reports of reliability and validity of scores on past uses. However, an experimental study plan also describes in detail the approach for manipulating the independent variables of interest:

- Thoroughly discuss the materials used for the manipulated variable(s) of interest. One group, for example, may participate in a special computer-assisted learning plan used by a teacher in a classroom. This plan might involve handouts, lessons, and special written instructions to help students in this experimental group learn how to study a subject using computers. A pilot test of these materials may also be discussed, as well as any training required to administer the materials in a standardized way.

- Often the researcher does not want participants to know what variables are being manipulated or the condition they have been assigned to (and sometimes what the primary outcome measures of interest are). It is important, then, to draft a *cover story* that will be used to explain the study and procedures to participants during the experiment. If any deception is used in the study, it is important to draft a suitable debriefing approach and to get all procedures and materials approved by your institution's IRB (see Chapter 4).

Experimental Procedures

The specific experimental design procedures also need to be identified. This discussion involves indicating the overall experiment type, citing reasons for the design, and advancing a visual model to help the reader understand the procedures.

- Identify the type of experimental design to be used in the proposed study. The types available in experiments are pre-experimental designs, quasi-experiments, and true experiments. With pre-experimental designs, the researcher studies a single group and implements an intervention during the experiment. This design does not have a control group to compare with the experimental group. In quasi-experiments, the investigator uses control and experimental groups, but the design may have partial or total lack of random assignment to groups. In a *true experiment,* the investigator randomly assigns the participants to treatment groups. A **single-subject design** or N of 1 design involves observing the behavior of a single individual (or a small number of individuals) over time.

- Identify what is being compared in the experiment. In many experiments, those of a type called between-subject designs, the investigator compares two or more groups (Keppel & Wickens, 2003; Rosenthal & Rosnow, 1991). For example, a factorial design experiment, a variation on the between-group design, involves using two or more treatment variables to examine the independent and simultaneous effects of these treatment variables on an outcome (Vogt & Johnson, 2015). This widely used experimental design explores the effects of each treatment separately and also the effects of variables used in combination, thereby providing a rich and revealing multidimensional view. In other experiments, the researcher studies only one group in what is called a within-group design. For example, in a repeated measures design, participants are assigned to different treatments at different times during the experiment. Another example of a within-group design would be a study of the behavior of a single individual over time in which the experimenter provides and withholds a treatment at different times in the experiment to determine its impact. Finally, studies that include both a between-subjects and a within-subjects variable are called mixed designs.

- Provide a diagram or a figure to illustrate the specific research design to be used. A standard notation system needs to be used in this figure. As a **research tip**, we recommend using the classic notation system provided by Campbell and Stanley (1963, p. 6):

  o *X* represents an exposure of a group to an experimental variable or event, the effects of which are to be measured.

  o *O* represents an observation or measurement recorded on an instrument.

  o *X*s and *O*s in a given row are applied to the same specific persons. *X*s and *O*s in the same column, or placed vertically relative to each other, are simultaneous.

  o The left-to-right dimension indicates the temporal order of procedures in the experiment (sometimes indicated with an arrow).

  o The symbol *R* indicates random assignment.

  o Separation of parallel rows by a horizontal line indicates that comparison groups are not equal (or equated) by random assignment. No horizontal line between the groups displays random assignment of individuals to treatment groups.

In Examples 8.2–8.5, this notation is used to illustrate pre-experimental, quasi-experimental, true experimental, and single-subject designs.

Example 8.2 Pre-experimental Designs

One-Shot Case Study

This design involves an exposure of a group to a treatment followed by a measure.

Group A X_____O

One-Group Pretest-Posttest Design

This design includes a pretest measure followed by a treatment and a posttest for a single group.

Group A O1————X————O2

Static Group Comparison or Posttest-Only With Nonequivalent Groups

Experimenters use this design after implementing a treatment. After the treatment, the researcher selects a comparison group and provides a posttest to both the experimental group(s) and the comparison group(s).

Group A X_____O

Group B _____O

Alternative Treatment Posttest-Only With Nonequivalent Groups Design

This design uses the same procedure as the Static Group Comparison, with the exception that the nonequivalent comparison group received a different treatment.

Group A X1_____O

Group B X2_____O

Example 8.3 Quasi-experimental Designs

Nonequivalent (Pretest and Posttest) Control-Group Design

In this design, a popular approach to quasi-experiments, the experimental Group A and the control Group B are selected without random assignment. Both groups take a pretest and posttest. Only the experimental group receives the treatment.

Group A O————X————O

_____

Group B O—————————O

Single-Group Interrupted Time-Series Design

In this design, the researcher records measures for a single group both before and after a treatment.

Group A O—O—O—O—X—O—O—O—O

Control-Group Interrupted Time-Series Design

This design is a modification of the Single-Group Interrupted Time-Series design in which two groups of participants, not randomly assigned, are observed over time. A treatment is administered to only one of the groups (i.e., Group A).

Group A O—O—O—O—X—O—O—O—O

_____

Group B O—O—O—O—O—O—O—O—O

Example 8.4 True Experimental Designs

Pretest–Posttest Control-Group Design

A traditional, classical design, this procedure involves random assignment of participants to two groups. Both groups are administered both a pretest and a posttest, but the treatment is provided only to experimental Group A.

Group A R————O————X————O

Group B R————O————————O

Posttest-Only Control-Group Design

This design controls for any confounding effects of a pretest and is a popular experimental design. The participants are randomly assigned to groups, a treatment is given only to the experimental group, and both groups are measured on the posttest.

Group A R————————X————O

Group B R————————————O

Solomon Four-Group Design

A special case of a 2 × 2 factorial design, this procedure involves the random assignment of participants to four groups. Pretests and treatments are varied for the four groups. All groups receive a posttest.

Group A R————O————X————O

Group B R————O————————O

Group C R————————X————O

Group D R————————————O

Example 8.5 Single-Subject Designs

A-B-A Single-Subject Design

This design involves multiple observations of a single individual. The target behavior of a single individual is established over time and is referred to as a baseline behavior. The baseline behavior is assessed, the treatment provided, and then the treatment is withdrawn.

Baseline A   Treatment B   Baseline A

O–O–O–O–O–X–X–X–X–X–O–O–O–O–O–O

Threats to Validity

There are several threats to validity that will raise questions about an experimenter's ability to conclude that the manipulated variable(s) of interest affect an outcome and not some other factor. Experimental researchers need to identify potential threats to the internal validity of their experiments and design them so that these threats will not likely arise or are minimized. There are two types of threats to validity: (a) internal threats and (b) external threats.

- Internal validity threats are experimental procedures, treatments, or experiences of the participants that threaten the researcher's ability to draw correct inferences from the data about the population in an experiment. Table 8.5 displays these threats, provides a description of each one of them, and suggests potential responses by the researcher so that the threat may not occur. There are those involving participants (i.e., history, maturation, regression, selection, and mortality), those related to the use of an experimental treatment that the researcher manipulates (i.e., diffusion, compensatory and resentful demoralization, and compensatory rivalry), and those involving procedures used in the experiment (i.e., testing and instruments).

Table 8.5 Types of Threats to Internal Validity

Type of Threat to Internal Validity	Description of Threat	In Response, Actions the Researcher Can Take
History	Because time passes during an experiment, events can occur that unduly influence the outcome beyond the experimental treatment.	The researcher can have both the experimental and control groups experience the same external events.
Maturation	Participants in an experiment may mature or change during the experiment, thus influencing the results.	The researcher can select participants who mature or change at the same rate (e.g., same age) during the experiment.
Regression to the mean	Participants with extreme scores are selected for the experiment. Naturally, their scores will probably change during the experiment. Scores, over time, regress toward the mean.	A researcher can select participants who do not have extreme scores as entering characteristics for the experiment.
Selection	Participants can be selected who have certain characteristics that predispose them to have certain outcomes (e.g., they are brighter).	The researcher can select participants randomly so that characteristics have the probability of being equally distributed among the experimental groups.
Mortality (also called study attrition)	Participants drop out during an experiment due to many possible reasons. The outcomes are thus unknown for these individuals.	A researcher can recruit a large sample to account for dropouts or compare those who drop out with those who continue—in terms of the outcome.
Diffusion of treatment (also called cross contamination of groups)	Participants in the control and experimental groups communicate with each other. This communication can influence how both groups score on the outcomes.	The researcher can keep the two groups as separate as possible during the experiment.
Compensatory/ resentful demoralization	The benefits of an experiment may be unequal or resented when only the experimental group receives the treatment (e.g., experimental group receives therapy and the control group receives nothing).	The researcher can provide benefits to both groups, such as giving the control group the treatment after the experiment ends or giving the control group some different type of treatment during the experiment.

Type of Threat to Internal Validity	Description of Threat	In Response, Actions the Researcher Can Take
Compensatory rivalry	Participants in the control group feel that they are being devalued, as compared to the experimental group, because they do not experience the treatment.	The researcher can take steps to create equality between the two groups, such as reducing the expectations of the control group or clearly explaining the value of the control group.
Testing	Participants become familiar with the outcome measure and remember responses for later testing.	The researcher can have a longer time interval between administrations of the outcome or use different items on a later test than were used in an earlier test.
Instrumentation	The instrument changes between a pretest and posttest, thus impacting the scores on the outcome.	The researcher can use the same instrument for the pretest and posttest measures.

Source: Adapted from Creswell (2012).

- Potential threats to external validity also must be identified and designs created to minimize these threats. **External validity threats** arise when experimenters draw incorrect inferences from the sample data to other persons, other settings, and past or future situations. As shown in Table 8.6, these threats arise because of the characteristics of individuals selected for the sample, the uniqueness of the setting, and the timing of the experiment. For example, threats to external validity arise when the researcher generalizes beyond the groups in the experiment to other racial or social groups not under study, to settings not examined, or to past or future situations. Steps for addressing these potential issues are also presented in Table 8.6.

- Other threats that might be mentioned in the method section are the threats to **statistical conclusion validity** that arise when experimenters draw inaccurate inferences from the data because of inadequate statistical power or the violation of statistical assumptions. Threats to construct validity occur when investigators use inadequate definitions and measures of variables.

Practical **research tips** for proposal writers to address validity issues are as follows:

- Identify the potential threats to validity that may arise in your study. A separate section in a proposal may be composed to advance this threat.

- Define the exact type of threat and what potential issue it presents to your study.

- Discuss how you plan to address the threat in the design of your experiment.

- Cite references to books that discuss the issue of threats to validity, such as Cook and Campbell (1979); Shadish, Cook, & Campbell (2001); and Tuckman (1999).

The Procedure

A researcher needs to describe in detail the sequential step-by-step procedure for conducting the experiment. A reader should be able to clearly understand the cover story, the design being used, the manipulated variable(s) and outcome variable(s), and the timeline of activities. It is also important to describe steps taken to minimize noise and bias in the experimental procedures (e.g., "To reduce the risk of experimenter bias, the experimenter was blind to the participant's study condition until all outcome measures were assessed.").

- Discuss a step-by-step approach for the procedure in the experiment. For example, Borg and Gall (2006) outlined steps typically used in the procedure for a pretest-posttest control group design with matching participants in the experimental and control groups:

  1. Administer measures of the dependent variable or a variable closely correlated with the dependent variable to the research participants.

Table 8.6 Types of Threats to External Validity

Types of Threats to External Validity	Description of Threat	In Response, Actions the Researcher Can Take
Interaction of selection and treatment	Because of the narrow characteristics of participants in the experiment, the researcher cannot generalize to individuals who do not have the characteristics of participants.	The researcher restricts claims about groups to which the results cannot be generalized. The researcher conducts additional experiments with groups with different characteristics.
Interaction of setting and treatment	Because of the characteristics of the setting of participants in an experiment, a researcher cannot generalize to individuals in other settings.	The researcher needs to conduct additional experiments in new settings to see if the same results occur as in the initial setting.
Interaction of history and treatment	Because results of an experiment are time-bound, a researcher cannot generalize the results to past or future situations.	The researcher needs to replicate the study at later times to determine if the same results occur as in the earlier time.

Source: Adapted from Creswell (2012).

2. Assign participants to matched pairs on the basis of their scores on the measures described in Step 1.

3. Randomly assign one member of each pair to the experimental group and the other member to the control group.

4. Expose the experimental group to the experimental treatment and administer no treatment or an alternative treatment to the control group.

5. Administer measures of the dependent variables to the experimental and control groups.

6. Compare the performance of the experimental and control groups on the posttest(s) using tests of statistical significance.

Data Analysis

Tell the reader about the types of statistical analyses that will be implemented on the dataset.

- Report the descriptive statistics. Some descriptive statistics that are commonly reported include frequencies (e.g., how many male and female participants were in the study?), means and standard deviations (e.g., what's the mean age of the sample; what are the group means and corresponding standard deviation values for the primary outcome measures?).

- Indicate the inferential statistical tests used to examine the hypotheses in the study. For experimental designs with categorical information (groups) on the independent variable and continuous information on the dependent variable, researchers use t tests or univariate analysis of variance (ANOVA), analysis of covariance (ANCOVA), or multivariate analysis of variance (MANOVA— multiple dependent measures). (Several of these tests are mentioned in Table 8.3, which was presented earlier.) In factorial designs where more than one independent variable is manipulated, you can test for main effects (of each independent variable) and interactions between independent variables. Also, indicate the practical significance by reporting effect sizes and confidence intervals.

- For single-subject research designs, use line graphs for baseline and treatment observations for abscissa (horizontal axis) units of time and the ordinate (vertical axis) target behavior. Researchers plot each data point separately on the graph, and connect the data points with lines (e.g., see Neuman & McCormick, 1995). Occasionally, tests of statistical significance, such as t tests, are used to compare the pooled mean of the baseline and the treatment phases, although such procedures may violate the assumption of independent measures (Borg & Gall, 2006).

Interpreting Results and Writing a Discussion Section

The final step in an experiment is to interpret the findings in light of the hypotheses or research questions and to draft a discussion section. In this interpretation, address whether the hypotheses or questions were supported or whether they were refuted. Consider whether the independent variable manipulation was effective (a manipulation check measure can be helpful in this regard). Suggest why the results were significant, or why they were not, linking the new evidence with past literature (Chapter 2), the theory used in the study (Chapter 3), or persuasive logic that might explain the results. Address whether the results might have been influenced by unique strengths of the approach, or weaknesses (e.g., threats to internal validity), and indicate how the results might be generalized to certain people, settings, and times. Finally, indicate the implications of the results, including implications for future research on the topic.

Example 8.6 is a description of an experimental method plan adapted from a value affirmation stress study published by Creswell and colleagues (Creswell et al., 2005).

Example 8.6   An Experimental Method Plan

This study tested the hypothesis that thinking about one's important personal values in a self-affirmation activity could buffer subsequent stress responses to a laboratory stress challenge task. The specific study hypothesis was that the self-affirmation group, relative to the control group, would have lower salivary cortisol stress hormone responses to a stressful performance task. Here we highlight a plan for organizing the methodological approach for conducting this study. For a full description of the study methods and findings, see the published paper (Creswell et al., 2005).

Method

Participants

A convenience sample of eighty-five undergraduates will be recruited from a large public university on the west coast, and compensated with course credit or $30. This sample

size is justified based on a power analysis conducted prior to data collection with the software program G*Power (Faul et al., 2007; Faul et al., 2009), based on [specific input parameters described here for the power analysis]. Participants will be eligible to participate if they meet the following study criteria [list study inclusion and exclusion criteria here]. All study procedures have been approved by the University of California, Los Angeles Institutional Review Board, and participants will provide written informed consent prior to participating in study related activities.

The study is a 2 × 4 mixed design, with value affirmation condition as a two-level between subjects variable (condition: value affirmation or control) and time as a four-level within-subjects variable (time: baseline, 20 minutes post-stress, 30 minutes post-stress, and 45 minutes post-stress). The primary outcome measure is the stress hormone cortisol, as measured by saliva samples.

Procedure

To control for the circadian rhythm of cortisol, all laboratory sessions will be scheduled between the hours of 2:30 pm and 7:30 pm. Participants will be run through the laboratory procedures one at a time. The cover story consists of telling participants that the study is interested in studying physiological responses to laboratory performance tasks.

Upon arrival all participants will complete an initial values questionnaire where they will rank order five personal values. After a 10-minute acclimation period, participants will provide a baseline saliva sample, for the assessment of salivary cortisol levels. Participants will then receive instructions on the study tasks and then will be randomly assigned by the experimenter (using a random number generator) to either a value affirmation or control condition, where they will be asked to [description of the value affirmation independent variable manipulation here, along with the subsequent manipulation check measure]. All participants will then complete the laboratory stress challenge task [description of the stress challenge task procedures for producing a stress response here]. After the stress task, participants will complete multiple post-stress task questionnaire measures [describe them here], and then provide saliva samples at 20, 30, and 45 minutes post-stress task onset. After providing the last saliva sample, participants will be debriefed, compensated, and dismissed.

SUMMARY

This chapter identified essential components for organizing a methodological approach and plan for conducting either a survey or an experimental study. The outline of steps for a survey study began with a discussion about the purpose, the identification of the population and sample, the survey instruments to be used, the relationship between the variables, the research questions, specific items on the survey, and steps to be taken in the analysis and the interpretation of the data from the survey. In the design of an experiment, the researcher identifies participants in the study, the variables—the manipulated variable(s) of interest and the outcome variables—and the instruments used. The design also includes the specific type of experiment, such as a pre-experimental, quasi-experimental, true experiment, or single-subject design. Then the researcher draws a figure to illustrate the design, using appropriate notation. This is followed by comments about potential threats to internal and external validity (and possibly statistical and construct validity) that relate to the experiment, the statistical analyses used to test the hypotheses or research questions, and the interpretation of the results.

Writing Exercises

1. Design a plan for the procedures to be used in a survey study. Review the checklist in Table 8.1 after you write the section to determine if all components have been addressed.

2. Design a plan for procedures for an experimental study. Refer to Table 8.4 after you complete your plan to determine if all questions have been addressed adequately.

Additional Readings

Campbell, D. T., & Stanley, J. C. (1963). Experimental and quasi-experimental designs for research. In N. L. Gage (Ed.), *Handbook of research on teaching* (pp. 1–76). Chicago: Rand McNally.

This chapter in the Gage *Handbook* is the classical statement about experimental designs. Campbell and Stanley designed a notation system for experiments that is still used today; they also advanced the types of experimental designs, beginning with factors that jeopardize internal and external validity, the pre-experimental design types, true experiments, quasi-experimental designs, and correlational and ex post facto designs. The chapter presents an excellent summary of types of designs, their threats to validity, and statistical procedures to test the designs. This is an essential chapter for students beginning their study of experimental studies.

Fowler, F. J. (2014). *Survey research methods* (5th ed.). Thousand Oaks, CA: Sage.

Floyd Fowler provides a useful text about the decisions that go into the design of a survey research project. He addresses use of alternative sampling procedures, ways of reducing nonresponse rates, data collection, design of good questions, employing sound interviewing techniques, preparation of surveys for analysis, and ethical issues in survey designs.

Keppel, G. & Wickens, T. D. (2003). *Design and analysis: A researcher's handbook* (4th ed.). Englewood Cliffs, NJ: Prentice Hall.

Geoffrey Keppel and Thomas Wickens provide a detailed, thorough treatment of the design of experiments from the principles of design to the statistical analysis of experimental data. Overall, this book is for the mid-level to advanced statistics student who seeks to understand the design and statistical analysis of experiments. The introductory chapter presents an informative overview of the components of experimental designs.

Kraemer, H. C., & Blasey, C. (2016). *How many subjects? Statistical power analysis in research.* Thousand Oaks: Sage.

This book provides guidance on how to conduct power analyses for estimating sample size. This serves as an excellent resource for both basic and more complex estimation procedures.

Lipsey, M. W. (1990). *Design sensitivity: Statistical power for experimental research.* Newbury Park, CA: Sage.

Mark Lipsey has authored a major book on the topics of experimental designs and statistical power of those designs. Its basic premise is that an experiment needs to have sufficient sensitivity to detect those effects it purports to investigate. The book explores statistical power and includes a table to help researchers identify the appropriate size of groups in an experiment.

Neuman, S. B., & McCormick, S. (Eds.). (1995). *Single-subject experimental research: Applications for literacy.* Newark, DE: International Reading Association.

Susan Neuman and Sandra McCormick have edited a useful, practical guide to the design of single-subject research. They present many examples of different types of designs, such as reversal designs and multiple-baseline designs, and they enumerate the statistical procedures that might be involved in analyzing the single-subject data. One chapter, for example, illustrates the conventions for displaying data on line graphs. Although this book cites many applications in literacy, it has broad application in the social and human sciences.

Thompson, B. (2006). *Foundations of behavioral statistics: An insight-based approach.* New York: The Guilford.

Bruce Thompson has organized a highly readable book about using statistics. He reviews the basics about descriptive statistics (location, dispersion, shape), about relationships among variables and statistical significance, about the practical significance of results, and about more advanced statistics such as regression, ANOVA, the general linear model, and logistic regression. Throughout the book, he brings in practical examples to illustrate his points.

⑤SAGE edge™

https://edge.sagepub.com/creswellrd5e

Students and instructors, please visit the companion website for videos featuring John W. Creswell, full-text SAGE journal articles, quizzes and activities, plus additional tools for research design.

Qualitative Methods

Qualitative methods demonstrate a different approach to scholarly inquiry than methods of quantitative research. Although the processes are similar, qualitative methods rely on text and image data, have unique steps in data analysis, and draw on diverse designs. Writing a method section for a proposal or study for qualitative research partly requires educating readers as to the intent of qualitative research, mentioning specific designs, carefully reflecting on the role the researcher plays in the study, drawing from an ever-expanding list of types of data sources, using specific protocols for recording data, analyzing the information through multiple steps of analysis, and mentioning approaches for documenting the methodological integrity or accuracy—or validity—of the data collected. This chapter addresses these important components of writing a good qualitative method section into a proposal or study. Table 9.1 presents a checklist for reviewing the qualitative methods section of your project to determine whether you have addressed important topics.

\

Table 9.1	A Checklist of Questions for Designing a Qualitative Procedure
_____	Are the basic characteristics of qualitative studies mentioned?
_____	Is the specific type of qualitative design to be used in the study mentioned? Is the history of, a definition of, and applications for the design mentioned?
_____	Does the reader gain an understanding of the researcher's role or reflexivity in the study (past historical, social, cultural experiences, personal connections to sites and people, steps in gaining entry, and sensitive ethical issues) and how they may shape interpretations made in the study?
_____	Is the purposeful sampling strategy for sites and individuals identified?
_____	Is a clear recruitment strategy for enrolling participants mentioned?
_____	Are the specific forms of data collection mentioned and a rationale given for their use?
_____	Are the procedures for recording information during the data collection detailed (such as protocols)?
_____	Are the data analysis steps identified?
_____	Is there evidence that the researcher has organized the data for analysis?
_____	Has the researcher reviewed the data generally to obtain a sense of the information?
_____	Are the ways that the data will be represented mentioned—such as in tables, graphs, and figures?

(Continued)

Table 9.1 (Continued)

_____	Has the researcher coded the data?
_____	Have the codes been developed to form a description and/or to identify themes?
_____	Are the themes interrelated to show a higher level of analysis and abstraction?
_____	Have the bases for interpreting the analysis been specified (personal experiences, the literature, questions, action agenda)?
_____	Has the researcher mentioned the outcome of the study (developed a theory, provided a complex picture of themes)?
_____	Have multiple strategies been cited for validating the findings?

The qualitative method section of a proposal requires attention to topics that are similar to a quantitative (or mixed methods) project. These involve telling the reader about the design being used in the study and, in this case, the use of qualitative research and its basic intent. It also involves discussing the sample for the study and the overall data collection and recording procedures. It further expands on the data analysis steps and the methods used for presenting the data, interpreting it, validating it, and indicating the potential outcomes of the study. In contrast to other designs, the qualitative approach includes comments by the researcher about their role and their self-reflection (or reflexivity, it is called), and the specific type of qualitative strategy being used. Further, because the writing structure of a qualitative project may vary considerably from study to study, the method section should also include comments about the nature of the final written product.

The Characteristics of Qualitative Research

For many years, qualitative writers had to discuss the characteristics of qualitative research and convince faculty and audiences as to their legitimacy. Now these discussions are less frequently found in the literature and there is some consensus as to what constitutes qualitative inquiry. Thus, our suggestions about the method section of a project or proposal are as follows:

- Review the needs of potential audiences for the proposal or study. Decide whether audience members are knowledgeable enough about the characteristics of qualitative research that this section is not necessary. For example, although qualitative research is typically accepted and well-known in the social sciences, it has emerged in the health sciences only in the last couple of decades. Thus, for health science audiences, a review of the basic characteristics will be important.

- If there is some question about the audience's knowledge, present the basic characteristics of qualitative research and consider discussing a recent qualitative research journal article (or study) to use as an example to illustrate the characteristics.

- If you present the basic characteristics, what ones should you mention? A number of authors of introductory texts convey these characteristics, such as Creswell (2016), Hatch (2002), and Marshall and Rossman (2016).

  - *Natural setting:* Qualitative researchers tend to collect data in the field at the site where participants experience the issue or problem under study. Researchers do not bring individuals into a lab (a contrived situation), nor do they typically send out instruments for individuals to complete. This up-close information gathered by actually talking directly to people and seeing them behave and act within their context is a major characteristic of qualitative research. In the natural setting, the researchers have face-to-face interaction, often extending over a prolonged period of time.

  - *Researcher as key instrument:* Qualitative researchers collect data themselves through examining documents, observing behavior, or interviewing participants. They may use a protocol—an instrument for recording data—but the researchers are the ones who actually gather the information and interpret it. They do not tend to use or rely on questionnaires or instruments developed by other researchers.

  - *Multiple sources of data:* Qualitative researchers typically gather multiple forms of data, such as interviews, observations, documents, and audiovisual information rather than rely on a single data source. These are all open-ended forms of data in which the participants share their ideas freely, not constrained by predetermined scales or instruments. Then the researchers review all of the data, make sense of it, and organize it into codes and themes that cut across all of the data sources.

  - *Inductive and deductive data analysis:* Qualitative researchers typically work inductively, building patterns, categories, and themes from the bottom up by organizing the data into increasingly more abstract units of information. This inductive process illustrates working back and forth between the themes and the database until the researchers have established a comprehensive set of themes. Then deductively, the researchers look back at their data from the themes to determine if more evidence can support each theme or whether they need to gather additional information. Thus, while the process begins inductively, deductive thinking also plays an important role as the analysis moves forward.

o *Participants' meanings:* In the entire qualitative research process, the researchers keep a focus on learning the meaning that the participants hold about the problem or issue, not the meaning that the researchers bring to the research or that writers express in the literature.

o *Emergent design:* The research process for qualitative researchers is emergent. This means that the initial plan for research cannot be tightly prescribed, and some or all phases of the process may change or shift after the researcher enters the field and begins to collect data. For example, the questions may change, the forms of data collection may shift, and the individuals studied and the sites visited may be modified. These shifts signal that the researchers are delving deeper and deeper into the topic or the phenomenon under study. The key idea behind qualitative research is to learn about the problem or issue from participants and to address the research to obtain that information.

o *Reflexivity:* In qualitative research, inquirers reflect about how their role in the study and their personal background, culture, and experiences hold potential for shaping their interpretations, such as the themes they advance and the meaning they ascribe to the data. This aspect of the methods is more than merely advancing biases and values in the study, but how the background of the researchers actually may shape the direction of the study.

o *Holistic account:* Qualitative researchers try to develop a complex picture of the problem or issue under study. This involves reporting multiple perspectives, identifying the many factors involved in a situation, and generally sketching the larger picture that emerges. This larger picture is not necessarily a linear model of cause and effect but rather a model of multiple factors interacting in different ways. This picture, qualitative researchers would say, mirrors real life and the ways that events operate in the real world. A visual model of many facets of a process or a central phenomenon aids in establishing this holistic picture (see, for example, Creswell & Brown, 1992).

Qualitative Designs

Beyond these general characteristics are more specific approaches (i.e., strategies of inquiry, designs, or procedures) in conducting qualitative research (Creswell & Poth, 2018). These approaches have emerged in the field of qualitative research since it has matured in the social sciences since the early 1990s. They include procedures for data collection, analysis, and writing, but they originated out of disciplines in the social sciences. Many approaches exist, such as the 28 identified by Tesch (1990), the 22 types in Wolcott's (2009) tree, and the five approaches to qualitative inquiry by Creswell and Poth (2018), and Creswell (2016). Marshall and Rossman (2016) discussed five types common across five different authors. As mentioned in Chapter 1, we recommend that qualitative researchers choose from among the possibilities, such as narrative, phenomenology, ethnography, case study, and grounded theory. We selected these five because they are popular across the social and health sciences today. Others exist that have been addressed adequately in qualitative books, such as participatory action research (Kemmis & Wilkinson, 1998), discourse analysis (Cheek, 2004), or participatory action research (Ivankova, 2015). In these approaches, researchers study individuals (narrative, phenomenology); explore processes, activities, and events (case study, grounded theory); or learn about broad culture-sharing behavior of individuals or groups (ethnography).

In writing a procedure for a qualitative proposal, consider the following research tips: •

- Identify the specific approach that you will be using and provide references to the literature that discusses the approach.

- Provide some background information about the approach, such as its discipline origin, the applications of it (preferably to your field), and a brief definition of it (see Chapter 1 for the five approaches or designs).

- Discuss why it is an appropriate strategy to use in the proposed study.

- Identify how the use of the approach will shape many aspects of the design process, such as the title, the problem, the research questions, the data collection and analysis, and the report write-up.

The Researcher's Role and Reflexivity

As mentioned in the list of characteristics, qualitative research is interpretative research; the inquirer is typically involved in a sustained and intensive experience with participants. This introduces a range of strategic, ethical, and personal issues into the qualitative research process (Locke, Spirduso, & Silverman, 2013). With these concerns in mind, inquirers explicitly identify reflexively their biases, values, and personal background, such as gender, history, culture, and socioeconomic status (SES) that shape their interpretations formed during a study. In addition, gaining entry to a research site and the ethical issues that might arise are also elements of the researcher's role.

Reflexivity requires commenting on two important points:

- *Past experiences.* Include statements about past experiences with the research problem or with the participants or setting that help the reader understand the connection between the researchers and the study. These experiences may involve participation in the setting, past educational or work experiences, or culture, ethnicity, race, SES, or other demographics that tie the researchers directly to the study.

- *How past experiences shape interpretations.* Be explicit, then, about how these experiences may potentially shape the interpretations the researchers make during the study. For example, the experiences may cause researchers to lean toward certain themes, to actively look for evidence to support their positions, and to create favorable or unfavorable conclusions about the sites or participants.

How can reflexive thinking be incorporated into your qualitative study (Creswell, 2016)? You can write notes about your personal experiences during the study. These notes might include observations about the process of data collection, hunches about what you are learning, and concerns about reactions of participants to the research process. These ideas can be written as **memos**—notes written during the research process that reflect on the process or that help shape the development of codes and themes. In writing these reflective notes, how do you know whether you are being sufficiently reflexive for a qualitative study? Sufficient reflexivity occurs when researchers record notes during the process of research, reflect on their own personal experiences, and consider how their personal experiences may shape their interpretation of results. Also, qualitative researchers need to limit their discussions about personal experiences so that they do not override the importance of the content or methods in a study.

Another aspect of reflecting on the role of the researcher is to be aware of connections between the researcher and the participants or the research sites that may unduly influence the researcher's interpretations. "Backyard" research (Glesne & Peshkin, 1992) involves studying the researcher's own organization, or friends, or immediate work setting. This often leads to compromises in the researcher's ability to disclose information and raises issues of an imbalance of power between the inquirer and the participants. When researchers collect data at their own workplaces (or when they are in a superior role to participants), the information may be convenient and easy to collect, but it may not be accurate information and it may jeopardize the roles of the researchers and the participants. If studying the backyard is essential, then the researcher is responsible for showing how the data will not be compromised and how such information will not place the participants (or the researchers) at risk. In addition, multiple strategies for validation (see approaches to validation later in this chapter) are necessary to demonstrate the accuracy of the information.

Further, indicate steps taken to obtain permission from the institutional review board (IRB) (see Chapter 4) to protect the rights of human participants. Attach, as an appendix, the approval letter from the IRB and discuss the process involved in securing permissions. Discuss steps taken to gain entry to the setting and to secure permissions to study the participants or situation (Marshall & Rossman, 2016). It is important to gain access to research or archival sites by seeking the approval of **gatekeepers**, individuals at the site who provide access to the site and allow or permit the research to be done. A brief proposal might need to be developed and submitted for review to gatekeepers. Bogdan and Biklen (1992) advanced topics that could be addressed in such a proposal:

- Why was the site chosen for study?

- What activities will occur at the site during the research study?

- Will the study be disruptive?

- How will the results be reported?

- What will the gatekeeper gain from the study?

Comment about sensitive ethical issues that may arise (see Chapter 4). For each issue raised, discuss how the research study will address it. For example, when studying a sensitive topic, it is necessary to mask names of people, places, and activities. In this situation, the process for masking information requires discussion in the proposal.

Data Collection Procedures

Comments about the role of the researcher set the stage for discussion of issues involved in collecting data. The data collection steps include setting the boundaries for the study through sampling and recruitment; collecting information through unstructured or semi-structured observations and interviews, documents, and visual materials; as well as establishing the protocol for recording information.

- Identify the purposefully selected sites or individuals for the proposed study. The idea behind qualitative research is to **purposefully select** participants or sites (or documents or visual material) that will best help the researcher understand the problem and the research question. This does not necessarily suggest random sampling or selection of a large number of participants and sites, as is typically found in quantitative research. A discussion of participants and the site might include four aspects identified by Miles and Huberman (1994): (a) the setting (i.e., where the research will take place), (b) the actors (i.e., who will be observed or interviewed), (c) the events (i.e., what the actors will be observed or interviewed doing), and (d) the process (i.e., the evolving nature of events undertaken by the actors within the setting).

- Discuss the strategies being used to recruit individual (or cases) to the study. This is a challenging aspect of research. Indicate ways of informing appropriate participants about the study, and cite the actual recruitment messages sent to them. Discuss ways to provide incentives for individuals to participate, and reflect on approaches that will be used if one method of recruitment is not successful.

- Comment on the number of participants and sites involved in the research. Aside from the small number that characterizes qualitative research, how many sites and participants should you have? First of all, there is no specific answer to this question; the literature contains a variety of perspectives (e.g., see Creswell & Poth, 2018). Sample size depends on the qualitative design being used (e.g., ethnography, case study). From a review of many qualitative research studies, we have some rough estimates to advance. Narrative includes one or two individuals; phenomenology involves a range of 3–10; grounded theory, 20–30; ethnography examines one single culture-sharing group with numerous artifacts, interviews, and observations; and case studies include about four to five cases. This is certainly one approach to the sample size issue. Another approach is equally viable. The idea of **saturation** comes from grounded theory. Charmaz (2006) said that one stops collecting data when the categories (or themes) are saturated: when gathering fresh data no longer sparks new insights or reveals new properties. This is when you have an adequate sample.

- Indicate the type or types of data to be collected. In many qualitative studies, inquirers collect multiple forms of data and spend a considerable time in the natural setting gathering information. The collection procedures in qualitative research involve four basic types and their strengths and limitations, as shown in Table 9.2.

  o A **qualitative observation** is when the researcher takes field notes on the behavior and activities of individuals at the research site. In these field notes, the researcher records, in an unstructured or semi-structured way (using some prior questions that the inquirer wants to know), activities at the research site. Qualitative observers may also engage in roles varying from a nonparticipant to a complete participant. Typically these observations are open-ended in that the researchers ask general questions of the participants allowing the participants to freely provide their views.

o   In **qualitative interviews,** the researcher conducts face-to-face interviews with participants, telephone interviews, or engages in focus group interviews with six to eight interviewees in each group. These interviews involve unstructured and generally open-ended questions that are few in number and intended to elicit views and opinions from the participants.

o   During the process of research, the investigator may collect **qualitative documents.** These may be public documents (e.g., newspapers, minutes of meetings, official reports) or private documents (e.g., personal journals and diaries, letters, e-mails).

o   A final category of qualitative data consists of **qualitative audiovisual and digital materials** (including social media materials). This data may take the form of photographs, art objects, videotapes, website main pages, e-mails, text messages, social media text, or any forms of sound. Include creative data collection procedures that fall under the category of visual ethnography (Pink, 2001) and which might include living stories, metaphorical visual narratives, and digital archives (Clandinin, 2007).

o   In a discussion about data collection forms, be specific about the types and include arguments concerning the strengths and weaknesses of each type, as discussed in Table 9.2. Typically, in good qualitative research the researchers draw on multiple sources of qualitative data to make interpretations about a research problem.

- Include data collection types that go beyond typical observations and interviews. These unusual forms create reader interest in a proposal and can capture useful information that observations and interviews may miss. For example, examine the compendium of types of data in Table 9.3 that can be used, to stretch the imagination about possibilities, such as gathering sounds or tastes, or using cherished items to elicit comments during an interview. Such stretching will be viewed positively by graduate committee members and by editors of journals.

Data Collection Types	Options Within Types	Advantages of the Type	Limitations of the Type
Observations	• Complete participant—researcher conceals role • Observer as participant—role of researcher is known • Participant as observer— observation role secondary to participant role • Complete observer—researcher observes without participating	• Researcher has a firsthand experience with participant. • Researcher can record information as it occurs. • Unusual aspects can be noticed during observation. • Useful in exploring topics that may be uncomfortable for participants to discuss.	• Researcher may be seen as intrusive. • Private information may be observed that researcher cannot report. • Researcher may not have good attending and observing skills. • Certain participants (e.g., children) may present special problems in gaining rapport.
Interviews	• Face-to-face—one-on-one, in-person interview • Telephone—researcher interviews by phone • Focus group—researcher interviews participants in a group • E-mail Internet interview	• Useful when participants cannot be directly observed. • Participants can provide historical information. • Allows researcher control over the line of questioning.	• Provides indirect information filtered through the views of interviewees. • Provides information in a designated place rather than the natural field setting. • Researcher's presence may bias responses. • Not all people are equally articulate and perceptive.
Documents	• Public documents—minutes of meetings or newspapers • Private documents—journals, diaries, or letters	• Enables a researcher to obtain the language and words of participants. • Can be accessed at a time convenient to researcher—an unobtrusive source of information. • Represents data to which participants have given attention. • As written evidence, it saves a researcher the time and expense of transcribing.	• Not all people are equally articulate and perceptive. • May be protected information unavailable to public or private access. • Requires the researcher to search out the information in hard-to-find places. • Requires transcribing or optically scanning for computer entry. • Materials may be incomplete. • The documents may not be authentic or accurate.

Table 9.2 Qualitative Data Collection Types, Options, Advantages, and Limitations

Data Collection Types	Options Within Types	Advantages of the Type	Limitations of the Type
Audiovisual digital materials	• Photographs • Videotapes • Art objects • Computer messages • Sounds • Film	• May be an unobtrusive method of collecting data. • Provides an opportunity for participants to directly share their reality. • It is creative in that it captures attention visually.	• May be difficult to interpret. • May not be accessible publicly or privately. • The presence of an observer (e.g., photographer) may be disruptive and affect responses.

Note: This table includes material adapted from Bogdan & Biklen (1992), Creswell & Poth (2018), and Merriam (1998).

Table 9.3   A List of Qualitative Data Collection Sources

Observations

- Conduct an observation as a participant or an observer.
- Conduct an observation shifting position from participant to observer (and vice versa).

Interviews

- Conduct one-on-one interviews in the same room, or virtually via web-based or e-mail platforms.
- Conduct a focus group interview in the same room, or virtually via web-based or e-mail platforms.

Documents

- Keep a research journal during the study, or have a participant keep a journal or diary.
- Examine personal documents (e.g., letters, e-mails, private blogs).
- Analyze organizational documents (e.g., reports, strategic plans, charts, medical records).
- Analyze public documents (e.g., official memos, blogs, records, archival information).
- Examine autobiographies and biographies.

Audiovisual and Digital Materials

- Have participants take photographs or record videos (i.e., photo elicitation).
- Use video or film in a social situation or of an individual.
- Examine photographs or videos.
- Examine websites, tweets, Facebook messages.
- Collect sounds (e.g., musical sounds, a child's laughter, car horns honking).
- Gather phone or computer-based messages.
- Examine possessions or ritual objects.

Source:

Data Recording Procedures

Before entering the field, qualitative researchers plan their approach to data recording. The qualitative proposal or project should identify the procedures the researcher will use for recording data.

- *Observation protocol.* Plan to develop and use a protocol for recording observations in a qualitative study. Researchers often engage in multiple observations during the course of a qualitative study and use an **observational protocol** for recording information while observing. This may be a single page with a dividing line down the middle to separate descriptive notes (portraits of the participants, a reconstruction of dialogue, a description of the physical setting, accounts of particular events, or activities) from reflexive notes (the researcher's personal thoughts, such as "speculation, feelings, problems, ideas, hunches, impressions, and prejudices"; Bogdan & Biklen, 1992, p. 121). Also written on this form might be demographic information about the time, place, and date of the field setting where the observation takes place.

- *Interview protocol.* Plan to develop and use an **interview protocol** for asking questions and recording answers during a qualitative interview. Researchers record information from interviews by making handwritten notes, by audiotaping, or by videotaping. Even if an interview is taped, we recommend that researchers take notes in the event that recording equipment fails. If audiotaping is used, researchers need to plan in advance for the transcription of the tape.

The interview protocol should be about two pages in length. There should be some spaces between the questions for the interviewer to write short notes and quotes in case the audio-recording device does not work. The total number of questions should be somewhere between 5 and 10, although no precise number can be given. It should be prepared in advance of the interview, and used consistently in all of the interviews. It is helpful for the interviewer to memorize the questions so that he or she does not appear to be simply reading the interview protocol. The interview protocol consists of several important components. These are basic information about the interview, an introduction, the interview content questions with probes, and closing instructions (see also Creswell, 2016). See Figure 9.1.

Data Analysis Procedures

A methods discussion in a qualitative proposal or study needs also to specify the steps in analyzing the various forms of qualitative data. In general, the intent is to make sense out of text and image data. It involves segmenting and taking apart the data (like peeling back the layers of an onion)

Figure 9.1 Sample Interview Protocol

○ *Basic information about the interview*. This is a section of the interview where the interviewer records basic information about the interview so that the database can be well organized. It should include the time and date of the interview, where the interview took place, and the names of both the interviewer and interviewee. The project length of the interview could also be noted as well as the file name for the digital copy of the audio recording and transcription.

○ *Introduction*. This section of the protocol provides the instructions to the interviewer so that useful information is not overlooked during a potentially anxious period of conducting the interview. The interviewer needs to introduce himself or herself, and to discuss the purpose of the study. This purpose can be written out in advance and simply read by the interviewer. It should also contain a prompt to the interviewer to collect a signed copy of the informed consent form (alternatively, the participant may have sent the form to the interviewer). The interviewer might also talk about the general structure of the interview (e.g., how it will begin, the number of questions, the time that it should take), and ask the interviewee if he or she has any questions before beginning the interview. Finally, before the interview begins, the interviewer may need to define some important terms that will be used in the interview.

○ *Opening question*. An important first step in an interview is to set the interviewee at ease. We typically begin with an ice-breaker type of question. This is a question where we ask participants to talk about themselves in a way that will not alienate them. We might ask them about their job, their role, or even how they spent the day. We do not ask personal questions (e.g., "What is your income?"). People like talking about themselves, and this opening question should be framed to accomplish this goal.

○ *Content questions*. These questions are the research sub-questions in the study, phrased in a way that seems friendly to the interviewee. They essentially parse the central phenomenon into its parts—asking about different facets of the central phenomenon. Whether the final question would be a restatement of the central question is open to debate. It is hoped that after the interviewee has answered all of the sub-questions, the qualitative researcher will have a good understanding as to how the central question has been answered.

○ *Using probes*. These content questions also need to include probes. Probes are reminders to the researcher of two types: to ask for more information, or to ask for an explanation of ideas. The specific wording might be as follows (and these words could be inserted into the interview protocol as a reminder to the interviewer):

- "Tell me more" (asking for more information)
- "I need more detail" (asking for more information)
- "Could you explain your response more?" (asking for an explanation)
- "What does 'not much' mean?" (asking for an explanation)

Sometimes beginning qualitative researchers are uncomfortable with a small number of questions and they feel that their interview may be quite short with only a few (5–10) questions. True, some people may have little to say (or little information to provide about the central phenomenon), but by including probes in the interview, the researcher can expand the duration of the interview as well as net useful information. A useful final question might be, "Who should I contact next to learn more?" or "Is there any further information that you would like to share that we have not covered?" These follow-up questions essentially net closure on the interview and show the researcher's desire to learn more about the topic of the interview.

○ *Closing instructions*. It is important to thank the interviewee for his or her time and respond to any final questions. Assure the interviewee of the confidentiality of the interview. Ask if you can follow-up with another interview if one is needed to clarify certain points. One question that may surface is how participants will learn about the results of your project. It is important to think through and provide a response to this question because it involves your time and resources. A convenient way to provide information to interviewees is to offer to send them an abstract of the final study. This brief communication of results is efficient and convenient for most researchers.

as well as putting it back together. The discussion in your study about qualitative data analysis might begin with several general points about the overall process:

- *Simultaneous procedures.* Data analysis in qualitative research will proceed hand-in-hand with other parts of developing the qualitative study, namely, the data collection and the write-up of findings. While interviews are going on, for example, researchers may be analyzing an interview collected earlier, writing memos that may ultimately be included as a narrative in the final report, and organizing the structure of the final report. This process is unlike quantitative research in which the investigator collects the data, then analyzes the information, and finally writes the report.

- *Winnowing the data.* Because text and image data are so dense and rich, all of the information cannot be used in a qualitative study. Thus, in the analysis of the data, researchers need to "winnow" the data (Guest, MacQueen, & Namey, 2012), a process of focusing in on some of the data and disregarding other parts of it. This process, too, is different from quantitative research in which researchers go to great lengths to preserve all of the data and reconstruct or replace missing data. In qualitative research, the impact of this process is to aggregate data into a small number of themes, something between five and seven themes (Creswell, 2013).

- *Using qualitative computer software programs for assistance.* Also specify whether you will use a qualitative computer data analysis program to assist you in analyzing the data (or whether you will hand code the data). Hand coding is a laborious and time-consuming process, even for data from a few individuals. Thus, qualitative software programs have become quite popular, and they help researchers organize, sort, and search for information in text or image databases (see Guest and colleagues' [2012] chapter on qualitative data analysis software). Several excellent computer software programs are available, and they have similar features: good tutorials and demonstration files, the ability to incorporate both text and image (e.g., photographs) data, the features of storing and organizing data, the search capacity of locating all text associated with specific codes, interrelated codes for making queries of the relationship among codes, and the import and export of qualitative data to *quantitative* programs, such as spreadsheets or data analysis programs. The basic idea behind these programs is that using the computer is an efficient means for storing and locating qualitative data. Although the researcher still needs to go through each line of text (as in hand coding by going through transcriptions) and assign codes, this process may be faster and more efficient than hand coding. Also, in large databases, the researcher can quickly locate all passages (or text segments) coded the same and determine whether participants are responding to a code idea in similar or different ways. Beyond this, the computer program can facilitate relating different codes (e.g., How do males and females—the first code of *gender*—differ in terms of their *attitudes to smoking*—a second code?). These are just a few features of the software programs that make them a logical choice for qualitative data analysis over hand coding. As with any software program, qualitative software programs require time and skill to learn and employ effectively, although books for learning the programs are widely available. Demos are available for six popular qualitative data analysis software programs: MAXqda (www.maxqda.com/), Atlas.ti (www.atlasti.com), Provalis and QDA Miner (https://provalisresearch.com/), Dedoose (www .dedoose.com/), and QSR NVivo (www.qsrinternational .com/). These programs are available for both the PC and MAC platforms.

- *Overview of the data analysis process* (see Figure 9.2). As a **research tip**, we urge researchers to look at qualitative data analysis as a process that requires sequential steps to be followed, from the specific to the general, and involving multiple levels of analysis:

Step 1. *Organize and prepare the data for analysis*. This involves transcribing interviews, optically scanning material, typing up field notes, cataloguing all of the visual material, and sorting and arranging the data into different types depending on the sources of information.

Step 2. *Read or look at all the data*. This first step provides a general sense of the information and an opportunity to reflect on its overall meaning. What general ideas are participants saying? What is the tone of the ideas? What is the impression of the overall depth, credibility, and use of the information? Sometimes qualitative researchers write notes in margins of transcripts or observational field notes, or start recording general thoughts about the data at this stage. For visual data, a sketchbook of ideas can begin to take shape.

Step 3. *Start coding all of the data*. **Coding** is the process of organizing the data by bracketing chunks (or text or image segments) and writing a word representing a category in the margins (Rossman & Rallis, 2012). It involves taking text data or pictures gathered during data collection, segmenting sentences (or paragraphs) or images into categories, and labeling those categories

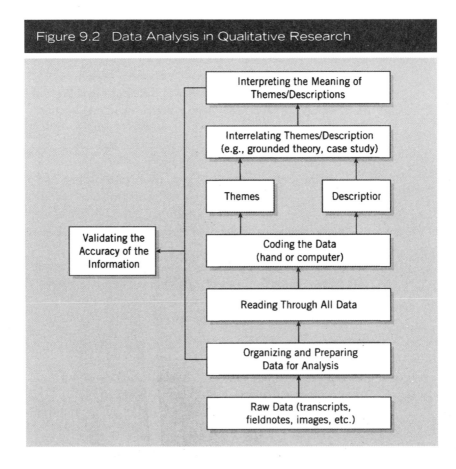

Figure 9.2 Data Analysis in Qualitative Research

Interpreting the Meaning of Themes/Descriptions

Interrelating Themes/Description (e.g., grounded theory, case study)

Themes

Descriptior

Validating the Accuracy of the Information

Coding the Data (hand or computer)

Reading Through All Data

Organizing and Preparing Data for Analysis

Raw Data (transcripts, fieldnotes, images, etc.)

with a term, often based in the actual language of the participant (called an *in vivo* term).

Step 4. *Generate a description and themes.* Use the coding process to generate a description of the setting or people as well as categories or themes for analysis. *Description* involves a detailed rendering of information about people, places, or events in a setting. Researchers can generate codes for this description. This analysis is useful in designing detailed descriptions for case studies, ethnographies, and narrative research projects. Use the coding as well for generating a small number of *themes* or categories— perhaps five to seven themes for a research study. These themes are the ones that appear as major findings in qualitative studies and are often used as headings in the findings sections of studies (or in the findings section of a dissertation or thesis). They should display multiple perspectives from individuals and be supported by diverse quotations and specific evidence. Beyond identifying the themes during the coding process, qualitative researchers can do much with themes to build additional layers of complex analysis. For example, researchers interconnect themes into a story line (as in narratives) or develop them into a theoretical model (as in grounded theory). Themes are analyzed for each individual case and across different cases (as in case studies) or shaped into a general description (as in phenomenology). Sophisticated qualitative studies go beyond description and theme identification and form complex theme connections.

Step 5. *Representing the description and themes.* Advance how the description and themes will be *represented* in the qualitative narrative. The most popular approach is to use a narrative passage to convey the findings of the analysis. This might be a discussion that mentions a chronology of events, the detailed discussion of several themes (complete with subthemes, specific illustrations, multiple perspectives from individuals, and quotations) or a discussion with interconnecting themes. Many qualitative researchers also use visuals, figures, or tables as adjuncts to the discussions. They present a process model (as in grounded theory), advance a drawing of the specific research site (as in ethnography), or convey descriptive information about each participant in a table (as in case studies and ethnographies).

- *Specific coding procedures.* As shown in Table 9.4, Tesch (1990) provided the eight steps typically used in forming codes. In addition, give some attention to the types of codes to develop when analyzing a text transcript or a picture (or other type of visual object).

We tend to think about codes as falling into three categories:

- *Expected codes.* Code on topics that readers would expect to find, based on the literature and common sense. When studying bullying in the schools, we might code some segments as "attitudes toward oneself." This code would be expected in a study about bullying in the schools.

- *Surprising codes.* Code on findings that are surprising and could not be anticipated before the study began. In a study of leadership in nonprofit organizations, we might learn about the impact of geo-warming on the building of the organization and how this shapes the location and proximity of individuals to one another. Without going out to the building before the study begins and looking at it, we would not necessarily think about the codes of geo-warming and location of offices in my study of leadership.

- *Codes of unusual or of conceptual interest.* Code unusual ideas, and those that are, in and of themselves, of conceptual interest to readers. We will use one of the codes that we discovered in our qualitative study of a campus's response to a gunman

Table 9.4　Tesch's Eight Steps in the Coding Process

1. Get a sense of the whole. Read all the transcriptions carefully. Perhaps jot down some ideas as they come to mind as you read.

2. Pick one document (i.e., one interview)—the most interesting one, the shortest, the one on the top of the pile. Go through it, asking yourself, "What is this about?" Do not think about the substance of the information but its underlying meaning. Write thoughts in the margin.

3. When you have completed this task for several participants, make a list of all topics. Cluster together similar topics. Form these topics into columns, perhaps arrayed as major, unique, and leftover topics.

4. Now take this list and go back to your data. Abbreviate the topics as codes and write the codes next to the appropriate segments of the text. Try this preliminary organizing scheme to see if new categories and codes emerge.

5. Find the most descriptive wording for your topics and turn them into categories. Look for ways of reducing your total list of categories by grouping topics that relate to each other. Perhaps draw lines between your categories to show interrelationships.

6. Make a final decision on the abbreviation for each category and alphabetize these codes.

7. Assemble the data material belonging to each category in one place and perform a preliminary analysis.

8. If necessary, recode your existing data.

(Asmussen & Creswell, 1995). We did not anticipate the code "retriggering" to emerge in our study, and it surfaced from the perspective of a psychologist called into the campus to assess the response. The fact that individuals were reminded of past traumatic incidents—retriggering—prompted us to use the term as an important code and ultimately a theme in our analysis.

- *On using predetermined codes.* Another issue about coding is whether the researcher should (a) develop codes *only* on the basis of the emerging information collected from participants, (b) use predetermined codes and then fit the data to them, or (c) use some combination of emerging and predetermined codes. The traditional approach in the social sciences is to allow the codes to emerge during the data analysis. In the health sciences, a popular approach is to use predetermined codes based on the theory being examined. In this case, the researchers might develop a **qualitative codebook,** a table that contains a list of predetermined codes that researchers use for coding the data. Guest and colleagues (2012) discussed and illustrated the use of codebooks in qualitative research. The intent of a codebook is to provide definitions for codes and to maximize coherence among codes—especially when multiple coders are involved. This codebook would provide a list of codes, a code label for each code, a brief definition of it, a full definition of it, information about when to use the code and when not to use it, and an example of a quote illustrating the code. This codebook can evolve and change during a study based on close analysis of the data when the researcher is not starting from an emerging code perspective. For researchers who have a distinct theory they want to test in their projects, we would recommend developing a preliminary codebook for coding the data and then permitting the codebook to develop and change based on the information learned during the data analysis.

- *Coding visual images.* As mentioned earlier, visual data are becoming used more frequently in qualitative research. These data sources represent images drawn from photographs, videos, film, and drawing (Creswell, 2016). Participants might be handed a camera and asked to take pictures of what they see. Alternatively, they may be asked to draw a picture of the phenomenon under study, or reflect on a favorite picture or object that would elicit responses. Challenges in using visual images do arise in qualitative research. Images may reflect trends of the culture or society rather than the perspectives of a single individual. It is difficult to respect anonymity when images of individuals and places represent qualitative data. Permissions are needed to respect the privacy of individuals providing visual data.

Despite these concerns, once the qualitative researcher obtains the visual data, the process of coding comes into play. These steps often follow this procedure:

Step 1. Prepare your data or analysis. If hand coding, print each image with a wide margin (or affix it to a larger piece of paper) to allow space to assign the code labels. If using a computer, import all images into the application.

Step 2. Code the image by tagging areas of the image and assigning code labels. Some codes might involve meta-details (e.g., the camera angle).

Step 3. Compile all of the codes for the images on a separate sheet.

Step 4. Review the codes to eliminate redundancy and overlap. This step also begins to reduce the codes to potential themes.

Step 5. Group codes into themes that represent a common idea.

Step 6. Assign the codes/themes to three groups: expected codes/themes, surprising codes/themes, and unusual codes/themes. This step helps to ensure the qualitative "findings" will represent diverse perspectives.

Step 7. Array the codes/themes into a conceptual map that shows the flow of ideas in the "findings" section. The flow might represent presenting the themes from a more general picture to a more specific picture.

Step 8. Write the narrative for each theme that will go into the "findings" section of a study or for a general summary that will go into the "discussion" section as the overall findings in the study. (Creswell, 2016, pp. 169–170).

- *Further data analysis by type of approach.* A helpful conceptualization to advance in the method section is that qualitative data analysis will proceed on two layers: (a) the first basic layer is the more general procedure (see above) in analyzing the data, and (b) the second more advanced layer would be the analysis steps embedded within specific qualitative designs. For example, narrative research employs restorying the participants' stories using structural devices, such as plot, setting, activities, climax, and denouement (Clandinin & Connelly, 2000). Phenomenological research uses the analysis of significant statements, the generation of meaning units, and the development of what Moustakas (1994) called an essence description. Grounded theory has systematic steps (Corbin & Strauss, 2015; Strauss & Corbin, 1990, 1998). These involve generating categories of information (open coding), selecting one of the categories and positioning it within a theoretical model (axial coding), and then explicating a story from the interconnection of these categories (selective coding). Case study and ethnographic research involve a detailed description of the setting or individuals, followed by analysis of the data for themes or issues (see Stake, 1995; Wolcott, 1994). A complete description of the data analysis in a proposal, when the inquirer is using one of these strategies, would be to first describe the general process of analysis followed by the specific steps within the strategy.

Interpretation

Interpretation in qualitative research involves several procedures: summarizing the overall findings, comparing the findings to the literature, discussing a personal view of the findings, and stating limitations and future research. In terms of overall findings, the question "What were the lessons learned?" captures the essence of this idea (Lincoln & Guba, 1985). These lessons could be the researcher's personal interpretation, couched in the understanding that the inquirer brings to the study from a personal culture, history, and experiences.

It could also be a meaning derived from a comparison of the findings with information gleaned from the literature or theories. In this way, authors suggest that the findings confirm past information or diverge from it. It can also suggest new questions that need to be asked—questions raised by the data and analysis that the inquirer had not foreseen earlier in the study. Ethnographers can end a study, Wolcott (1994) said, by stating further questions. The questioning approach is also used in transformative approaches to qualitative research. Moreover, when qualitative researchers use a theoretical lens, they can form interpretations that call for action agendas for reform and change. Researchers might describe how the narrative outcome will be compared with theories and the general literature on the topic. In many qualitative articles, researchers also discuss the literature at the end of the study (see Chapter 2). Thus, interpretation in qualitative research can take many forms; be adapted for different types of designs; and be flexible to convey personal, research-based, and action meanings.

Finally, part of interpretation involves suggesting limitations in a project and advancing future research directions. Limitations often attach to the methods of a study (e.g., inadequate sample size, difficulty in recruitment), and they represent weaknesses in the research that the author acknowledges so that future studies will not suffer from the same problems. Suggestions for future research propose research themes that studies might address to advance the literature, to remedy some of the weaknesses in the present study, or to advance new leads or directions that can point to useful applications or knowledge.

Validity and Reliability

Although validation of findings occurs throughout the steps in the research process, this discussion focuses on how the researcher writes a passage in a proposal or study on the procedures to be undertaken to validate the proposed study's findings. Researchers need to convey the steps they will take in their studies to check for the accuracy and credibility of their findings. Validity does not carry the same connotations in qualitative research that it does in quantitative research; nor is it a companion to reliability (examining stability) or generalizability (the external validity of applying results to new settings, people, or samples), topics discussed in Chapter 8. **Qualitative validity** means that the researcher checks for the accuracy of the findings by employing certain procedures, whereas **qualitative reliability** indicates that the researcher's approach is consistent across different researchers and among different projects (Gibbs, 2007).

- *Defining qualitative validity.* Validity is one of the strengths of qualitative research and is based on determining whether the findings are accurate from the standpoint of the researcher, the participant, or the readers of an account (Creswell & Miller, 2000).

Terms abound in the qualitative literature that address validity, such as *trustworthiness, authenticity*, and *credibility* (Creswell & Miller, 2000), and it is a much-discussed topic (Lincoln, Lynham, & Guba, 2011).

- *Using multiple validity procedures.* A procedural perspective that we recommend for research proposals is to identify and discuss one or more strategies available to check the accuracy of the findings. Researchers should actively incorporate **validity strategies** into their proposals. We recommend the use of multiple approaches, which should enhance the researcher's ability to assess the accuracy of findings as well as convince readers of that accuracy. There are eight primary strategies, organized from those used most frequently and easiest to implement to those used occasionally and more difficult to implement:

  o *Triangulate* different data sources by examining evidence from the sources and using it to build a coherent justification for themes. If themes are established based on converging several sources of data or perspectives from participants, then this process can be claimed as adding to the validity of the study.

  o Use *member checking* to determine the accuracy of the qualitative findings by taking the final report or specific descriptions or themes back to participants and determining whether these participants feel that they are accurate. This does not mean taking back the raw transcripts to check for accuracy; instead, the researcher takes back parts of the polished or semi-polished product, such as the major findings, the themes, the case analysis, the grounded theory, the cultural description, and so forth. This procedure can involve conducting a follow-up interview with participants in the study and providing an opportunity for them to comment on the findings.

  o Use a *rich, thick description* to convey the findings. This description may transport readers to the setting and give the discussion an element of shared experiences. When qualitative researchers provide detailed descriptions of the setting, for example, or offer many perspectives about a theme, the results become more realistic and richer. This procedure can add to the validity of the findings.

  o Clarify the *bias* the researcher brings to the study. This self-reflection creates an open and honest narrative that will resonate well with readers. Reflexivity has already been mentioned as a core characteristic of qualitative research. Good qualitative research contains comments by the researchers about how their interpretation of the findings is shaped by their background, such as their gender, culture, history, and socioeconomic origin.

○ Present *negative* or *discrepant information* that runs counter to the themes. Because real life is composed of different perspectives that do not always coalesce, discussing contrary information adds to the credibility of an account. A researcher can accomplish this by discussing evidence about a theme. Most evidence will build a case for the theme; researchers can also present information that contradicts the general perspective of the theme. By presenting this contradictory evidence, the account becomes more realistic and more valid.

○ Spend *prolonged time* in the field. In this way, the researcher develops an in-depth understanding of the phenomenon under study and can convey detail about the site and the people that lends credibility to the narrative account. The more experience that a researcher has with participants in their settings, the more accurate or valid will be the findings.

○ Use *peer debriefing* to enhance the accuracy of the account. This process involves locating a person (a peer debriefer) who reviews and asks questions about the qualitative study so that the account will resonate with people other than the researcher. This strategy—involving an interpretation beyond the researcher and invested in another person—adds validity to an account.

○ Use an *external auditor* to review the entire project. As distinct from a peer debriefer, this auditor is not familiar with the researcher or the project and can provide an objective assessment of the project throughout the process of research or at the conclusion of the study. The role is similar to that of a fiscal auditor, and specific questions exist that auditors might ask (Lincoln & Guba, 1985). The procedure of having an independent investigator look over many aspects of the project (e.g., accuracy of transcription, the relationship between the research questions and the data, the level of data analysis from the raw data through interpretation) enhances the overall validity of a qualitative study.

• *Using qualitative reliability.* How do qualitative researchers check to determine if their approaches are reliable (i.e., consistent or stable)? Yin (2009) suggested that qualitative researchers need to document the procedures of their case studies and to document as many of the steps of the procedures as possible. He also recommended setting up a detailed case study protocol and database, so that others can follow the procedures. Gibbs (2007) suggested several qualitative reliability procedures:

- ○ Check transcripts to make sure that they do not contain obvious mistakes made during transcription.

- ○ Make sure that there is not a drift in the definition of codes, a shift in the meaning of the codes during the process of coding. This can be accomplished by continually comparing data with the codes and by writing memos about the codes and their definitions (see the discussion on a qualitative codebook).

- ○ For team research, coordinate the communication among the coders by regular documented meetings and by sharing the analysis.

- ○ Cross-check codes developed by different researchers by comparing results that are derived independently. Proposal writers need to include several of these procedures as evidence that they will have consistent results in their proposed study. We recommend that several procedures be mentioned in a proposal and that single researchers find another person who can cross-check their codes for what is called **intercoder agreement** (or cross-checking) (also see Guest et al., 2012; Creswell, 2016). Such an agreement might be based on whether two or more coders agree on codes used for the same passages in the text. It is not that they code the same passage of text; rather they determine whether another coder would code it with the same or a similar code. Reliability subprograms in qualitative computer software packages can then be used to determine the level of consistency of coding. Miles and Huberman (1994) recommended that the consistency of the coding be in agreement at least 80% of the time for good qualitative reliability.

- Qualitative generalization is a term used in a limited way in qualitative research, since the intent of this form of inquiry is not to generalize findings to individuals, sites, or places outside of those under study (see Gibbs, 2007, for his cautionary note about qualitative generalizability). In fact, the value of qualitative research lies in the particular description and themes developed in the context of a specific site. Particularity rather than generalizability (Greene & Caracelli, 1997) is the hallmark of good qualitative research. However, there are a few discussions in the qualitative literature about generalizability, especially as applied to case study research in which the inquirer studies several cases. Yin (2009), for example, felt that qualitative case study results can be generalized to some broader theory. The generalization occurs when qualitative researchers study additional cases and generalize findings to the new cases. It is the same as the replication logic used in experimental research. However, to repeat a case study's findings in a new case setting requires good documentation of qualitative procedures, such as a protocol for documenting the problem in detail and the development of a thorough case study database.

Writing the Qualitative Report

A plan for qualitative methods should end with some comments about the narrative that will emerge from the data analysis. Numerous varieties of narratives exist, and examples from scholarly journals illustrate these models. In a plan for a study, consider advancing several points about the narrative:

- The basic procedure in reporting the results of a qualitative study are to develop descriptions and themes from the data (see Figure 9.1), to present these descriptions and themes that convey multiple perspectives from participants and detailed descriptions of the setting or individuals. Using a qualitative strategy of inquiry, these results may also provide a chronological narrative of an individual's life (narrative research), a detailed description of their experiences (phenomenology), a theory generated from the data (grounded theory), a detailed portrait of a culture-sharing group (ethnography), or an in-depth analysis of one or more cases (case study).

- Given these different strategies, the findings and interpretation sections of a plan for a study might discuss how the sections will be presented: as objective accounts, fieldwork experiences (Van Maanen, 1988), a chronology, a process model, an extended story, an analysis by cases or across cases, or a detailed descriptive portrait.

- At the specific level, there might be some inclusion in the proposal or project about writing strategies that will be used to convey the qualitative research. These might include the following:

  o Quotes: From short to long embedded passages

  o Dialogue that reflects the culture of participants, their language, and a sensitivity to their culture or ethnicity, and the interweaving of words from participants and the author's interpretations

  o Varied narrative forms, such as matrices, comparison tables, and diagrams

  o First person "I" or collective "we" pronouns in the narration

  o Metaphors and analogies (see, for example, Richardson, 1990)

  o Narrative forms associated with specific qualitative strategies (e.g., description in case studies and ethnographies, a detailed story in narrative research)

Example 9.1 is a complete qualitative method section that was included in a proposal by Miller (1992). It contains most of the topics for a good qualitative method section addressed in this chapter.

Example 9.1   Qualitative Procedures

Miller's project was an ethnographic study of first-year experiences of the president of a 4-year college. As we present this discussion, we refer back to the sections addressed in this chapter and highlight them in boldfaced type. Also, we have maintained Miller's use of the term *informant,* although today, the more appropriate term *participant* should be used.

The Qualitative Research Paradigm

The qualitative research paradigm has its roots in cultural anthropology and American sociology (Kirk & Miller, 1986). It has only recently been adopted by educational researchers (Borg & Gall, 1989). The intent of qualitative research is to understand a particular social situation, event, role, group, or interaction (Locke, Spirduso, & Silverman, 1987). It is largely an investigative process where the researcher gradually makes sense of a social phenomenon by contrasting, comparing, replicating, cataloguing and classifying the object of study (Miles & Huberman, 1984). Marshall and Rossman (1989) suggest that this entails immersion in the everyday life of the setting chosen for the study; the researcher enters the informants' world and through ongoing interaction, seeks the informants' perspectives and meanings. *[Qualitative assumptions are mentioned.]*

Scholars contend that qualitative research can be distinguished from quantitative methodology by numerous unique characteristics that are inherent in the design. The following is a synthesis of commonly articulated assumptions regarding characteristics presented by various researchers.

1. Qualitative research occurs in natural settings, where human behavior and events occur.

2. Qualitative research is based on assumptions that are very different from quantitative designs. Theory or hypotheses are not established a priori.

3. The researcher is the primary instrument in data collection rather than some inanimate mechanism (Eisner, 1991; Fraenkel & Wallen, 1990; Lincoln & Guba, 1985; Merriam, 1988).

4. The data that emerge from a qualitative study are descriptive. That is, data are reported in words (primarily the participant's words) or pictures, rather than in numbers (Fraenkel & Wallen, 1990; Locke et al., 1987; Marshall & Rossman, 1989; Merriam, 1988).

5. The focus of qualitative research is on participants' perceptions and experiences, and the way they make sense of their lives (Fraenkel & Wallen, 1990; Locke et al., 1987; Merriam, 1988). The attempt is therefore to understand not one, but multiple realities (Lincoln & Guba, 1985).

6. Qualitative research focuses on the process that is occurring as well as the product or outcome. Researchers are particularly interested in understanding how things occur (Fraenkel & Wallen, 1990; Merriam, 1988).

7. Idiographic interpretation is utilized. In other words, attention is paid to particulars; and data is interpreted in

regard to the particulars of a case rather than generalizations.

8. Qualitative research is an emergent design in its negotiated outcomes. Meanings and interpretations are negotiated with human data sources because it is the subjects' realities that the researcher attempts to reconstruct (Lincoln & Guba, 1985; Merriam, 1988).

9. This research tradition relies on the utilization of tacit knowledge (intuitive and felt knowledge) because often the nuances of the multiple realities can be appreciated most in this way (Lincoln & Guba, 1985). Therefore, data are not quantifiable in the traditional sense of the word.

10. Objectivity and truthfulness are critical to both research traditions. However, the criteria for judging a qualitative study differ from quantitative research. First and foremost, the researcher seeks believability, based on coherence, insight and instrumental utility (Eisner, 1991) and trustworthiness (Lincoln & Guba, 1985) through a process of verification rather than through traditional validity and reliability measures. [Qualitative characteristics are mentioned.]

The Ethnographic Research Design

This study will utilize the ethnographic research tradition. This design emerged from the field of anthropology, primarily from the contributions of Bronislaw Malinowski, Robert Park and Franz Boas (Jacob, 1987; Kirk & Miller, 1986). The intent of ethnographic research is to obtain a holistic picture of the subject of study with emphasis on portraying the everyday experiences of individuals by observing and interviewing them and relevant others (Fraenkel & Wallen, 1990). The ethnographic study includes in-depth interviewing and continual and ongoing participant observation of a situation (Jacob, 1987) and in attempting to capture the whole picture reveals how people describe and structure their world (Fraenkel & Wallen, 1990). [The author used the ethnographic approach.]

The Researcher's Role

Particularly in qualitative research, the role of the researcher as the primary data collection instrument necessitates the identification of personal values, assumptions and biases at the outset of the study. The investigator's contribution to the research setting can be useful and positive rather than detrimental (Locke et al., 1987). My perceptions of higher education and the college presidency have been shaped by my personal experiences. From August 1980 to May 1990 I served as a college administrator on private campuses of 600 to 5,000 students. Most recently (1987–1990), I served as the Dean for Student Life at a small college in the Midwest. As a member of the President's cabinet, I was involved with all top level administrative cabinet activities and decisions and worked closely with the faculty, cabinet officers, president and board of trustees. In addition to reporting to the president, I worked with him through his first year in office. I believe this understanding of the context and role enhances my awareness, knowledge and sensitivity

(Continued)

to many of the challenges, decisions and issues encountered as a first year president and will assist me in working with the informant in this study. I bring knowledge of both the structure of higher education and of the role of the college presidency. Particular attention will be paid to the role of the new president in initiating change, relationship building, decision making, and providing leadership and vision.

Due to previous experiences working closely with a new college president, I bring certain biases to this study. Although every effort will be made to ensure objectivity, these biases may shape the way I view and understand the data I collect and the way I interpret my experiences. I commence this study with the perspective that the college presidency is a diverse and often difficult position. Though expectations are immense, I question how much power the president has to initiate change and provide leadership and vision. I view the first year as critical; filled with adjustments, frustrations, unanticipated surprises and challenges. *[Author reflected on her role in the study.]*

Bounding the Study

Setting

This study will be conducted on the campus of a state college in the Midwest. The college is situated in a rural Midwestern community. The institution's 1,700 students nearly triple the town's population of 1,000 when classes are in session.

The institution awards associate, bachelor and master's degrees in 51 majors.

Actors

The informant in this study is the new President of a state college in the Midwest. The primary informant in this study is the President. However, I will be observing him in the context of administrative cabinet meetings. The president's cabinet includes three Vice Presidents (Academic Affairs, Administration, Student Affairs) and two Deans (Graduate Studies and Continuing Education).

Events

Using ethnographic research methodology, the focus of this study will be the everyday experiences and events of the new college president, and the perceptions and meaning attached to those experiences as expressed by the informant. This includes the assimilation of surprising events or information, and making sense of critical events and issues that arise.

Processes

Particular attention will be paid to the role of the new president in initiating change, relationship building, decision making, and providing leadership and vision. *[Author mentioned data collection boundaries.]*

Ethical Considerations

Most authors who discuss qualitative research design address the importance of ethical considerations (Locke et al.,

1982; Marshall & Rossman, 1989; Merriam, 1988; Spradley, 1980). First and foremost, the researcher has an obligation to respect the rights, needs, values, and desires of the informant(s). To an extent, ethnographic research is always obtrusive. Participant observation invades the life of the informant (Spradley, 1980) and sensitive information is frequently revealed. This is of particular concern in this study where the informant's position and institution are highly visible. The following safeguards will be employed to protect the informant's rights: 1) the research objectives will be articulated verbally and in writing so that they are clearly understood by the informant (including a description of how data will be used), 2) written permission to proceed with the study as articulated will be received from the informant, 3) a research exemption form will be filed with the Institutional Review Board (Appendixes B1 and B2), 4) the informant will be informed of all data collection devices and activities, 5) verbatim transcriptions and written interpretations and reports will be made available to the informant, 6) the informant's rights, interests and wishes will be considered first when choices are made regarding reporting the data, and 7) the final decision regarding informant anonymity will rest with the informant. *[Author addressed ethical issues and IRB review.]*

Data Collection Strategies

Data will be collected from February through May, 1992. This will include a minimum of bi-monthly, 45 minute recorded interviews with the informant (initial interview questions, Appendix C), bimonthly two hour observations of administrative cabinet meetings, bi-monthly two hour observations of daily activities and bi-monthly analysis of the president's calendar and documents (meeting minutes, memos, publications). In addition, the informant has agreed to record impressions of his experiences, thoughts and feelings in a taped diary (guidelines for recorded reflection, Appendix D). Two follow-up interviews will be scheduled for the end of May 1992 (See Appendix E for proposed timeline and activity schedule). *[The author proposed to use face-to-face interviews, participate as observer, and obtain private documents.]*

To assist in the data collection phase I will utilize a field log, providing a detailed account of ways I plan to spend my time when I am on-site, and in the transcription and analysis phase (also comparing this record to how time is actually spent). I intend to record details related to my observations in a field notebook and keep a field diary to chronicle my own thinking, feeling, experiences and perceptions throughout the research process. *[The author recorded descriptive and reflective information.]*

Data Analysis Procedures

Merriam (1988) and Marshall and Rossman (1989) contend that data collection and data analysis must be a simultaneous process in qualitative

(Continued)

(Continued)

research. Schatzman and Strauss (1973) claim that qualitative data analysis primarily entails classifying things, persons, and events and the properties which characterize them. Typically throughout the data analysis process ethnographers index or code their data using as many categories as possible (Jacob, 1987). They seek to identify and describe patterns and themes from the perspective of the participant(s), then attempt to understand and explain these patterns and themes (Agar, 1980). During data analysis the data will be organized categorically and chronologically, reviewed repeatedly, and continually coded. A list of major ideas that surface will be chronicled (as suggested by Merriam, 1988). Taped interviews and the participant's taped diary will be transcribed verbatim. Field notes and diary entries will be regularly reviewed. *[Author described steps in data analysis.]*

In addition, the data analysis process will be aided by the use of a qualitative data analysis computer program called HyperQual. Raymond Padilla (Arizona State University) designed HyperQual in 1987 for use with the Macintosh computer. HyperQual utilizes HyperCard software and facilitates the recording and analysis of textual and graphic data. Special stacks are designated to hold and organize data. Using HyperQual the researcher can directly "enter field data, including interview data, observations, researcher's memos, and illustrations . . . (and) tag (or code) all or part of the source data so that chunks of data can be pulled out and then be reassembled in a new and illuminating configuration" (Padilla, 1989, pp. 69–70). Meaningful data chunks can be identified, retrieved, isolated, grouped and regrouped for analysis. Categories or code names can be entered initially or at a later date. Codes can be added, changed or deleted with HyperQual editor and text can be searched for key categories, themes, words or phrases. *[Author mentions the proposed use of computer software for data analysis.]*

Verification

In ensuring internal validity, the following strategies will be employed:

1. Triangulation of data—Data will be collected through multiple sources to include interviews, observations and document analysis;

2. Member checking—The informant will serve as a check throughout the analysis process. An ongoing dialogue regarding my interpretations of the informant's reality and meanings will ensure the truth value of the data;

3. Long terms and repeated observations at the research site—Regular and repeated observations of similar phenomena and settings will occur on-site over a four month period of time;

4. Peer examination—a doctoral student and graduate assistant in the Educational Psychology Department will serve as a peer examiner;

5. Participatory modes of research—The informant will be involved in

most phases of this study, from the design of the project to checking interpretations and conclusions; and

6. Clarification of researcher bias—At the outset of this study researcher bias will be articulated in writing in the dissertation proposal under the heading, "The Researcher's Role."

The primary strategy utilized in this project to ensure external validity will be the provision of rich, thick, detailed descriptions so that anyone interested in transferability will have a solid framework for comparison (Merriam, 1988). Three techniques to ensure reliability will be employed in this study. First, the researcher will provide a detailed account of the focus of the study, the researcher's role, the informant's position and basis for selection, and the context from which data will be gathered (LeCompte & Goetz, 1984). Second, triangulation or multiple methods of data collection and analysis will be used, which strengthens reliability as well as internal validity (Merriam, 1988). Finally, data collection and analysis strategies will be reported in detail in order to provide a clear and accurate picture of the methods used in this study. All phases of this project will be subject to scrutiny by an external auditor who is experienced in qualitative research methods. *[Author identified strategies of validity to be used in the study.]*

Reporting the Findings

Lofland (1974) suggests that although data collection and analysis strategies are similar across qualitative methods, the way the findings are reported is diverse. Miles and Huberman (1984) address the importance of creating a data display and suggest that narrative text has been the most frequent form of display for qualitative data. This is a naturalistic study. Therefore, the results will be presented in descriptive, narrative form rather than as a scientific report. Thick description will be the vehicle for communicating a holistic picture of the experiences of a new college president. The final project will be a construction of the informant's experiences and the meanings he attaches to them. This will allow readers to vicariously experience the challenges he encounters and provide a lens through which readers can view the subject's world. *[Outcomes of the study were mentioned.]*

SUMMARY

This chapter explored the components that go into developing and writing a qualitative method section for a proposal. Recognizing the variation that exists in qualitative studies, the chapter advances a general guideline for procedures. This guideline includes a discussion about the general characteristics of qualitative research if audiences are not familiar with this approach to research.

These characteristics are that the research takes place in the natural setting, relies on the researcher as the instrument for data collection, employs multiple methods of data collection, is both inductive and deductive, is based on participants' meanings, includes researcher reflexivity, and is holistic. The guideline recommends discussing a research design, such as the study of individuals (narrative, phenomenology); the exploration of processes, activities, and events (case study, grounded theory); or the examination of broad culture-sharing behavior of individuals or groups (ethnography). The choice of design needs to be presented and defended. Further, the proposal or study needs to address the role of the researcher: past experiences, history, culture, and how this potentially shapes interpretations of the data. It also includes a discussion about personal connections to the site, steps to gain entry, and anticipation of sensitive ethical issues. Discussion of data collection should advance the purposeful sampling approach and the forms of data to be collected (i.e., observations, interviews, documents, and audiovisual and digital materials). It is useful to also indicate the types of data recording protocols that will be used.

Data analysis is an ongoing process during research. It involves analyzing participant information, and researchers typically employ general analysis steps as well as those steps found within a specific design. More general steps include organizing and preparing the data; an initial reading through the information; coding the data; developing from the codes a description and thematic analysis; using computer programs; representing the findings in tables, graphs, and figures; and interpreting the findings. These interpretations involve stating lessons learned, comparing the findings with past literature and theory, raising questions, offering personal perspective, stating limitations, and advancing an agenda for reform. The project should also contain a section on the expected outcomes for the study. Finally, an additional important step in planning a proposal is to mention the strategies that will be used to validate the accuracy of the findings and demonstrate the reliability of codes and themes.

Writing Exercises

1. Write a plan for the procedure to be used in your qualitative study. After writing the plan, use Table 9.1 as a checklist to determine the comprehensiveness of your plan.

2. Develop a table that lists, in a column on the left, the steps you plan to take to analyze your data. In a column on the right, indicate the steps as they apply directly to your project, the research strategy you plan to use, and data that you have collected.

Additional Readings

Creswell, J. W. (2016). *The 30 essential skills for the qualitative researcher.* Thousand Oaks, CA: Sage.

This is John Creswell's most applied book. It includes specific steps for conducting many of the most important qualitative inquiry procedures. It discusses the essential nature of qualitative research, specific procedures for conducting an observation and interview, the detailed procedures of data analysis, the uses of computer programs for assisting in qualitative data analysis, validity strategies, and procedures for intercoder agreement checks.

Creswell, J. W., & Poth, C. N. (2018). *Qualitative inquiry and research design: Choosing among five approaches* (4th ed.). Thousand Oaks, CA: Sage.

The basic premise of this book is that all qualitative research is not the same, and, over time, variations in procedures of conducting qualitative inquiry have evolved. This book discusses five approaches to qualitative research: (a) narrative research, (b) phenomenology, (c) grounded theory, (d) ethnography, and (e) case studies. A process approach is taken throughout the book in which the reader proceeds from broad philosophical assumptions and on through the steps of conducting a qualitative study (e.g., developing research questions, collecting and analyzing data, and so forth). The book also presents comparisons among the five approaches so that the qualitative research can make an informed choice about what strategy is best for a particular study.

Flick, U. (Ed.). (2007). *The Sage qualitative research kit.* Thousand Oaks, CA: Sage.

This is an eight-volume kit—edited by Uwe Flick—that is authored by different world-class qualitative researchers and was created to collectively address the core issues that arise when researchers actually do qualitative research. It addresses how to plan and design a qualitative study, the collection and production of qualitative data, the analysis of data (e.g., visual data, discourse analysis), and the issues of quality. Overall, it presents a recent, up-to-date window into the field of qualitative research.

Guest, G., MacQueen, K. M., & Namey, E. E. (2012). *Applied thematic analysis.* Thousand Oaks, CA: Sage.

This book provides a practical and detailed study of themes and data analysis in qualitative research. It contains detailed passages about the development of codes, codebooks, and themes, as well as approaches to enhancing the validity and reliability (including intercoder agreement) in qualitative research. It explores data reduction techniques and a comparison of themes. It presents useful information about qualitative data analysis software tools as well as procedures for integrating quantitative and qualitative data.

Marshall, C., & Rossman, G. B. (2011). *Designing qualitative research* (5th ed.). Thousand Oaks, CA: Sage.

Catherine Marshall and Gretchen Rossman introduce the procedures for designing a qualitative study and a qualitative proposal. The topics covered are comprehensive. They include building a conceptual framework around a study; the logic and assumptions of the overall design and methods; methods of data collection and procedures for managing, recording, and analyzing qualitative data; and the resources needed for a study, such as time, personnel, and funding. This is a comprehensive and insightful text from which both beginners and more experienced qualitative researchers can learn.

CHAPTER 10

Mixed Methods Procedures

How would you write a mixed methods procedure section for your proposal or study? Up until this point, we have considered collected quantitative data and qualitative data. We have not discussed "mixing" or combining the two forms of data in a study. We can start with the assumption that both forms of data provide different types of information (open-ended data in the case of qualitative and closed-ended data in the case of quantitative). If we further assume that each type of data collection has both limitations and strengths, we can consider how the strengths can be combined to develop a stronger understanding of the research problem or questions (and, as well, overcome the limitations of each). In a sense, more *insight* into a problem is to be gained from mixing or integration of the quantitative and qualitative data. This "mixing" or integrating of data, it can be argued, provides a stronger understanding of the problem or question than either by itself. Mixed methods research, therefore, is simply "mining" the databases more by integrating them. This idea is at the core of a new methodology called "mixed methods research."

Conveying the nature of mixed methods research and its essential characteristics needs to begin a good mixed methods procedure. Start with the assumption that mixed methods is a methodology in research and that the readers need to be educated as to the basic intent and definition of the design, the reasons for choosing the procedure, and the value it will lend to a study. Then, decide on a mixed methods design to use. There are several from which to choose; consider the different possibilities and decide which one is best for your proposed study. With this choice in hand, discuss the data collection, the data analysis, and the data interpretation, discussion, and validation procedures within the context of the design. Finally, end with a discussion of potential ethical issues that need to be anticipated in the study, and suggest an outline for writing the final study. These are all standard methods procedures, and they are framed in this chapter as they apply to mixed methods research. Table 10.1 shows a checklist of the mixed methods procedures addressed in this chapter.

Components of Mixed Methods Procedures

Mixed methods research has evolved into a set of procedures that proposal developers and study designers can use in planning a mixed methods study. In 2003, the *Handbook of Mixed Methods in the Social* and *Behavior Sciences*

Table 10.1	A Checklist of Questions for Designing a Mixed Methods Procedure

_____	Is a basic definition of mixed methods research provided?
_____	Are the reasons (or justification) given for using both quantitative and qualitative data in your study?
_____	Does the reader have a sense for the potential use of mixed methods research?
_____	Are the criteria identified for choosing a mixed methods design?
_____	Is the mixed methods design identified?
_____	Is a visual model (a diagram) presented that illustrates the research strategy?
_____	Are procedures of data collection and analysis mentioned as they relate to the chosen design?
_____	Are the sampling strategies for both quantitative and qualitative data collection mentioned for the design?
_____	Are specific data analysis procedures indicated for the design?
_____	Are the procedures for validation mentioned for the design and for the quantitative and qualitative research?
_____	Is the narrative structure of the final study or dissertation or thesis mentioned, and does it relate to the type of mixed methods design being used?

(Tashakkori & Teddlie, 2003) was published (and later added to in a second edition, see Tashakkori & Teddlie, 2010), providing a comprehensive overview of this approach. Now several journals emphasize mixed methods research, such as the _Journal of Mixed Methods Research, Quality and Quantity, Field Methods_, and the _International Journal of Multiple Research Approaches_. Additional journals actively encourage this form of inquiry (e.g., _International Journal of Social Research Methodology, Qualitative Health Research, Annals of Family Medicine_). Numerous published research studies have incorporated mixed methods research in the social and human sciences in diverse fields such as occupational therapy (Lysack & Krefting, 1994), interpersonal communication (Boneva, Kraut, & Frohlich, 2001), AIDS prevention (Janz et al., 1996), dementia caregiving (Weitzman & Levkoff, 2000), occupational health (Ames, Duke, Moore, & Cunradi, 2009), mental health (Rogers, Day, Randall, & Bentall, 2003), and in middle school science (Houtz, 1995). New books arrive each year solely devoted to mixed methods research (Bryman, 2006; Creswell, 2015; Creswell & Plano Clark, 2018; Greene, 2007; Morse & Niehaus, 2009; Plano Clark & Creswell, 2008; Tashakkori & Teddlie, 1998, 2010; Teddlie & Tashakkori, 2009).

Describe Mixed Methods Research

Because mixed methods research is still somewhat unknown in the social and human sciences as a distinct research approach, it is useful to convey a basic definition and description of the approach in a method section of a proposal. This might include the following:

- *A definition.* Begin by defining mixed methods. Recall the definition provided in Chapter 1. Elements in this definition can now be enumerated so that a reader has a complete set of core characteristics that describe mixed methods (see a more expanded view of defining mixed methods research in Johnson, Onwuegbuzie, & Turner, 2007):

  o It involves the *collection* of both qualitative (open-ended) and quantitative (closed-ended) data in response to research questions or hypotheses.

  o It includes the *rigorous methods* (i.e., data collection, data analysis, and interpretation) of both quantitative and qualitative data.

  o The two forms of data are *integrated* in the design analysis through merging the data, explaining the data, building from one database to another, or embedding the data within a larger framework.

  o These procedures are incorporated into a distinct *mixed methods design* that indicates the procedures to be used in a study.

  o These procedures are often informed by a philosophy (or worldview) and a theory (see Chapter 3).

- *Terminology.* Explain that many different terms are used for this approach, such as *integrating, synthesis, quantitative and qualitative methods, multimethod, mixed research,* or *mixed methodology* but that recent writings, such as the *SAGE Handbook of Mixed Methods in the Social & Behavioral Sciences* and SAGE's *Journal of Mixed Methods Research,* tend to use the term *mixed methods* (Bryman, 2006; Creswell, 2015; Tashakkori & Teddlie, 2010).

- *Background of methodology.* Educate the reader about the background of mixed methods by reviewing briefly the history of this approach to research. It can be seen as a methodology originating around the late 1980s and early 1990s in its current form based on work from individuals in diverse fields such as evaluation, education, management, sociology, and health sciences. It has gone through several periods of development and growth, and it continues to evolve, especially in procedures. Several texts outline these developmental phases (e.g., Creswell & Plano Clark, 2011, 2018; Teddlie & Tashakkori, 2009). This section could also include a brief discussion about the importance or rise of mixed methods today through indicators such as federal funding initiatives, dissertations, and the discipline-specific discussions about mixed methods found in journals across the social and health sciences (see Creswell, 2010, 2011, 2015).

- *Reasons for choosing mixed methods research.* Follow this section with statements about the value and rationale for the choice of mixed methods as an approach for your project. At a *general level,* mixed methods is chosen because of its strength of drawing on both qualitative and quantitative research and minimizing the limitations of both approaches. At a *practical level,* mixed methods provides a sophisticated, complex approach to research that appeals to those on the forefront of new research procedures. It also can be an ideal approach if the researcher has access to both quantitative and qualitative data. At a *procedural level,* it is a useful strategy to have a more complete understanding of research problems and questions, such as the following:

  o Comparing different perspectives drawn from quantitative and qualitative data

  o Explaining quantitative results with a qualitative follow-up data collection and analysis

  o Developing better contextualized measurement instruments by first collecting and analyzing qualitative data and then administrating the instruments to a sample

  o Augmenting experiments or trials by incorporating the perspectives of individuals

  o Developing cases (i.e., organizations, units, or programs) or documenting diverse cases for comparisons

  o Developing a more complete understanding of changes needed for a marginalized group through the combination of qualitative and quantitative data

  o Evaluating both the processes and the outcomes of a program, an experimental intervention, or a policy decision

- Indicate the type of *mixed methods design* that will be used in the study and the rationale for choosing it. A detailed discussion of the primary strategies available will be discussed shortly. Include a figure or diagram of these procedures.

- *Challenges to design.* Note the challenges this form of research poses for the inquirer. These include the need for extensive data collection, the time-intensive nature of analyzing both qualitative and quantitative data, and the requirement for the researcher to be familiar with both quantitative and qualitative forms of research. The complexity of the design also calls for clear, visual models to understand the details and the flow of research activities in this design.

Types of Mixed Methods Designs

There have been several typologies for classifying and identifying types of mixed methods strategies that proposal developers might use in their proposed mixed methods study. Creswell and Plano Clark (2018) identified several classification systems drawn from the fields of evaluation, nursing, public health, education policy and research, and social and behavioral research. In these classifications, authors used diverse terms for their types of designs, and a substantial amount of overlap of types existed in the typologies. For purposes of clarifying the design discussion in the mixed methods field, we will identify *three core mixed methods designs* (as shown in Figures 10.1 and 10.2)—the convergent design, the explanatory sequential design, and the exploratory sequential design—and then briefly mention more complex designs (i.e., the mixed methods experimental design, the mixed methods case study design, the mixed methods participatory–social justice design, and the mixed methods evaluation design) in which the core designs can be embedded. Each approach will be discussed in terms of a description of the design, the forms of data collection and data analysis and integration, interpretation, and validity challenges.

Convergent Mixed Methods Design

- *Description of the design.* The convergent mixed methods design is probably the most familiar of the core and complex mixed methods approaches. Researchers new to mixed methods typically first think of this approach because they feel that mixed methods only consists of combining the quantitative and qualitative data. In this single-phase approach, a researcher collects both quantitative and qualitative data, analyzes them separately, and then compares the results to see if the findings confirm or disconfirm each other (see Figure 10.1). The key assumption of this approach is that both qualitative and quantitative data provide different types of information—often detailed views of participants qualitatively and scores on instruments quantitatively—and together they yield results that should be the same. It builds off the historic concept of the multimethod, multitrait idea from Campbell and Fiske (1959), who felt that a psychological trait could best be understood by gathering different forms of data. Although the Campbell and Fiske conceptualization included only quantitative data, the mixed methods researchers extended the idea to include the collection of both quantitative and qualitative data.

Figure 10.1 Three Core Mixed Methods Designs

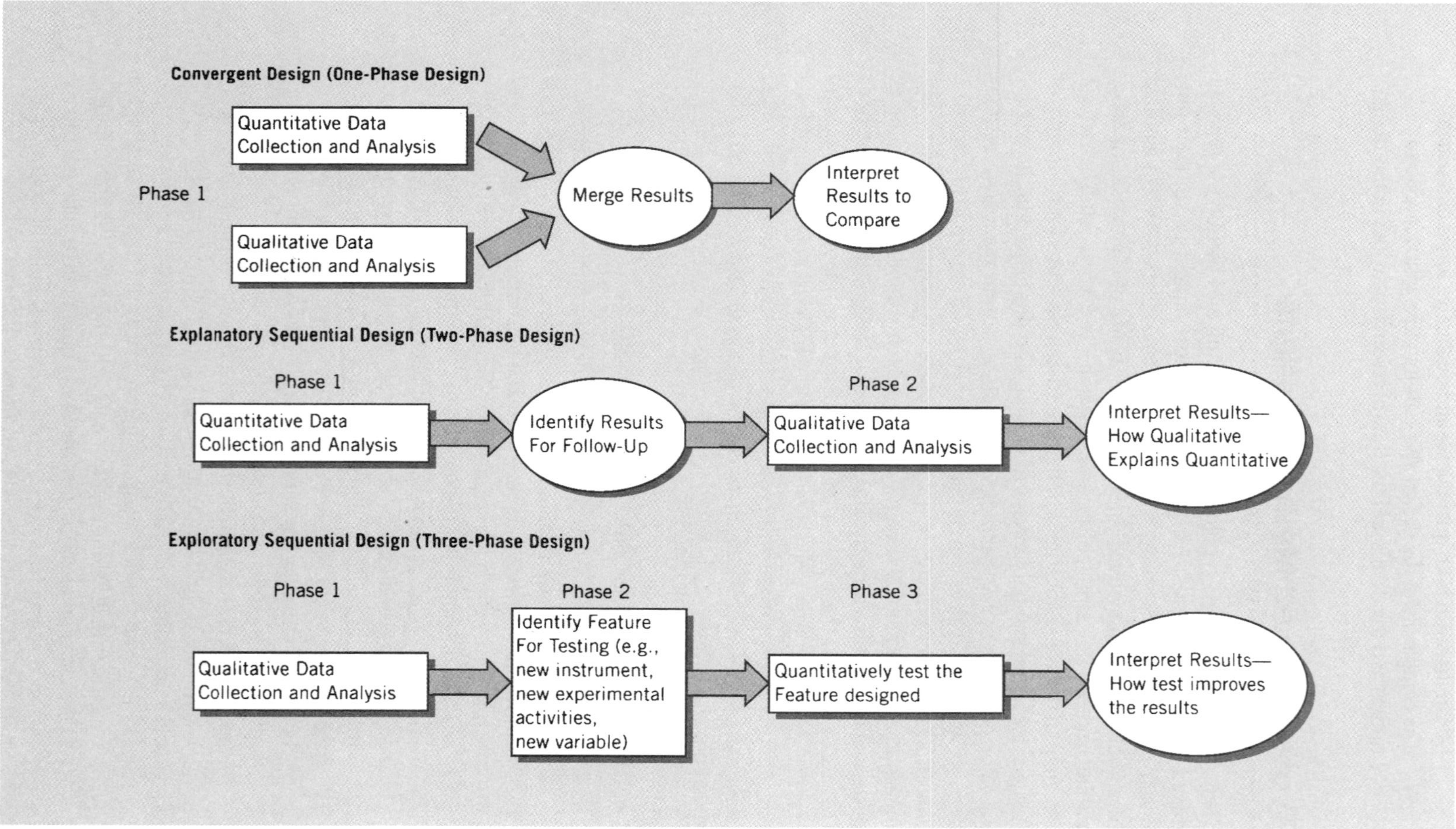

Convergent Design (One-Phase Design)

Quantitative Data Collection and Analysis

Qualitative Data Collection and Analysis

Phase 1

Merge Results → Interpret Results to Compare

Explanatory Sequential Design (Two-Phase Design)

Phase 1

Quantitative Data Collection and Analysis → Identify Results For Follow-Up

Phase 2

Qualitative Data Collection and Analysis → Interpret Results— How Qualitative Explains Quantitative

Exploratory Sequential Design (Three-Phase Design)

Phase 1

Qualitative Data Collection and Analysis

Phase 2

Identify Feature For Testing (e.g., new instrument, new experimental activities, new variable)

Phase 3

Quantitatively test the Feature designed → Interpret Results— How test improves the results

- *Data collection.* The qualitative data can assume any of the forms discussed in Chapter 9, such as interviews, observations, documents, and records. The quantitative data can be instrument data, observational checklists, or numeric records, such as census data, as discussed in Chapter 8. Ideally, the key idea with this design is to collect both forms of data using the *same or parallel variables, constructs, or concepts.* In other words, if the concept of self-esteem is being measured during quantitative data collection, the same concept is asked during the qualitative data collection process, such as in an open-ended interview. Some researchers will use this design to associate certain themes with statistical data using different forms of data for the quantitative and qualitative data collection. For instance, Shaw et al. (2013) compared quality improvement practices in family medicine clinics with colorectal cancer screening rates. Another data collection issue is the sample size for both the qualitative and quantitative data collection process. Unquestionably, the data for the qualitative data collection will be smaller than that for the quantitative data collection. This is because the intent of data collection for qualitative data is to locate and obtain information from a small sample but to gather extensive information from this sample; whereas, in quantitative research, a large N is needed in order to infer meaningful statistical results from samples to a population.

  How is this inequality resolved in a convergent mixed methods design? Sometimes mixed methods researchers will collect information from the same number of individuals on both the qualitative and quantitative databases. This means that the qualitative sample will be increased, and it will limit the amount of data collected from any one individual. Another approach would be to weight the qualitative cases so that they equal the N in the quantitative database. One other approach taken by some mixed methods researchers is not to consider the unequal sample sizes a problem. They would argue that the intent of qualitative and quantitative research differs (one to gain an in-depth perspective and the other, to generalize to a population) and that each provides an adequate count. Another issue in sampling is whether the individuals for the sample of qualitative participants should also be individuals in the quantitative sample. Typically, mixed methods researchers would include the sample of qualitative participants in the larger quantitative sample, because ultimately researchers make a comparison between the two databases and the more they are similar, the better the comparison.

- *Data analysis and integration.* Data analysis in a convergent design consists of three phases. First, analyze the qualitative database by coding the data and collapsing the codes into broad themes. Second, analyze the quantitative database in terms of statistical results. Third comes the mixed methods data analysis. This is the analysis that consists of integrating the two databases.

This integration consists of merging the results from both the qualitative and the quantitative findings. One challenge in this design is how to actually merge the two databases since bringing together a numeric quantitative database with a text qualitative database is not intuitive. There are several ways to merge the two databases:

o The first approach is called a side-by-side comparison. These comparisons can be seen in the discussion sections of mixed methods studies. The researcher will first report the quantitative statistical results and then discuss the qualitative findings (e.g., themes) that either confirm or disconfirm the statistical results. Alternatively, the researcher might start with the qualitative findings and then compare them to the quantitative results. Mixed methods writers call this a side-by-side approach because the researcher makes the comparison within a discussion, presenting first one set of findings and then the other. A good example of this can be seen in the Classen and colleagues' (2007) study.

o Researchers can also merge the two databases by changing or transforming qualitative codes or themes into quantitative variables and then combining the two quantitative databases—a procedure in mixed methods research called data transformation. The researcher takes the qualitative themes or codes and counts them (and possibly groups them) to form quantitative measures. Some useful procedures that mixed methods researchers have used can be found in Onwuegbuzie and Leech (2006). This approach is popular among researchers trained in quantitative research who may not value or see the worth of an independent qualitative interpretive database.

o A final procedure involves merging the two forms of data in a table or a graph. This is called a **joint display** of data, and it can take many different forms. It might be a table that arrays the themes on the horizontal axis and a categorical variable (e.g., different types of providers such as nurses, physician assistants, and doctors) on the vertical axis. It might be a table with key questions or concepts on the vertical axis and then two columns on the horizontal axis indicating qualitative responses and quantitative responses to the key questions or concepts (Li, Marquart, & Zercher, 2000). The basic idea is for the researcher to jointly display both forms of data—effectively merging them—in a single visual and then make an interpretation of the display (see Guetterman, Fetters, & Creswell, 2015).

• *Interpretation.* The interpretation in the convergent approach is typically written into a discussion section of the study. Whereas the results section reports on the findings from the analysis of both the quantitative and qualitative databases, the discussion section includes a discussion comparing the results from the two databases and notes whether there is convergence or divergence between the two sources of information. Typically the comparison does not yield a clean convergent or divergent situation, and differences exist on a few concepts, themes, or scales. When divergence occurs, steps for follow-up need to be taken. The researcher can state divergence as a limitation in the study without further follow-up. This approach represents a weak solution. Alternatively, mixed methods researchers can return to the analyses and further explore the databases, collect additional information to resolve the differences, or discuss the results from one of the databases as possibly limited (e.g., the constructs were not valid quantitatively or the qualitative themes did not match the open-ended questions). Whatever approach the researcher takes, the key point in a convergent design is to further discuss and probe results when divergent findings exist.

- *Validity.* Validity using the convergent approach should be based on establishing both quantitative validity (e.g., construct) and qualitative validity (e.g., triangulation) for each database. Is there a special form of mixed methods validity that needs to be addressed? There are certainly some potential threats to validity in using the convergent approach, and several of these have already been mentioned. Unequal sample sizes may provide less of a picture on the qualitative side than the larger N on the quantitative side. Generally we find the use of unequal sample sizes in a convergent design study, with the researcher acknowledging the different perspectives on size taken by quantitative and qualitative researchers. The use of different concepts or variables on both sides, quantitative and qualitative, may yield incomparable and difficult-to-merge findings. Our recommended approach is to use the same concepts for both the quantitative and qualitative arms of the research study, but we acknowledge that some researchers use the convergent design to associate different qualitative and quantitative concepts. A lack of follow-up on conclusions when the scores and themes diverge also represents an invalid strategy of inquiry. In this discussion we have recommended several ways to probe divergence in more detail and would recommend the use of one or more of these strategies in a convergent design project.

Explanatory Sequential Mixed Methods Design

- *Description of the design.* The explanatory sequential mixed methods approach is a design in mixed methods that appeals to individuals with a strong quantitative background or from fields relatively new to qualitative approaches. It involves a two-phase data collection project in which the researcher collects quantitative data in the first phase, analyzes the results, and then uses the results to plan (or build on to) the second, qualitative phase. The quantitative results typically inform the types of participants to be purposefully selected for the qualitative phase and the types of questions that will be asked of the participants. The overall intent of this design is to have the qualitative data help explain in more detail the initial quantitative results, thus it is important to tie together or to connect the quantitative results to the qualitative data collection. A typical procedure might involve collecting survey data in the first phase, analyzing the data, and then following up with qualitative interviews to help explain confusing, contradictory, or unusual survey responses.

- *Data collection.* The data collection proceeds in two distinct phases with rigorous quantitative sampling in the first phase and with purposeful sampling in the second, qualitative phase. One challenge in this strategy is to plan adequately what quantitative results to follow up on and what participants to gather qualitative data from in the second phase. The key idea is that the qualitative data collection builds directly on the quantitative results. The quantitative results that then are built on may be extreme or outlier cases, significant predictors, significant results relating variables, insignificant results, or even demographics. For example, when using demographics, the researcher could find in the initial quantitative phase that individuals in different socioeconomic levels respond differently to the dependent variables. Thus, the follow-up qualitatively may group respondents to the quantitative phase into different categories and conduct qualitative data collection with individuals representing each of the categories. Another challenge is whether the qualitative sample should be individuals that are in the initial quantitative sample. The answer to this question should be that they are the same individuals, because the intent of the design is to follow up the quantitative results and explore the results in more depth. The idea of explaining the mechanism—how the variables interact—in more depth through the qualitative follow-up is a key strength of this design.

- *Data analysis and integration.* The quantitative and the qualitative databases are analyzed separately in this approach. Then the researcher combines the two databases by the form of integration called connecting the quantitative results to the qualitative data collection. This is the point of integration in an explanatory sequential design. Thus, the quantitative results are then used to *plan* the qualitative follow-up. One important area is that the quantitative results cannot only inform the sampling procedure but it can also point toward the types of qualitative questions to ask participants in the second phase. These questions, like all good qualitative research questions, are general and open-ended. Because analysis proceeds independently for each phase, this design is useful for student research and perhaps easier to accomplish (than the convergent design) because one database explains the other and the data collection can be spaced out over time.

- *Interpretation.* The mixed methods researcher interprets the follow up results in a discussion section of the study. This interpretation follows the form of first reporting the quantitative, first-phase results and then the qualitative, second phase results. However, this design then employs a third form of interpretation: how the qualitative findings help to explain the quantitative results. A common misstep at this point by beginning researchers is to merge the two databases. While this approach may be helpful, the intent of the design is to have the qualitative data help to provide more depth, more insight into the quantitative results. Accordingly, in the interpretation section, after the researcher presents the general quantitative and then qualitative results, a discussion should follow that specifies how the qualitative results help to expand or explain the quantitative results. Because the qualitative database questions narrows the scope of the quantitative questions, a direct comparison of the overall results of the two databases is not recommended.

- *Validity.* As with all mixed methods studies, the researcher needs to establish the validity of the scores from the quantitative measures and to discuss the validity of the qualitative findings. In the explanatory sequential mixed methods approach, additional validity concerns arise. The accuracy of the overall findings may be compromised because the researcher does not consider and weigh all of the options for following up on the quantitative results. We recommend that researchers consider all options for identifying results to follow up on before settling on one approach. Attention may focus only on personal demographics and overlook important explanations that need further understanding. The researcher may also contribute to invalidated results by drawing on different samples for each phase of the study. If explaining the quantitative results in more depth, then it makes sense to select the qualitative sample from individuals who participated in the quantitative sample. This maximizes the importance of one phase explaining the other. These are a few of the challenges that need to be built into the planning process for a good explanatory sequential mixed methods study.

Exploratory Sequential
Mixed Methods Design

- *Description of the design.* If we reverse the explanatory sequential approach and start with a qualitative phase first followed by a quantitative phase, we have an exploratory sequential approach. A three-phase exploratory sequential mixed methods is a design in which the researcher first begins by exploring with qualitative data and analysis, then builds a feature to be tested (e.g., a new survey instrument, experimental procedures, a website, or new variables) and tests this feature in a quantitative third phase. Like the explanatory sequential approach, the second feature builds on the results of the initial database. The intent of this design is to explore with a sample first so that a later quantitative phase can be tailored to meet the needs of the individuals being studied. Sometimes this quantitative feature will include developing a contextually sensitive measurement instrument and then testing it with a sample. Other times it may involve developing new variables not available in the literature or attuned to a specific population being studied, or designing a website or an Internet application shaped to the needs of the individuals being studied. This design is popular in global health research when, for example, investigators need to understand a community or population before administering English-language instruments.

  In this design, the researcher would first collect focus group data, analyze the results, develop an instrument (or other quantitative feature such as a website for testing), and then administer it to a sample of a population. In this case, there may not be adequate instruments to measure the concepts with the sample the investigator wishes to study. In effect, the researcher employs a three-phase procedure with the first phase as exploratory, the second as instrument (or quantitative feature) development, and the third as administering and testing the instrument feature to a sample of a population.

- *Data collection.* In this strategy, the data collection would occur at two points in the design: the initial qualitative data collection and the test of the quantitative feature in the third phase of the project. The challenge is how to use the information from the initial qualitative phase to build or identify the quantitative feature in the second phase. This is the integration point in an exploratory sequential design.

  Several options exist, and we will use the approach of developing a culturally sensitive instrument as an illustration. The qualitative data analysis can be used to develop an instrument with good psychometric properties (i.e., validity, reliability). The qualitative data analysis will yield quotes, codes, and themes (see Chapter 9). The development of an instrument can proceed by using the quotes to write items for an instrument, the codes to develop variables that group the items, and themes that group the codes into scales. This is a useful procedure for moving from qualitative data analysis to scale development (the quantitative feature developed in the second phase). Scale development also needs to follow good procedures for instrument design, and the steps for this include ideas such as item discrimination, construct validity, and reliability estimates (see DeVellis, 2012).

Developing a good psychometric instrument that fits the sample and population under study is not the only use of this design. A researcher can analyze the qualitative data to develop new variables that may not be present in the literature, to identify the types of scales that might exist in current instruments or to form categories of information that will be explored further in a quantitative phase. The question arises if the sample for the qualitative phase is the same for the quantitative phase. This cannot be, because the qualitative sample is typically much smaller than a quantitative sample needed to generalize from a sample to a population. Sometimes mixed methods researchers will use entirely different samples for the qualitative (first phase) and quantitative components (third phase) of the study. However, a good procedure is to draw both samples from the same population but make sure that the individuals for both samples are not the same. To have individuals help develop an instrument and then to survey them in the quantitative phase would introduce confounding factors into the study.

- *Data analysis and integration.* In this strategy the researcher analyzes the two databases separately and uses the findings from the initial exploratory database to build into a feature that can be analyzed quantitatively. So integration in this design involves using the qualitative findings (or results) to inform the design of a quantitative phase of the research such as the development of a measurement instrument or new variables. This means that the researcher needs to pay careful attention to the qualitative data analysis steps and determine what findings to build on. If, for example, the researcher uses grounded theory (see Chapter 9), the theoretical model generated may provide a model to be tested in the second, quantitative phase. A qualitative case study can yield different cases that become the focus of important variables in the second quantitative phase.

- *Interpretation.* Researchers interpret the mixed methods results in a discussion section of a study. The order of interpretation is to first report the qualitative findings, the development or design of the feature to be tested (e.g., the development of an instrument, the development of new quantitative measures), and then the quantitative test in the final phase of the study. It does not make sense to compare the two databases, because they are typically drawn from different samples (as noted above in the data collection discussion) and the intent of the strategy is to determine if the qualitative themes in the first phase can be generalized to a larger sample.

- *Validity.* Researchers using this strategy need to check for the validity of the qualitative data as well as the validity of the quantitative scores. Special validity concerns arise, however, in using this design that need to be anticipated by the proposal or mixed methods report developer. One concern is that the researcher may not use appropriate steps to develop a good psychometric instrument. Developing a good instrument is not easy, and adequate steps need to be put in place. Another concern is that a researcher may develop an instrument or measures that do not take advantage of the richness of the qualitative findings. This occurs when the qualitative data lacks rigor or occurs simply at the theme level without the further data analysis steps associated with using one of the qualitative design-types, such as ethnography, grounded theory, or case study procedures. Finally, as previously mentioned, the sample in the qualitative phase should not be included in the quantitative phase as this will introduce undue duplication of responses. It is best to have the sample of qualitative participants provide information for scale, instrument, or variable (or website) design, but the same individuals should not complete the follow-up instruments. This sample strategy, therefore, differs from the sampling strategy needed for an explanatory sequential design.

Several Complex Mixed Methods Designs

After working with these three core designs—convergent, explanatory sequential, and exploratory sequential—that are the foundation of good mixed methods research, we have now branched out to incorporate more designs that typically fit complex projects. By complex we mean that the designs involve more steps and procedures than are embodied in the three core designs. These mixed methods designs are not more "advanced." They simply involve more steps and incorporate the core designs into "processes" of research. We have come to this position based on key readings in the mixed methods literature that have surfaced in the past few years. The first step involved isolating and thinking about the types of more complex features that the core designs could be embedded within.

A useful typology emerged in the work of Plano Clark and Ivankova (2016). Their book was helpful in conceptualizing the many types of applications of complex designs. In an entire chapter they discussed the intersection of mixed methods with other approaches to form "advanced applications" (p. 136). They recommended a framework for considering the possibilities of these complex applications:

- *Intersecting a secondary method (mixed methods) within a primary quantitative or qualitative research design.* A *research design* is a set of formal procedures for collecting, analyzing, and interpreting data such as those found in a quantitative experiment or qualitative case study. In this framework, a mixed methods core design could be embedded as a secondary (or supportive) method within a primary quantitative or qualitative design. The typical form of this application is to embed qualitative data collection and analysis within a quantitative experimental or intervention design.

- *Intersecting mixed methods within another methodology.* A *methodology* is a set of procedures that guide the use of design. These procedures exist in the research at a more practical level than the design. In this framework, a mixed methods core design could be added to another methodological approach. For example, a core design could be added to a case study, an evaluation approach, action research, social network analysis, longitudinal research, Q methodology, phenomenology, or grounded theory.

- *Intersecting mixed methods within a theoretical framework.* A *theoretical framework* advances an abstract and formalized set of assumptions to guide the design and conduct of the research. In this framework, a mixed methods core design could be intersected with an established theory. This theoretical lens could be drawn from perspectives such as social justice, feminism, critical theory, participatory involvement, or other conceptual frameworks that advance the needs and involvement of special populations and often call for action or change.

These three types of complex designs deserve additional attention because many researchers are conducting evaluations, using theoretical orientations such as gender or social inequality theories, and conducting experiments or interventions using mixed methods. In our discussion of mixed methods, we simply need to account for these complex applications and assess how core designs might be embedded within them.

Another step forward in designs appeared in Nastasi and Hitchcock (2016). Their book brought forth several ideas that we now incorporate into our complex designs. They suggested that distinct "processes" occur in research in which both quantitative and qualitative data might be used in distinct steps in the overall process. Their book focused on two ideas: the use of mixed methods in program evaluation and its use in experimental, intervention trials. It also relied heavily on the authors' mixed methods study in Sri Lanka that addressed the mental health of youth, and they advanced the steps in their evaluation process and embedded into these steps the use of qualitative and quantitative data in multiple core designs. From their work we then have some practical examples of incorporating core designs into the complex procedures of an evaluation and an experimental, intervention trial.

Specifically, we see embedding the core designs into larger processes. As in Creswell and Plano Clark (2018), here we briefly discuss four examples of complex designs and then discuss a general model for embedding the core designs in these processes:

- *Mixed methods experimental (intervention) design.* The **mixed methods experimental (or intervention) design** involves the researcher collecting and analyzing both quantitative and qualitative data and integrating the information within an experiment or intervention trial (see Figure 10.2). This design adds qualitative data collection into an experiment or intervention so that the personal experiences of participants can be included in the research. Thus the qualitative data become a secondary source of data embedded in the experimental pre- and posttest data collection. It requires the researcher to understand experiments and to be able to design them in a rigorous way (e.g., a randomized controlled trial). As shown in Figure 10.2, researchers add the qualitative data to the experiment in different ways: before the experiment begins, during the experiment, or after the experiment (Sandelowsi, 1996). The basic ideas are to embed the core exploratory sequential design into the experiment to carry out exploration before conducting the experiment; to embed a convergent core design during the experiment to assess participants' experiences with the intervention; or to add an explanatory sequential design into the experiment after the study to follow up on the experimental outcomes. The points at which the qualitative data collection and findings connect to the experiment represent the integration in the mixed methods study. In this design it is important to be explicit about the reasons for adding the qualitative data. We enumerated several important reasons in Figure 10.2. These lists are representative of the examples of mixed methods research we have found in the literature. The qualitative data collection can occur at a single point in time or at multiple points in time depending on the resources available to the researcher. This type of mixed methods use has become popular in the health sciences.

Figure 10.2 Mixed Methods Intervention Design

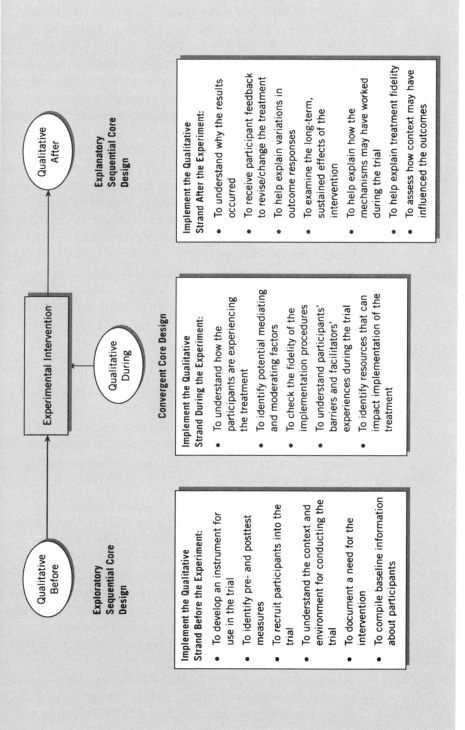

Qualitative
Before

Exploratory
Sequential Core
Design

Experimental Intervention

Qualitative
During

Convergent Core Design

Qualitative
After

Explanatory
Sequential Core
Design

**Implement the Qualitative
Strand Before the Experiment:**

• To develop an instrument for
  use in the trial

• To identify pre- and posttest
  measures

• To recruit participants into the
  trial

• To understand the context and
  environment for conducting the
  trial

• To document a need for the
  intervention

• To compile baseline information
  about participants

**Implement the Qualitative
Strand During the Experiment:**

• To understand how the
  participants are experiencing
  the treatment

• To identify potential mediating
  and moderating factors

• To check the fidelity of the
  implementation procedures

• To understand participants'
  barriers and facilitators'
  experiences during the trial

• To identify resources that can
  impact implementation of the
  treatment

**Implement the Qualitative
Strand After the Experiment:**

• To understand why the results
  occurred

• To receive participant feedback
  to revise/change the treatment

• To help explain variations in
  outcome responses

• To examine the long-term,
  sustained effects of the
  intervention

• To help explain how the
  mechanisms may have worked
  during the trial

• To help explain treatment fidelity

• To assess how context may have
  influenced the outcomes

Source: Adapted from Sandelowski (1996). .

- *Case study design.* The **mixed methods case study design** involves the use of one or more core designs (i.e., convergent, explanatory sequential, exploratory sequential) within the framework of a single or multiple case study design. The intent of this design is to develop or generate cases based on both quantitative and qualitative results and their integration. We have found two basic variants of this design. One is a deductive approach where researchers establish the cases at the outset of the study and document the differences in the cases through the qualitative and quantitative data. A second is more of an inductive approach where the researcher collects and analyzes both quantitative and qualitative data and then forms cases—often multiple cases— and then makes comparisons among the cases. Regardless of the approach, the challenge is to identify the cases before the study begins or to generate cases based on the evidence collected. Another challenge is to understand case study research (Stake, 1995; Yin, 2014) and effectively intersect case study design with mixed methods. The type of core design embedded within this approach can vary, but we can find good illustrations of the design using a convergent design (Shaw, Ohman-Strickland, & Piasecki, 2013). Within this framework, the typical mixed methods case study design is one where both types of data are gathered concurrently in a convergent core design and the results are merged together to examine a case and/or compare multiple cases. This type of mixed methods case study design is shown in Figure 10.3. In this hypothetical example, the researcher gathers both survey quantitative data and qualitative interview data at roughly the same time. Analysis of both databases produces results that can be merged to identify specific cases. These cases portray different profiles found in the databases, and they can be compared in a cross-case comparison.

- *Participatory-social justice design.* The **mixed methods participatory-social justice design** is a mixed methods design in which the researcher adds a core design within a larger participatory and/or social justice theoretical or conceptual framework (see Figure 10.4). The intent of this design is to give voice to participants and collaborate with them in shaping the research and to build evidence from both quantitative and qualitative data. As a complex design, these frameworks span the entire mixed methods study. The framework can be, for example, a feminist theory or a racial theory. It might also be a participatory theory of the involvement of stakeholders in many aspects of the mixed methods study (Ivankova, 2015), although it could be debated as to whether participatory action research exists in a

Figure 10.3 Mixed Methods Case Study Design

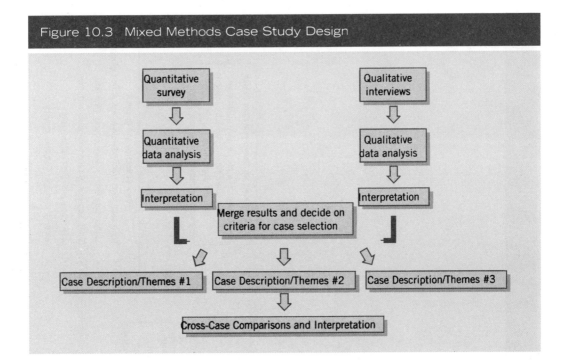

study as a conceptual framework or as methodological procedures. This aside, in addition to seeing the strong placement of this theory in the study, we can also identify one or more of the core designs operating. Within a feminist mixed methods study, for example, we can see both the flow of the theory into many aspects of the project (e.g., informing the problem, shaping the research questions, highlighting the outcomes) as well as an embedded core design such as an explanatory sequential design where an initial survey is followed by one-on-one interviews. In Figure 10.4, we see this type of core design embedded within a participatory-social justice framework. This is a study discussing the transition of homeless individuals from a hospital to a shelter (Greysen, 2012). The element that makes this study participatory research is the substantial involvement of community personnel in many aspects of the study. What makes the project mixed methods is the collection and analysis of both quantitative and qualitative data. As shown in Figure 10.4, we see that multiple core designs were embedded within the study. An exploratory sequential core design connected identifying the research priorities and developing a survey. Then, the data collection and analysis portrayed a convergent design with the combination of themes and statistical results.

Figure 10.4 Mixed Methods Participatory-Social Justice Design

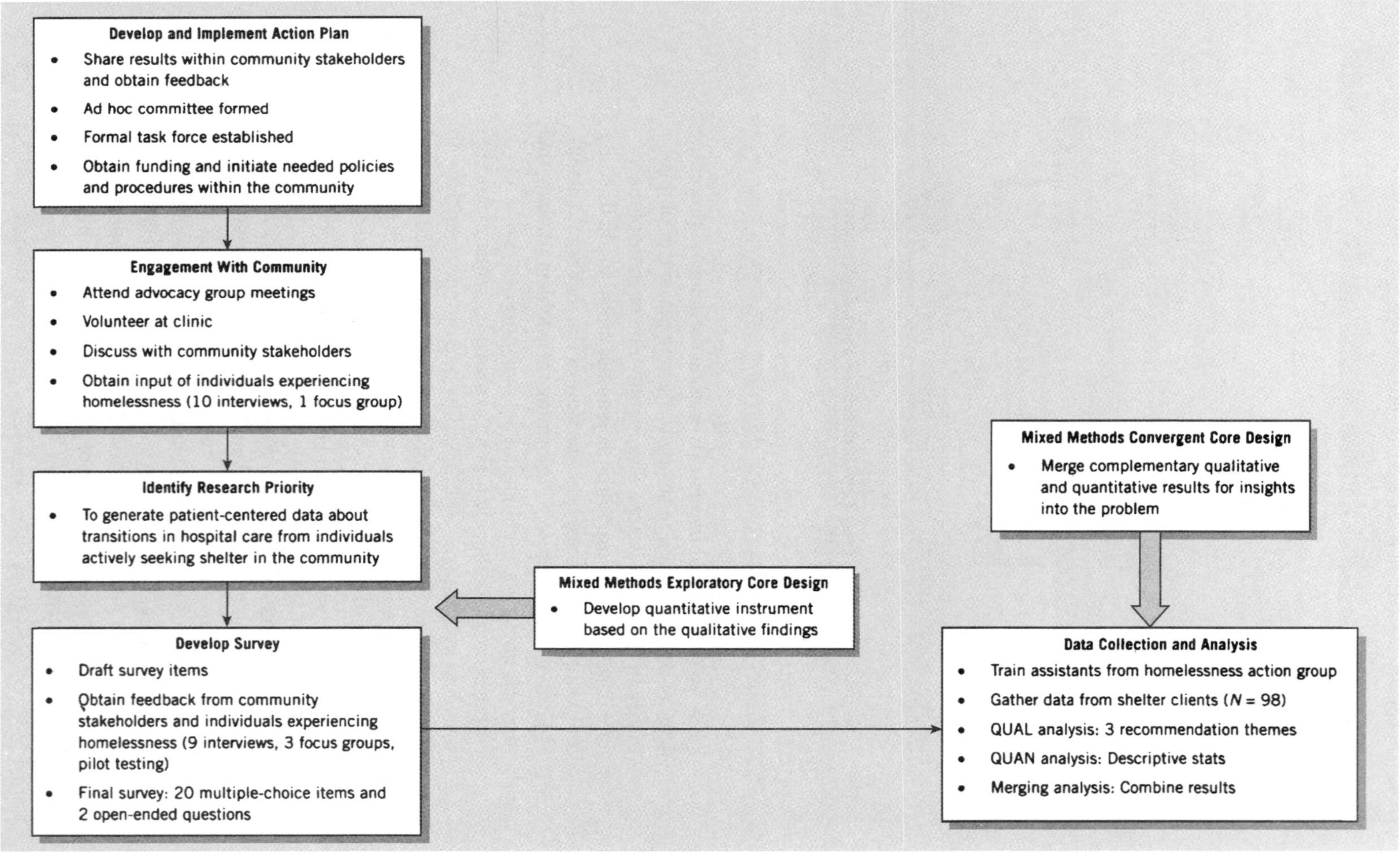

Develop and Implement Action Plan
- Share results within community stakeholders and obtain feedback
- Ad hoc committee formed
- Formal task force established
- Obtain funding and initiate needed policies and procedures within the community

Engagement With Community
- Attend advocacy group meetings
- Volunteer at clinic
- Discuss with community stakeholders
- Obtain input of individuals experiencing homelessness (10 interviews, 1 focus group)

Identify Research Priority
- To generate patient-centered data about transitions in hospital care from individuals actively seeking shelter in the community

Develop Survey
- Draft survey items
- Obtain feedback from community stakeholders and individuals experiencing homelessness (9 interviews, 3 focus groups, pilot testing)
- Final survey: 20 multiple-choice items and 2 open-ended questions

Mixed Methods Exploratory Core Design
- Develop quantitative instrument based on the qualitative findings

Mixed Methods Convergent Core Design
- Merge complementary qualitative and quantitative results for insights into the problem

Data Collection and Analysis
- Train assistants from homelessness action group
- Gather data from shelter clients ($N = 98$)
- QUAL analysis: 3 recommendation themes
- QUAN analysis: Descriptive stats
- Merging analysis: Combine results

Source: Adapted from Greysen et al. (2012); reported in Creswell & Plano Clark (2018).

- *Evaluation design.* The mixed methods evaluation design consists of one or more core designs added to the steps in an evaluation procedure typically focused on evaluating the success of an intervention, a program, or a policy (see Figure 10.5). The intent of this design is to engage in a process of research in which both quantitative and qualitative data and their integration shapes one or more of the steps in the process. This complex design illustrates a core design within another methodology. This approach is typically used in program evaluation where quantitative and qualitative approaches are used over time to support the development, adaptation, and evaluation of programs, experiments, or policies. We often find multiple core designs occurring throughout these projects. For example, researchers might start by conducting a qualitative needs assessment study to understand the meaning of smoking and health from the perspective of adolescents in this community. Using these results, the researchers might develop an instrument and quantitatively assess the prevalence of different attitudes across the community. In a third phase, the researchers might develop a program based on what they have learned and then examine both the process and the outcomes of this intervention program. Across these phases the researchers would make use of exploratory (phase 1 to phase 2), explanatory (phase 2 to phase 3), and convergent (phase 3) core designs.

Examine Figure 10.5. This mixed methods evaluation design was used in a study of the mental health of youth in Sri Lanka (Nastasi & Hitchcock, 2016). In the outer circle we see the general steps in the evaluation process. Within boxes in the circle we also find the combination of quantitative and qualitative research. In short, looking across these boxes within the circle, we see that the authors have incorporated multiple core designs at different stages in the evaluation process. The figure also shows within the boxes the dates on which the data were collected.

A Procedure for Embedding Core Designs Into Complex Designs

In the mixed methods evaluation design example in Figure 10.5, we see that core designs can be embedded within a process of evaluation. This provides important clues as to how to embed the core designs within complex procedures such as other designs, theories, or methodologies. It also speaks to how to draw a diagram of the mixed methods procedures. In our

Figure 10.5   Mixed Methods Evaluation Design

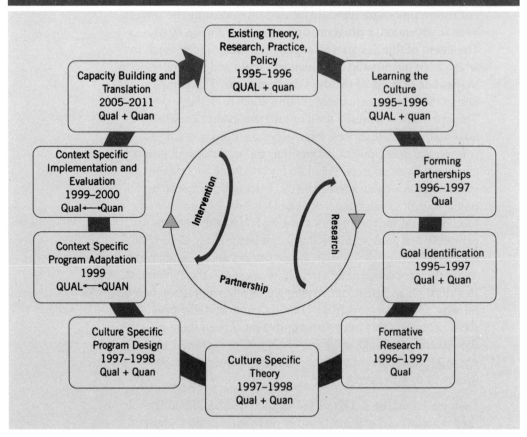

Source: Nastasi & Hitchcock (2016). Used with permission from SAGE Publishing.

thinking, we embed the core designs into more complex procedures using these steps:

1. Identify the quantitative and qualitative data collection in your study. Refer to whether the data source is closed-ended (quantitative) or open-ended (qualitative).

2. Draw a diagram of the steps in the procedure. These steps (represented by boxes) may be the phases in an experimental design, the generation of cases, or the phases of an evaluation.

3. Look into the steps (boxes) and ask yourself at what steps in the procedure you have an opportunity to collect both quantitative and qualitative data. Such data collection, you will recall from Chapter 1, represents a core defining characteristic of mixed methods research.

4. In those boxes where you are collecting both forms of data, ask yourself further how the databases are being connected. Are they being merged (as in a convergent mixed methods design) or connected (as in an explanatory sequential mixed methods design or an exploratory sequential mixed methods design).

5. Discuss the procedures of using the core mixed methods designs, paying attention to how the data are being integrated in each step.

As is evident in our discussion, we believe in drawing diagrams of procedures, whether of core designs or more complex designs. Besides thinking about how to draw these diagrams, you might consider some of the notations that have emerged in the field of mixed methods research. **Mixed methods notation** provides shorthand labels and symbols that convey important aspects of mixed methods research, and they provide a way that mixed methods researchers can easily communicate their procedures (see Table 10.2). Morse (1991) first developed the notation, and it has been added to by writers such as Tashakkori and Teddlie (1998) and Plano Clark (2005) who suggest the following:

- QUAL and QUAN capitalization indicates an emphasis or priority on the quantitative or qualitative data, analysis, and interpretation in the study. In a mixed methods study, the qualitative and quantitative data may be equally emphasized, or one may be more emphasized than the other. Capitalization indicates that an approach or method is emphasized. Lowercase indicates lesser priority or emphasis on the method.

- Quan and Qual stand for *quantitative* and *qualitative*, respectively, and they use the same number of letters to indicate equality between the forms of data.

- A plus sign—+—indicates a convergent or merging integration of data collection—with both quantitative and qualitative data collected at same time.

- An arrow—→—indicates a sequential form of data collection; one form (e.g., qualitative data) builds or connects with the other (e.g., quantitative data).

- Parentheses—( )—indicate that one form of data collection is embedded within another or embedded within a larger design.

- Double arrows—→←—mean that the flow of activities can go both ways.

- Also in the figures we see boxes that highlight important major components of the design—such as data collection or data analysis.

Table 10.2 Notation Used in Mixed Methods Research

Notation	What It Indicates	Example	Citation Establishing Notation
Uppercase letters	Greater emphasis given to a method	QUAN, QUAL	Morse (1991)
Lowercase letters	Lesser emphasis given to a method	quan, qual	Morse (1991)
+	Convergent methods	QUAN + QUAL	Morse (1991)
→	Sequential methods	QUAL→quan	Morse (1991)
( )	Embed within a design or framework	QUAN(qual)	Plano Clark (2005)
→←	Recursive	QUAL→←QUAN	Nastasi et al. (2007)
[ ]	Study within a series	QUAL → [QUAN + qual]	Morse & Niehaus (2009)

Factors Important in Choosing a Mixed Methods Design

The choice of a particular mixed methods design is based on several factors that relate to the intent of the procedures as well as practical considerations. We will begin with the procedural reasons for choosing a particular mixed methods strategy. It should be recognized that many variations exist in mixed methods designs, and the particular approach an investigator has in mind may not conform exactly to the approaches specified here. However, these designs represent the common underlying features of many designs, and, with modification, researchers can find their own strategy. To choose a design for your project, consider the following factors:

- *Choice based on outcomes expected or intent.* Earlier in this chapter, we reviewed the reasons for choosing mixed methods research. In Table 10.3, we repeat the reasons but this time link them to expected outcomes of a mixed methods project and the type of mixed methods strategy. This thinking calls for the researcher to determine the outcome anticipated at the end of the mixed methods study and then to link it to the types. These outcomes are, in turn, shaped by the intention behind including and integrating both quantitative and qualitative data.

- *Choice based on integrating the data together.* To choose a mixed methods strategy beyond considering the outcome anticipated, the researcher needs to consider whether mixed methods integration of the two databases will be *merged* (convergent mixed methods design), *explaining* (explanatory sequential design), *building*

Table 10.3 Choosing a Mixed Methods Project, Expected Outcomes, Type of Design

Reasons for Choosing Mixed Methods	Expected Outcomes	Recommended Mixed Methods Design
Comparing different perspectives drawn from quantitative and qualitative data	Merging the two databases to show how the data converge or diverge	Convergent mixed methods design
Explaining quantitative results with qualitative data	A more in-depth understanding of the quantitative results (often cultural relevance)	Explanatory sequential mixed methods design
Developing better measurement instruments	A test of better measures for a sample of a population	Exploratory sequential mixed methods design
Understanding experimental results by incorporating perspectives of individuals	An understanding of participant views within the context of an experimental intervention	Mixed methods experimental (intervention design)
Comparing one or more case studies	An understanding of the differences and similarities among several cases	Mixed methods case study design
Developing an understanding of needed changes for a marginalized group	A call for action	Mixed methods participatory-social justice design
Understanding the need for an impact of a program, intervention, or policy	A formative and summative evaluation	Mixed methods evaluation design

(exploratory sequential design), or *embedded* (the complex designs). Merging the data involves combining the quantitative and qualitative data through the procedures of a side-by-side comparison, data transformation, or a joint display. Connecting the data means that the analysis of one data set is used to lead into or build into the second data set. In short, the data analysis of one data set informs the data collection of the other data set. In embedding, one data set—involving quantitative, qualitative, or combined data—is embedded within a larger design, theory, or methodology.

For example, in a convergent design the two are considered to be independent and the data collection and analysis for each database proceed separately. In an embedded experimental design, the qualitative data may be collected independently of the experiment and used to support or augment the larger design, the experiment. Alternatively, the two databases may be connected, with one building on the other. This is a sequential type of design (explanatory sequential design or an exploratory sequential design), and one database does not stand in isolation of the other database. In these sequential designs, the data collection in the second phase cannot be conducted until the first phase results are in. In short, the follow-up data collection builds directly on the results of the initial data collection.

- *Choice based on the timing of the data collection.* A related factor is timing in mixed methods data collection—whether the two databases are collected concurrently, at roughly the same time, or with one following the other, sequentially. A convergent strategy typically involves collecting data concurrently while the explanatory sequential and the exploratory sequential strategies means that the data will be collected in sequence. Sometimes this criterion is difficult to identify in published mixed methods studies, but it should go into the thinking about choosing a mixed methods strategy. In complex designs, the timing may vary and be included at multiple time points in the design.

- *Choice based on the emphasis placed on each database.* Like timing, the emphasis placed on each databasein mixed methods research is also somewhat difficult to determine and to apply to the question of choice. A mixed methods study can illustrate an equal emphasis (or priority or weight) on both databases, or an unequal emphasis. For example, a mixed methods project can stress the qualitative phase of the research and give minimal attention to the quantitative phase. How can we tell? We can look at the number of pages in a study to determine emphasis, how the study begins (e.g., with a strong quantitative theory orientation or personal qualitative stories), the amount of depth and sophistication given to the qualitative and quantitative data collection and analysis, or even the background training of the investigator. As mentioned earlier in the section on notation, capital letters may be used in the notation for greater emphasis (e.g., QUAN) and lowercase letters for less emphasis (e.g., quan). The emphasis can help determine the choice of a mixed methods strategy. Typically if the researcher seeks to emphasize both databases, a convergent approach is best. Alternatively, if a stronger emphasis is sought for the quantitative approach, then an explanatory sequential strategy is used because it began with the quantitative component of the study. If a qualitative approach is to be emphasized, then an exploratory sequential strategy is chosen. These are not firm guidelines, but they may play into the overall decision about a choice of strategy.

- *Choice based on type of design most suited for a field.* On a practical level, the choice of a strategy depends on the inclination of fields toward certain mixed methods designs. For quantitatively oriented fields, the explanatory sequential approach seems to work well because the study begins (and perhaps is driven) by the quantitative phase of the research. In qualitatively oriented fields, the exploratory sequential approach may be more appealing because it begins with an exploration using qualitative research. However, in this approach, an outcome may be a measurement instrument that is tested so that the outcome, a quantitative outcome, outweighs in importance how the study began. In some fields, the choice of approach may be dependent on collecting data efficiently, and this would argue for a convergent mixed methods study in which both quantitative and qualitative data are typically collected at roughly the same time rather than at different times that require more visits to the research site.

- *Choice based on a single researcher or team.* A final practical reason for a choice of a strategy depends on whether a single researcher (e.g., graduate student) conducts the study or a team of researchers (e.g., funded long-term investigation). If the investigator is a single researcher, the sequential strategies of an explanatory sequential or exploratory sequential approach are best because the investigation can be divided into two manageable tasks rather than multiple data collection and analysis procedures. The study can be projected out over a period of time rather than collecting multiple forms of data at the same time as in a convergent approach. When time is a problem, we encourage students to think about a convergent design. In this design, both forms of data are gathered at roughly the same time, and it does not require repeated visits to the field to gather data. Complex designs are well-suited for a team of researchers who assist in the multiple phases of the research and for well-funded projects that unfold over several years.

We recommend that students find a published mixed methods journal article that uses their design and introduce it to advisers and faculty committees so that they have a working model to understand the design. Since we are at the early stage of adopting mixed methods research in many fields, a published example of research in a field will help to create both legitimacy for mixed methods research and the idea that it is a feasible approach to research for graduate committees or other audiences. If a research team is conducting the study, multiple forms of data collection at the same time or over a long period of time are possible, such as in an embedded or a multiphase design. Although a single researcher can conduct a participatory–social justice study, the labor-intensive nature of collecting data in the field involving participants as collaborators typically suggests more of a team approach than the inquiry by a single investigator.

Examples of Mixed Methods Procedures

Examples 10.1–10.4 illustrate mixed methods studies that use both the sequential and convergent strategies and procedures.

Example 10.1   A Convergent Parallel
Mixed Methods Design

Classen et al. (2007) studied older driver safety in order to develop a health promotion intervention based on modifiable factors influencing motor vehicle crashes with older drivers (age 65 and older). It was a good example of a convergent mixed methods study. The central purpose of the study was identified in the abstract:

> This study provided an explicit socio-ecological view explaining the interrelation of possible causative factors, an integrated summary of these causative factors, and empirical guidelines for developing public health interventions to promote older driver safety. Using a mixed methods approach, we were able to compare and integrate main findings from a national crash dataset with perspectives of stakeholders. (p. 677)

This purpose statement identified the use of both quantitative (i.e., a national crash data set) and qualitative (i.e., stakeholders' perspectives) data. From one of the research questions in the study, we learned that the authors compared the qualitative stakeholder perspectives, needs, and goals for safe and unsafe driving with the quantitative results of the factors that influenced driving injuries. So the *expected outcome* was to compare the findings. The method section commented on the quantitative national data set, the statistical analysis of this data set, and then the qualitative data set and its analysis. Although not stated explicitly, the data were *used together* to form results, not used for one database to build on another, and the *timing* was to look at both databases concurrently. A diagram illustrated the procedures involved in both collecting and analyzing the information. A results section first reported the quantitative results and then the qualitative results. More *emphasis* was given to the quantitative results, leading to the conclusion that this study favored the quantitative research. However, these reports on the results from the two databases were followed by an analysis of key findings in which the quantitative and qualitative results were compared for supportive and non-supportive findings. In this discussion section, the researchers merged the two databases in a side-by-side comparison. Looking more broadly at the topic and the authors, we saw that the quantitative emphasis would probably be better accepted in the field of occupational therapy than qualitative research. Also, a scan of the authors' biographical sketches showed that this mixed methods study was completed by a *team of researchers* drawn from individuals with quantitative and qualitative expertise.

As suggested by this statement, the *expected outcome* of the study was projected to be a detailed picture of resilience and the personal perspectives of the survivors as learned through qualitative data. Also, the authors

Example 10.2 An Explanatory Sequential Mixed Methods Design

In 2007, Banyard and Williams conducted an explanatory sequential mixed methods study examining how women recover from childhood sexual abuse. The quantitative component of the study consisted of structured interviews (with 136 girls in 1990 and a subset of 61 girls in 1997) looking at resilience, correlates of resilience, over time across 7 years of early adulthood. The qualitative aspect consisted of interviews with a subset of 21 girls about their life events, coping, recovery, and resilience. The intent of the mixed methods study was to use the qualitative interviews to "explore and make sense" of the quantitative findings (p. 277). Here was the purpose statement:

> Multiple methods are used to examine aspects of resilience and recovery in the lives of female survivors of child sexual abuse (CSA) across

7 years of early adulthood. First quantitative changes in measures of resilience over time were examined. To what extent did women stay the same, increase, or decrease in functioning in a variety of sphere across 7 years during early adulthood? Next, the role of re-traumatization as an impediment to ongoing resilience and correlates of growth or increased well-being over time were examined. Finally, because resilient processes in adulthood have not been the focus of much research and require further description, qualitative data from a subset of participants was used to examine survivors' own narratives about recovery and healing to learn about key aspects of resilience in women's own words. (p. 278)

intended to probe the quantitative findings, to explain them in more detail through the qualitative data. With this intent, the study set up as a sequential approach, with the *two databases connected* and one building on the other. Also, with this approach, the *timing* illustrated the qualitative data collection followed the quantitative results. It was difficult to discern whether this study placed greater *emphasis* on the quantitative or qualitative component of the project. The project began with a quantitative longitudinal phase with extensive discussions of the measures used to gather data. The authors detailed the quantitative results. However, the qualitative findings illustrated many themes that emerged from the interviews with the women. These themes pointed toward new issues that helped to develop the concept of resilience, such as the turning points in the women's lives, the ongoing nature of recovery, and the role of spirituality in recovery. The study was conducted by a *team* of researchers from psychology and criminal justice and supported by the National Institutes of Health (NIH).

In this mixed methods study, the *expected outcome* was clearly to develop good psychometric measures and then to use the measures as outcomes in an experimental project. It was also to use the qualitative data to develop hypotheses that might be tested using the intervention in the experiment.

Example 10.3 An Exploratory Sequential
Mixed Methods Design

A good example of an exploratory sequential study with an experimental test outcome is found in Betancourt et al. (2011). This study used mixed methods research to adapt and evaluate a family strengthening intervention in Rwanda. The investigators sought to examine the mental health problems facing HIV-affected children in Rwanda. They first began with an exploratory, qualitative first phase of interviews with children and their caregivers. From a qualitative thematic analysis of the data, they then performed an extensive review of the literature to locate standardized measures that matched their qualitative findings. They found some measures and added some new ones to develop a survey instrument. This instrument went through several refinements following rigorous procedures of instrument-scale development (e.g., backward and forward translations, a discussion of items, reliability and validity) to develop good construct validity for the measures. These measures (e.g., family communication, good parenting, and others) then became the pretest and posttest assessments in an experimental (intervention) study. For the intervention in the study, the researchers were led to a strengths-based, family-based prevention program that was hypothesized to be related to the measures. The final step in the mixed methods process was to use the validated measures within a program that featured the prevention program. At various points in this study, the researchers also collaborated with stakeholders to help to develop good measures. Thus, this study illustrated a good, complex mixed methods project with an initial qualitative phase, an instrument development phase, and an experimental phase. It shows how an initial exploration qualitatively can be used to support a later quantitative testing phase. They stated the purpose of the study as follows:

> In the multi-step process used in this mental health services research, we aimed to (1) carefully unpack locally-relevant indicators of mental health problems and protective resources using qualitative methods; (2) apply qualitative findings to the adaptation of mental health measures and the development of a locally-informed intervention; (3) validate the selected mental health measures; and (4) apply the measures to rigorous evaluation research on the effectiveness of the intervention chosen through the mixed methods process. (p. 34)

The initial phase qualitative data collection was *connected* to the subsequent quantitative measures and their rigorous testing for scores on validity and reliability. The entire project was *timed* for the quantitative phase to follow the qualitative phase, and the quantitative phase could be stated as the development of the measures (and survey) and the experimental intervention study. If we were to diagram this project, it would be qual → QUAN → QUAN. As this notation shows, the *emphasis* in the project favored quantitative research, and the project could be seen as pointing toward the program intervention test at the end of the article. Recognizing that the researchers came from public health, an organization called Partners in Health, and a children's hospital, the strong quantitative orientation of the project makes sense. Overall, this mixed methods study illustrated both the core exploratory sequential design and the more advanced embedded experimental design with a sequential focus. To conduct such a complex project, the study involved a *team* of researchers both in the United States and in Rwanda.

Example 10.4   A Social Justice Design

The final example is a feminist study using a mixed methods social-justice explanatory sequential study by Hodgkin (2008). This study investigated the concept of social capital for men and women in households in a regional city in Australia. Social capital described norms and networks that enabled people to work collectively together to address and resolve common problems (e.g., through social activities, the community, and civic participation). The basic mixed methods approach was an explanatory sequential design with an initial survey, a quantitative phase, followed by an interview, qualitative phase. As stated by the author, "the qualitative study elaborated on and enhanced some of the results from the quantitative study" (p. 301). In addition, the author declared that this was a feminist mixed methods project. This means that Hodgkin used a feminist framework (see Chapter 3) to encase the entire mixed methods project. She also referred to the Merten's transformative research paradigm (Mertens, 2007) that gave voice to women, used a range of data collection methods, and bridged the subjective and objective ways of knowing (see the epistemology discussion in Chapter 3). The purpose of the study was this:

> The author will provide examples of quantitative data to demonstrate the existence of different social capital profiles for men and women. Stories will also be presented to provide a picture of gender inequality and expectation. The author will conclude by arguing that despite reluctance on the part of feminists to embrace quantitative methods, the big picture accompanied by the personal story can bring both depth and texture to a study. (p. 297)

Thus, in this mixed methods study, the *expected outcome* for the study was to help explain the initial survey results in more depth with qualitative interview data. Added to this would be the transformative perspective of seeking to provide a picture of gender inequality and expectations. The databases were used *sequentially* with the qualitative interviews following and expanding on the quantitative surveys. While the surveys were sent to both men and women in households ($N = 1431$), the interviews included only women in the survey sample ($N = 12$). The women interviewed were of different ages, they varied in terms of their work activities (inside and outside the home), they were mothers, and they varied in their educational level of attainment. The *timing* of the data collection was in two phases with the second-phase qualitative interviews building on the results from the first-phase quantitative surveys. In fact, the survey data indicated that men and women differed in terms of their level of social participation in groups, and in community group participation. The *emphasis* in this study seemed to be equal between the quantitative and qualitative components, and clearly the *sole author* of the study sought to provide a good example of mixed methods research that used a feminist framework.

How was this framework used? The author announced at the beginning of the study that "the aim of this article is to demonstrate the use of mixed methods in feminist research" (p. 296). Then the author discussed the lack of qualitative research in the empirical studies of social capital and noted the White, middle-class notion of community that dominated the discussions of social capital. Further, the author talked about lifting up the voices of those disenfranchised by gender and engaged in a study that first pointed out gender differences in social, community, and civic participation within a large sample of men and women, and then focused a qualitative follow-up on only women to understand the women's role in more depth. The qualitative findings then addressed themes that influence women's participation, such as wanting to be a "good mother," wanting to avoid isolation, and wanting to be a good citizen. A summary of the qualitative findings indicates specifically how the qualitative data helped to enhance the findings of the initial survey results. Unlike many feminist mixed methods studies, the conclusion did not indicate a strong call for action to change the inequality. It only mentioned in passing that the mixed methods study provided a powerful voice to gender inequality.

SUMMARY

In designing the procedures for a mixed methods discussion, begin by defining mixed methods research and its core characteristics, briefly mentioning its historical evolution; discuss your chosen mixed methods design; and note the challenges in using the design. Convey a diagram of your procedures that includes good notation to help the reader understand the flow of activities. As you discuss your design, convey the elements that go into it, such as the procedures used in a convergent parallel, an explanatory sequential, or an exploratory sequential mixed methods study. Also consider whether you will overlay your project with a more complex procedure that embeds the data within a larger design, theoretical framework, or methodology. Finally, consider factors that play into your choice of a mixed methods design. These involve considering the intent of the design, what outcomes you expect from the study, the integration of the databases, the timing of them, the emphasis placed on each database, the choice of design that matches your field, and the conduct of the project either by yourself or a team of researchers.

Writing Exercises

1. Design a combined qualitative and quantitative study that employs two phases sequentially. Discuss and provide rationales for why the phases are ordered in the sequence you propose.

2. Design a combined qualitative and quantitative study that gives emphasis to qualitative data collection and less emphasis to quantitative data collection. Discuss the approach to be taken in writing the introduction, the purpose statement, the research questions, and the specific forms of data collection.

3. Develop a figure and specific procedures that illustrate the use of a theoretical lens, such as a feminist perspective. Use the procedures of either an explanatory or exploratory design for conducting the study. Use appropriate notation in the figure.

Additional Readings

Creswell, J. W., & Plano Clark, V. L. (2018). *Designing and conducting mixed methods research* (3rd ed.) Thousand Oaks, CA: Sage.

John Creswell and Vicki Plano Clark provide two chapters on mixed methods research designs. Chapter 3 discusses the three core mixed methods designs: convergent mixed methods designs, explanatory sequential mixed methods design, and exploratory sequential mixed methods designs. Chapter 4 advances the four examples of complex designs: mixed methods intervention designs, mixed methods case study designs, mixed methods participatory–social justice designs, and mixed methods evaluation designs. The authors provide examples and diagrams of each type of design and detail important characteristics such as their integrative features.

Greene, J. C., Caracelli, V. J., & Graham, W. F. (1989). Toward a conceptual framework for mixed-method evaluation designs. *Educational Evaluation and Policy Analysis, 11*(3), 255–274.

Jennifer Greene and associates undertook a study of 57 mixed methods evaluation studies reported from 1980 to 1988. From this analysis, they developed five different mixed methods purposes and seven design characteristics. They found the purposes of mixed methods studies to be based on seeking convergence (triangulation), examining different facets of a phenomenon (complementarity), using the methods sequentially (development), discovering paradox and fresh perspectives (initiation), and adding breadth and scope to a project (expansion). They also found that the studies varied in terms of the assumptions, strengths, and limitations of the method and whether they addressed different phenomena or the same phenomena; were implemented within the same or different paradigms; were given equal or different weight in the study; and were implemented independently, concurrently, or sequentially. Using the purposes and the design characteristics, the authors have recommended several mixed methods designs.

Morse, J. M. (1991). Approaches to qualitative-quantitative methodological triangulation. *Nursing Research, 40*(1), 120–123.

Janice Morse suggests that using qualitative and quantitative methods to address the same research problem leads to issues of weighing each method and their sequence in a study. Based on these ideas, she then advances two forms of methodological triangulation: (a) simultaneous, using both methods at the same time, and (b) sequential, using the results of one method for planning the next method. These two forms are described using a notation of capital and lowercase letters that signify relative weight as well as sequence. The different approaches to triangulation are then discussed in the light of their purpose, limitations, and approaches.

Plano Clark, V. L. & Creswell, J. W. (2008). *The mixed methods reader.* Thousand Oaks, CA: Sage.

Creswell and Plano Clark have developed a comprehensive guide to designing the steps in conducting mixed methods research. This design theme is carried forward in specific examples of published mixed methods studies in this *reader.* Examples are provided of the convergent design, the explanatory sequential design, and the exploratory sequential design.

Also, the book contains key articles throughout the years that have informed the development of the field of mixed methods.

Tashakkori, A., & Teddlie, C. (Eds.). (2010). *SAGE handbook of mixed methods in social & behavioral research* (2nd ed.). Thousand Oaks, CA: Sage.

This handbook, edited by Abbas Tashakkori and Charles Teddlie, represents a major effort to map the field of mixed methods research. The chapters provide an introduction to mixed methods, illustrates methodological and analytic issues in its use, identifies applications in the social and human sciences, and plots future directions. For example, separate chapters illustrate the use of mixed methods research in evaluation, management and organization, health sciences, nursing, psychology, sociology, and education.

⑨SAGE edge™

https://edge.sagepub.com/creswellrd5e

Students and instructors, please visit the companion website for videos featuring John W. Creswell, full-text SAGE journal articles, quizzes and activities, plus additional tools for research design.

Glossary

Abstract in a literature review is a brief review of the literature (typically in a short paragraph) that summarizes major elements to enable a reader to understand the basic features of the article.

Attention or interest thoughts in writing are sentences whose purposes are to keep the reader on track, organize ideas, and keep an individual's attention.

Big thoughts in writing are sentences containing specific ideas or images that fall within the realm of umbrella thoughts and serve to reinforce, clarify, or elaborate upon the umbrella thoughts.

Case studies are a qualitative design in which the researcher explores in depth a program, event, activity, process, or one or more individuals. The case(s) are bounded by time and activity, and researchers collect detailed information using a variety of data collection procedures over a sustained period of time.

Central phenomenon is the key idea or concept being explored in a qualitative study.

Central question in qualitative research is a broad question posed by the researcher that asks for an exploration of the central phenomenon or concept in a study.

Code of ethics is the ethical rules and principles drafted by professional associations that govern scholarly research in the disciplines.

Coding is the process of organizing the material into chunks or segments of text and assigning a word or phrase to the segment in order to develop a general sense of it.

Coherence in writing means that the ideas tie together and logically flow from one sentence to another and from one paragraph to another.

Computer databases of the literature are now available in libraries, and they provide quick access to thousands of journals, conference papers, and materials.

Confidence interval is an estimate in quantitative research of the range of upper and lower statistical values that are consistent with the observed data and are likely to contain the actual population mean.

Construct validity occurs when investigators use adequate definitions and measures of variables.

Convergent mixed methods design is a mixed methods strategy in which a researcher collects both quantitative and qualitative data, analyzes them separately, and then compares the results to see if the findings confirm or disconfirm each other.

Deficiencies in past literature may exist because topics have not been explored with a particular group, sample, or population; the literature may need to be replicated or repeated to see if the same findings hold, given new samples of people or new sites for study; or the voice of underrepresented groups have not been heard in published literature.

Deficiencies model of an introduction is an approach to writing an introduction to a research study that builds on gaps existing in the literature. It includes the elements of stating the research problem, reviewing past studies about the problem, indicating deficiencies in the study, and advancing the significance of the study.

Definition of terms is a section that may be found in a research proposal that defines terms that readers may not understand.

Descriptive analysis of data for variables in a study includes describing the results through means, standard deviations, and range of scores.

Directional hypothesis, as used in quantitative research, is one in which the researcher makes a prediction about the expected direction or outcomes of the study.

Effect size identifies the strength of the conclusions about group differences or the relationships among variables in quantitative studies.

Emphasis placed on each database in mixed methods is the priority given to the quantitative or qualitative data (or equal priority).

Ethnography is a qualitative strategy in which the researcher studies an intact cultural group in a natural setting over a prolonged period of time by collecting primarily observational and interview data.

An **experimental design** in quantitative research tests the impact of a treatment (or an intervention) on an outcome, controlling for all other factors that might influence that outcome.

Experimental research seeks to determine if a specific treatment influences an outcome in a study. Researchers assess this impact by providing a specific treatment to one group and withholding it from another group and then determining how both groups score on an outcome.

Explanatory sequential mixed methods is a mixed methods design that involves a two-phase project in which the researcher collects quantitative data in the first phase, analyzes the results, and then uses a qualitative phase to help explain the quantitative results.

Exploratory sequential mixed methods is a mixed methods strategy that involves a three-phase project in which the researcher first collects qualitative data and analyzes it, then designs a quantitative feature based on the qualitative results (e.g., new variables, an experimental intervention, a website), and finally, tests the quantitative feature.

External validity threats arise when experimenters draw incorrect inferences from the sample data to other persons, other settings, and past or future situations.

Fat in writing refers to words added to prose that are unnecessary to convey the intended meaning.

Gatekeepers are individuals at research sites who provide access to the site and allow or permit a qualitative research study to be undertaken.

Grounded theory is a qualitative strategy in which the researcher derives a general, abstract theory of a process, action, or interaction grounded in the views of participants in a study.

Habit of writing is scholarly writing in a regular and continuous way rather than in binges or in on-and-off again times.

Inferential questions or hypotheses relate variables or compare groups in terms of variables so that inferences can be drawn from the sample to a population.

Informed consent forms are those that participants sign before they engage in research. This form acknowledges that participants' rights will be protected during data collection.

Institutional review board (IRB) is a committee on a college and university campus that reviews research to determine to what extent the research could place participants at risk during the study. Researchers file applications with the IRB to approve their project and they use informed consent forms to have participants acknowledge the level of risk they agree to by participating in the study.

Intercoder agreement (or cross-checking) is when two or more coders agree on codes used for the same passages in the text. It is not that they code the same text but whether another coder would code a similar passage with the same or a similar code. Statistical procedures or reliability subprograms in qualitative computer software packages can be used to determine the level of consistency of coding.

Internal validity threats are experimental procedures, treatments, or experiences of the participants that threaten the researcher's ability to draw correct inferences from the data about the population in an experiment.

Interpretation in qualitative research means that the researcher draws meaning from the findings of data analysis. This meaning may result in lessons learned, information to compare with the literature, or personal experiences.

Interpretation in quantitative research means that the researcher draws conclusions from the results for the research questions, hypotheses, and the larger meaning of the study.

Interview protocol is a form used by a qualitative researcher for recording and writing down information obtained during an interview.

Joint displays are tables or graphs that array the quantitative or qualitative data collection and analysis side by side so that researchers can view and interpret their comparison or integration in a mixed methods study. Researchers can develop specific displays for each type of mixed methods design.

Literature map is a visual picture (or figure) of the research literature on a topic that illustrates how a particular study contributes to the literature.

Manipulation check measure is a measure of the intended manipulated variable of interest.

Mediating variables are variables in quantitative research that "stand between" the independent and dependent variables in the causal link. The logic is that the independent variable probably causes the mediating variable, which, in turn, influences the dependent variable.

Memos are notes written during the research process that reflect on the process or that help shape the development of codes and themes.

Mixed methods case study design is the use of one or more core designs (i.e., convergent, explanatory sequential, exploratory sequential) within the framework of a single or multiple case study design.

Mixed methods evaluation design consists of one or more core designs added to the steps in an evaluation procedure typically focused on evaluating the success of an intervention, a program or a policy.

Mixed methods experimental (or intervention) design occurs when the researcher collects and analyzes both quantitative and qualitative data from core designs and embeds them within an experiment or intervention trial.

Mixed methods integration occurs in mixed methods designs when data are merged, connected (used to explain or build), or embedded in a design.

Mixed methods notation provides shorthand labels and symbols that convey important aspects of mixed methods research, and they provide a way that mixed methods researchers can easily communicate their procedures.

Mixed methods participatory-social justice design is a mixed methods design in which the researcher adds a core design within a larger participatory and/or social justice theoretical or conceptual framework.

Mixed methods purpose statements contain the overall intent of the study, information about both the quantitative and qualitative strands of the study, and a rationale of incorporating both strands to study the research problem.

Mixed methods research is an approach to inquiry that combines or integrates both qualitative and quantitative forms of research. It involves philosophical assumptions, the use of qualitative and quantitative approaches, and the mixing or integrating of both approaches in a study.

Mixed methods research question is a special question posed in a mixed methods study that directly addresses the mixing of the quantitative and qualitative strands of the research. This is the question that will be answered in the study based on the mixing.

Moderating variables are variables in quantitative research that moderate the effect of independent variables in a study. They are variables created by the researcher who takes one independent variable times another (typically a demographic variable) to construct a new independent variable.

Narrative hook is a term drawn from English composition, meaning words that are used in the opening sentence of an introduction that serve to draw, engage, or hook the reader into the study.

Narrative research is a qualitative strategy in which the researcher studies the lives of individuals and asks one or more individuals to provide stories about their lives. This information is then often retold or restoried by the researcher into a narrative chronology.

Nondirectional hypothesis in a quantitative study is one in which the researcher makes a prediction, but the exact form of differences (e.g., higher, lower, more, or less) is not specified because the researcher does not know what can be predicted from past literature.

Null hypothesis in quantitative research represents the traditional approach to writing hypotheses: It

makes a prediction that, in the general population, no relationship or no significant difference exists between groups on a variable.

Observational protocol is a form used by a qualitative researcher for recording and writing down information while observing.

Phenomenological research is a qualitative strategy in which the researcher identifies the essence of human experiences about a phenomenon as described by participants in a study.

Postpositivists reflect a deterministic philosophy about research in which causes probably determine effects or outcomes. Thus, the problems studied by postpositivists reflect issues that need to identify and assess the causes that influence the outcomes, such as found in experiments.

Pragmatism as a worldview or philosophy arises out of actions, situations, and consequences rather than antecedent conditions (as in postpositivism). There is a concern with applications—what works—and solutions to problems. Instead of focusing on methods, researchers emphasize the research problem and use all approaches available to understand it.

A **purpose statement** in a research proposal or project sets the objectives, the intent, and the major idea for the study.

To **purposefully select** participants or sites (or documents or visual material) means that qualitative researchers select individuals who will best help them understand the research problem and the research questions.

Qualitative audiovisual digital materials take the form of photographs, art objects, videotapes, and sounds.

Qualitative codebook is a means for organizing qualitative data using a list of predetermined codes that are used for coding the data. This codebook might be composed with the names of codes in one column, a definition of codes in another column, and then specific instances (e.g., line numbers) in which the code is found in the transcripts.

Qualitative documents are public documents (e.g., newspapers, minutes of meetings, official reports) or private documents (e.g., personal journals and diaries, letters, e-mails).

Qualitative interviews means that the researcher conducts face-to-face interviews with participants, interviews participants by telephone, on the Internet, or engages in focus group interviews with six to eight interviewees in each group. These interviews involve unstructured and generally open-ended questions that are few in number and intended to elicit views and opinions from the participants.

Qualitative observation means that the researcher takes field notes on the behavior and activities of individuals at the research site and records observations.

Qualitative purpose statements contain information about the central phenomenon explored in the study, the participants in the study, and the research site. It also conveys an emerging design and research words drawn from the language of qualitative inquiry.

Qualitative reliability indicates that a particular approach is consistent across different researchers and different projects.

Qualitative research is a means for exploring and understanding the meaning individuals or groups ascribe to a social or human problem. The process of research involves emerging questions and procedures; collecting data in the participants' setting; analyzing the data inductively, building from particulars to general themes; and making interpretations of the meaning of the data. The final written report has a flexible writing structure.

Qualitative validity means that the researcher checks for the accuracy of the findings by employing certain procedures.

Quantitative hypotheses are predictions the researcher makes about the expected relationships among variables.

Quantitative purpose statements include the variables in the study and their relationship, the participants in a study, and the site for the research. It also includes language associated with quantitative research and the deductive testing of relationships or theories.

Quantitative research is a means for testing objective theories by examining the relationship among variables. These variables can be measured, typically on instruments, so that numbered data can be analyzed using statistical procedures. The final written report has a set structure consisting of introduction, literature and theory, methods, results, and discussion.

Quantitative research questions are interrogative statements that raise questions about the relationships among variables that the investigator seeks to answer.

Quasi-experiment is a form of experimental research in which individuals are not randomly assigned to groups.

Random sampling is a procedure in quantitative research for selecting participants. It means that each individual has an equal probability of being selected from the population, ensuring that the sample will be representative of the population.

Reflexivity means that researchers reflect about their biases, values, and personal background, such as gender, history, culture, and socioeconomic status, and how this background shapes their interpretations formed during a study.

Reliability refers to whether scores to items on an instrument are internally consistent (i.e., are the item responses consistent across constructs?), stable over time (test-retest correlations), and whether there was consistency in test administration and scoring.

Research approaches are plans and the procedures for research that span the decisions from broad assumptions to detailed methods of data collection and analysis. It involves the intersection of philosophical assumptions, designs, and specific methods.

Research designs are types of inquiry within qualitative, quantitative, and mixed methods approaches that provide specific direction for procedures in a research study.

Research methods involve the forms of data collection, analysis, and interpretation that researchers propose for their studies.

Research problems are problems or issues that lead to the need for a study.

Research tips are approaches or techniques that have worked well in research for authors.

Response bias is the effect of nonresponses on survey estimates, and it means that if nonrespondents had responded, their responses would have substantially changed the overall results of the survey.

Reviewing studies in an introduction justifies the importance of the study and creates distinctions between past studies and a proposed study.

Saturation is when, in qualitative data collection, the researcher stops collecting data because fresh data no longer sparks new insights or reveals new properties.

Script, as used in this book, is a template of a few sentences that contains the major words and ideas for particular parts of a research proposal or report (e.g., purpose statement or research question) and provides space for researchers to insert information that relates to their projects.

Significance of the study in an introduction conveys the importance of the problem for different audiences that may profit from reading and using the study.

Single-subject design or *N* of 1 design involves observing the behavior of a single individual (or a small number of individuals) over time.

Social constructivists hold the assumption that individuals seek understanding of the world in which they live and work. Individuals develop subjective meanings of their experiences, meanings directed toward certain objects or things.

Social science theory is a theory framework that researchers use in designs. This theory may inform many aspects of a study from the issue, to the problem, the findings, and the final suggestions for revising the theory.

Statistical conclusion validity arises when experimenters draw inaccurate inferences from the data because of inadequate statistical power or the violation of statistical assumptions.

Statistical significance testing reports an assessment as to whether the observed scores reflect a pattern other than chance. A statistical test is considered to be of significance if the results are unlikely by chance to have occurred, and the null hypothesis of "no effect" can be rejected.

Style manuals provide guidelines for creating a scholarly style of a manuscript, such as a consistent format for citing references, creating headings, presenting tables and figures, and using nondiscriminatory language.

Survey designs provide plans for a quantitative or numeric description of trends, attitudes, or opinions of a population by studying a sample of that population.

Survey research provides a quantitative or numeric description of trends, attitudes, or opinions of a population by studying a sample of that population.

Theoretical lens or perspective in qualitative research provides an overall orienting lens that is used to study questions of gender, class, and race (or other issues of marginalized groups). This lens becomes an advocacy perspective that shapes the types of questions asked, informs how data are collected and analyzed, and provides a call for action or change.

Theories in mixed methods research provide an orienting lens that shapes the types of questions asked, who participates in the study, how data are collected, and the implications made from the study (typically for change and advocacy). They present an overarching perspective used with research designs.

Theory in quantitative research is the use of an interrelated set of constructs (or variables) formed into propositions, or hypotheses, that specify the relationship among variables (typically in terms of magnitude or direction) and predicts the outcomes of a study.

Theory use in mixed methods studies may include theory deductively in quantitative theory testing and verification or inductively, as in an emerging qualitative theory or pattern. It also has distinctive features of providing a framework within which researchers collect, analyze, and integrate both quantitative and qualitative data. This framework has taken two forms: (a) the use of a social science framework and (b) the use of a transformative framework.

Timing in mixed methods data collection refers to the sequence of data collection in a study and whether the researcher collects the data concurrently at roughly the same time or collects the data sequentially with one database gathered prior to the other database.

Topic is the subject or subject matter of a proposed study that a researcher identifies early in the preparation of a study.

Transformative worldview is a philosophical position in which the researcher identifies one of the qualitative frameworks (e.g., indigenous populations, females, racial and ethnic groups, disabled individuals, and so forth) and uses the framework to advocate for the underrepresented populations and to help create a better, just society for them (Mertens, 2010).

True experiment is a form of experimental research in which individuals are randomly assigned to groups.

Validity in quantitative research refers to whether one can draw meaningful and useful inferences from scores on particular instruments.

Validity strategies in qualitative research are procedures (e.g., member checking, triangulating data sources) that qualitative researchers use to demonstrate the accuracy of their findings and convince readers of this accuracy.

Variable refers to a characteristic or attribute of an individual or an organization that can be measured or observed and that varies among the people or organization being studied. A variable typically will vary in two or more categories or on a continuum of scores, and it can be measured.

Worldview is defined as "a basic set of beliefs that guide action" (Guba, 1990, p. 17).

References

Aikin, M. C. (Ed.). (1992). *Encyclopedia of educational research* (6th ed.). New York: Macmillan.

American Psychological Association. (2010). *Publication Manual of the American Psychological Association* (6th ed.). Washington, DC: Author.

Ames, G. M., Duke, M. R., Moore, R. S., & Cunradi, C. B. (2009). The impact of occupational culture on drinking behavior of young adults in the U.S. Navy. *Journal of Mixed Methods Research, 3*(2), 129–150.

Anderson, E. H., & Spencer, M. H. (2002). Cognitive representation of AIDS. *Qualitative Health Research, 12*(10), 1338–1352.

Annual Review of Psychology. (1950–). Palo Alto, CA: Annual Reviews.

Asmussen, K. J., & Creswell, J. W. (1995). Campus response to a student gunman. *Journal of Higher Education, 66,* 575–591.

Babbie, E. (2015). *The practice of social research* (14th ed.). Belmont, CA: Wadsworth/Thomson.

Bachman, R. D., & Schutt, R. K. (2017). *Fundamentals of research in criminology and criminal justice* (4th ed.). Los Angeles, CA: Sage.

Bailey, E. P. (1984). *Writing clearly: A contemporary approach.* Columbus, OH: Charles Merrill.

Banyard, V. L., & Williams, L. M. (2007). Women's voices on recovery: A multi-method study of the complexity of recovery from child sexual abuse. *Child Abuse & Neglect, 31,* 275–290.

Bean, J., & Creswell, J. W. (1980). Student attrition among women at a liberal arts college. *Journal of College Student Personnel, 3,* 320–327.

Beisel, N. (February, 1990). Class, culture, and campaigns against vice in three American cities, 1872–1892. *American Sociological Review, 55,* 44–62.

Bem, D. (1987). Writing the empirical journal article. In M. Zanna & J. Darley (Eds.), *The compleat academic: A practical guide for the beginning social scientist* (pp. 171–201). New York: Random House.

Berg, B. L. (2001). *Qualitative research methods for the social sciences* (4th ed.). Boston: Allyn & Bacon.

Berger, P. L., & Luckmann, T. (1967). *The social construction of reality: A treatise in the sociology of knowledge.* Garden City, NJ: Anchor.

Betancourt, T. S., Meyers-Ohki, S. E., Stevenson, A., Ingabire, C., Kanyanganzi, F., Munyana, M., et al. (2011). Using mixed-methods research to adapt and evaluate a family strengthening intervention in Rwanda. *African Journal of Traumatic Stress, 2*(1), 32–45.

Blalock, H. (1969). *Theory construction: From verbal to mathematical formulations.* Englewood Cliffs, NJ: Prentice Hall.

Blalock, H. (1985). *Causal models in the social sciences.* New York: Aldine.

Blalock, H. (1991). Are there any constructive alternatives to causal modeling? *Sociological Methodology, 21,* 325–335.

Blase, J. J. (1989, November). The micropolitics of the school: The everyday political orientation of teachers toward open school principals. *Educational Administration Quarterly, 25*(4), 379–409.

Boeker, W. (1992). Power and managerial dismissal: Scapegoating at the top. *Administrative Science Quarterly, 37,* 400–421.

Bogdan, R. C., & Biklen, S. K. (1992). *Qualitative research for education: An introduction to theory and methods.* Boston: Allyn & Bacon.

Boice, R. (1990). *Professors as writers: A self-help guide to productive writing.* Stillwater, OK: New Forums.

Boneva, B., Kraut, R., & Frohlich, D. (2001). Using e-mail for personal relationships. *American Behavioral Scientist, 45*(3), 530–549.

Boote, D. N., & Beile, P. (2005). Scholars before researchers: On the centrality of the dissertation literature review in research preparation. *Educational Researcher, 34*(6), 3–15.

Booth-Kewley, S., Edwards, J. E., & Rosenfeld, P. (1992). Impression management, social desirability, and computer administration of attitude questionnaires: Does the computer make a difference? *Journal of Applied Psychology, 77*(4), 562–566.

Borg, W. R., & Gall, M. D. (2006). *Educational research: An introduction* (8th ed.). New York: Longman.

Bryman, A. (2006). *Mixed methods: A four-volume set.* Thousand Oaks, CA: Sage.

Buck, G., Cook, K., Quigley, C., Eastwood, J., & Lucas, Y. (2009). Profiles of urban, low SES, African American girls' attitudes toward science: A sequential explanatory mixed methods study. *Journal of Mixed Methods Research, 3*(1), 386–410.

Bunge, N. (1985). *Finding the words: Conversations with writers who teach.* Athens: Swallow Press, Ohio University Press.

Cahill, S. E. (1989). Fashioning males and females: Appearance management and the social reproduction of gender. *Symbolic Interaction, 12*(2), 281–298.

Campbell, D., & Stanley, J. (1963). Experimental and quasi-experimental designs for research. In N. L. Gage (Ed.), *Handbook of research on teaching* (pp. 1–76). Chicago: Rand McNally.

Campbell, D. T., & Fiske, D. (1959). Convergent and discriminant validation by the multitrait-multimethod matrix. *Psychological Bulletin, 56,* 81–105.

Carroll, D. L. (1990). *A manual of writer's tricks.* New York: Paragon.

Carstensen, L. W., Jr. (1989). A fractal analysis of cartographic generalization. *The American Cartographer, 16*(3), 181–189.

Castetter, W. B., & Heisler, R. S. (1977). *Developing and defending a dissertation proposal.* Philadelphia: University of Pennsylvania, Graduate School of Education, Center for Field Studies.

Charmaz, K. (2006). *Constructing grounded theory.* Thousand Oaks, CA: Sage.

Cheek, J. (2004). At the margins? Discourse analysis and qualitative research. *Qualitative Health Research, 14,* 1140–1150.

Cherryholmes, C. H. (1992, August–September). Notes on pragmatism and scientific realism. *Educational Researcher,* 13–17.

Clandinin, D. J. (Ed.). (2007). *Handbook of narrative inquiry: Mapping a methodology.* Thousand Oaks, CA: Sage.

Clandinin, D. J., & Connelly, F. M. (2000). *Narrative inquiry: Experience and story in qualitative research.* San Francisco: Jossey-Bass.

Classen, S., Lopez, D. D. S., Winter, S., Awadzi, K. D., Ferree, N., & Garvan, C. W. (2007). Population-based health promotion perspective for older driver safety: Conceptual framework to intervention plan. *Clinical Intervention in Aging 2*(4), 677–693.

Cohen, J. (1977). *Statistical power analysis for the behavioral sciences.* New York: Academic Press.

Cohen, S., Kamarck, T., & Mermelstein, R. (1983). A global measure of perceived stress. *Journal of Health and Social Behavior, 24,* 385–396.

Cook, T. D., & Campbell, D. T. (1979). *Quasi-experimentation: Design and analysis issues for field settings.* Chicago: Rand McNally.

Cooper, H. (2010). *Research synthesis and meta-analysis: A step-by-step approach* (4th ed.). Thousand Oaks, CA: Sage.

Cooper, J. O., Heron, T. E., & Heward, W. L. (2007). *Applied behavior analysis.* Upper Saddle River, NJ: Pearson/Merrill-Prentice Hall.

Corbin, J. M., & Strauss, J. M. (2007). *Basics of qualitative research: Techniques and procedures for developing grounded theory* (3rd ed.). Thousand Oaks, CA: Sage.

Corbin, J. M., & Strauss, J. M. (2015). *Techniques and procedures for developing grounded theory* (4th ed.). Thousand Oaks, CA: Sage.

Creswell, J. D., Welch, W. T., Taylor, S. E., Sherman, D. K., Gruenewald, T. L., & Mann, T. (2005). Affirmation of personal values buffers neuroendocrine and psychological stress responses. *Psychological Science, 16,* 846–851.

Creswell, J. W. (2010). Mapping the developing landscape of mixed methods research. In A. Tashakkori & C. Teddlie (Eds.), *SAGE handbook of mixed methods in social & behavioral research* (2nd ed., pp. 45–68). Thousand Oaks, CA: Sage.

Creswell, J. W. (2011). Controversies in mixed methods research. In N. Denzin & Y. Lincoln (Eds.), *The SAGE handbook on qualitative research* (4th ed., pp. 269–284). Thousand Oaks, CA: Sage.

Creswell, J. W. (2012). *Educational research: Planning, conducting, and evaluating quantitative and qualitative research* (4th ed.). Upper Saddle River, NJ: Merrill.

Creswell, J. W. (2013). *Qualitative inquiry and research design: Choosing among five approaches* (3rd ed.). Thousand Oaks, CA: Sage.

Creswell, J. W. (2014). *Research design: Qualitative, quantitative, and mixed methods approaches* (4th ed.). Thousand Oaks, CA: Sage.

Creswell, J. W. (2015). *A concise introduction to mixed methods research.* Thousand Oaks, CA: Sage.

Creswell, J. W. (2016). *30 essential skills for the qualitative researcher.* Thousand Oaks, CA: Sage.

Creswell, J. W., & Brown, M. L. (1992, Fall). How chairpersons enhance faculty research: A grounded theory study. *The Review of Higher Education, 16*(1), 41–62.

Creswell, J. W., & Guetterman, T. (in press). *Educational research: Planning, conducting, and evaluating quantitative and qualitative research* (6th ed.). Upper Saddle River, NJ: Pearson.

Creswell, J. W., & Miller, D. (2000). Determining validity in qualitative inquiry. *Theory Into Practice, 39*(3), 124–130.

Creswell, J. W., & Plano Clark, V. L. (2011). *Designing and conducting mixed methods research* (2nd ed.). Thousand Oaks, CA: Sage.

Creswell, J. W., & Plano Clark, V. L. (2018). *Designing and conducting mixed methods research* (3rd ed.). Thousand Oaks, CA: Sage.

Creswell, J. W., & Poth, C. N. (2018). *Qualitative inquiry and research design: Choosing among five approaches* (4th ed.). Thousand Oaks, CA: Sage.

Creswell, J. W., Seagren, A., & Henry, T. (1979). Professional development training needs of department chairpersons: A test of the Biglan model. *Planning and Changing, 10,* 224–237.

Crotty, M. (1998). *The foundations of social research: Meaning and perspective in the research process.* Thousand Oaks, CA: Sage.

Crutchfield, J. P. (1986). *Locus of control, interpersonal trust, and scholarly productivity.* Unpublished doctoral dissertation, University of Nebraska-Lincoln.

Daum, M. (2010). *Life would be perfect if I lived in that house.* New York: Knopf.

DeGraw, D. G. (1984). *Job motivational factors of educators within adult correctional institutions from various states.* Unpublished doctoral dissertation, University of Nebraska-Lincoln.

Denzin, N. K., & Lincoln, Y. S. (Eds.). (2011). *The SAGE handbook of qualitative research* (4th ed.). Thousand Oaks, CA: Sage.

Denzin, N. K., & Lincoln, Y. S. (Eds.). (2018). *The SAGE handbook of qualitative research* (5th ed.). Los Angeles, CA: Sage.

DeVellis, R. F. (2012). *Scale development: Theory and application* (3rd ed.). Thousand Oaks, CA: Sage.

DeVellis, R. F. (2017). *Scale development: Theory and application* (4th ed.). Los Angeles, CA: Sage.

Dillard, A. (1989). *The writing life.* New York: Harper & Row.

Dillman, D. A. (2007). *Mail and Internet surveys: The tailored design method* (2nd ed.). New York: John Wiley.

Duncan, O. D. (1985). Path analysis: Sociological examples. In H. M. Blalock, Jr. (Ed.), *Causal models in the social sciences* (2nd ed., pp. 55–79). New York: Aldine.

Educational Resources Information Center. (1975). *Thesaurus of ERIC descriptors* (12th ed.). Phoenix, AZ: Oryx.

Elbow, P. (1973). *Writing without teachers.* London: Oxford University Press.

Enns, C. Z., & Hackett, G. (1990). Comparison of feminist and nonfeminist women's reactions to variants of nonsexist and feminist counseling. *Journal of Counseling Psychology, 37*(1), 33–40.

Faul, F., Erdfelder, E., Buchner, A., & Lang, A.-G. (2009). Statistical power analyses using G*Power 3.1: Tests for correlation and regression analyses. *Behavior Research Methods, 41,* 1149–1160.

Faul, F., Erdfelder, E., Lang, A.-G., & Buchner, A. (2007). G*Power 3: A flexible statistical power analysis program for the social, behavioral, and biomedical sciences. *Behavior Research Methods, 39,* 175–191.

Fay, B. (1987). *Critical social science.* Ithaca, NY: Cornell University Press.

Fetterman, D. M. (2010). *Ethnography: Step by step* (3rd ed.). Thousand Oaks, CA: Sage.

Fink, A. (2016). *How to conduct surveys* (6th ed.). Thousand Oaks, CA: Sage.

Firestone, W. A. (1987). Meaning in method: The rhetoric of quantitative and qualitative research. *Educational Researcher, 16,* 16–21.

Flick, U. (Ed.). (2007). *The Sage qualitative research kit.* Thousand Oaks, CA: Sage.

Flinders, D. J., & Mills, G. E. (Eds.). (1993). *Theory and concepts in qualitative research: Perspectives from the field.* New York: Columbia University, Teachers College Press.

Fowler, F. J. (2008). *Survey research methods* (4th ed.). Thousand Oaks, CA: Sage.

Fowler, F. J. (2014). *Survey research methods* (5th ed.). Thousand Oaks, CA: Sage.

Franklin, J. (1986). *Writing for story: Craft secrets of dramatic nonfiction by a two-time Pulitzer prize-winner.* New York: Atheneum.

Gamson, J. (2000). Sexualities, queer theory, and qualitative research. In N. K. Denzin & Y. S. Lincoln (Eds.), *Handbook of qualitative research* (pp. 347–365). Thousand Oaks, CA: Sage.

Gibbs, G. R. (2007). Analyzing qualitative data. In U. Flick (Ed.), *The Sage qualitative research kit*. Thousand Oaks, CA: Sage.

Giordano, J., O'Reilly, M., Taylor, H., & Dogra, N. (2007). Confidentiality and autonomy: The challenge(s) of offering research participants a choice of disclosing their identity. *Qualitative Health Research, 17*(2), 264–275.

Giorgi, A. (2009). *The descriptive phenomenological method in psychology: A modified Husserlian approach*. Pittsburgh, PA: Duquesne University Press.

Glesne, C. (2015). *Becoming qualitative researchers: An introduction* (5th ed.). White Plains, NY: Longman.

Glesne, C., & Peshkin, A. (1992). *Becoming qualitative researchers: An introduction*. White Plains, NY: Longman.

Gravetter, F. J., & Wallnau, L. B. (2012). *Statistics for the behavioural sciences* (9th ed.). Belmont, CA: Wadsworth.

Greene, J. C. (2007). *Mixed methods in social inquiry*. San Francisco: Jossey-Bass.

Greene, J. C., & Caracelli, V. J. (Eds.). (1997). *Advances in mixed-method evaluation: The challenges and benefits of integrating diverse paradigms*. (New Directions for Evaluation, No. 74). San Francisco: Jossey-Bass.

Greene, J. C., Caracelli, V. J., & Graham, W. F. (1989). Toward a conceptual framework for mixed-method evaluation designs. *Educational Evaluation and Policy Analysis, 11*(3), 255–274.

Greysen, S. R., Allen, R., Lucas, G. I., Wang, E. A., Rosenthal, M. S. (2012). *J. Gen Intern Med.* doi:10.1007/s11606-012-2117-2.

Guba, E. G. (1990). The alternative paradigm dialog. In E. G. Guba (Ed.), *The paradigm dialog* (pp. 17–30). Newbury Park, CA: Sage.

Guest, G., MacQueen, K. M., & Namey, E. E. (2012). *Applied thematic analysis*. Thousand Oaks, CA: Sage.

Guetterman, T., Fetters, M. D., & Creswell, J. W. (2015). Integrating quantitative and qualitative results in health science mixed methods research through joint displays. *Annals of Family Medicine, 13*(6), 554–561.

Harding, P. (2009). *Tinkers*. New York: NYU School of Medicine, Bellevue Literary Press.

Hatch, J. A. (2002). *Doing qualitative research in educational settings*. Albany: State University of New York Press.

Heron, J., & Reason, P. (1997). A participatory inquiry paradigm. *Qualitative Inquiry, 3*, 274–294.

Hesse-Biber, S. N., & Leavy, P. (2011). *The practice of qualitative research* (2nd ed.). Thousand Oaks, CA: Sage.

Hodgkin, S. (2008). Telling it all: A story of women's social capital using mixed methods approach. *Journal of Mixed Methods Research, 2*(3), 296–316.

Homans, G. C. (1950). *The human group*. New York: Harcourt, Brace.

Hopkins, T. K. (1964). *The exercise of influence in small groups*. Totowa, NJ: Bedmister.

Houtz, L. E. (1995). Instructional strategy change and the attitude and achievement of seventh- and eighth-grade science students. *Journal of Research in Science Teaching, 32*(6), 629–648.

Huber, J., & Whelan, K. (1999). A marginal story as a place of possibility: Negotiating self on the professional knowledge landscape. *Teaching and Teacher Education, 15*, 381–396.

Humbley, A. M., & Zumbo, B. D. (1996). A dialectic on validity: Where we have been and where we are going. *The Journal of General Psychology, 123*, 207–215.

Isaac, S., & Michael, W. B. (1981). *Handbook in research and evaluation: A collection of principles, methods, and strategies useful in the planning, design, and evaluation of studies in education and the behavioral sciences* (2nd ed.). San Diego, CA: EdITS.

Israel, M., & Hay, I. (2006). *Research ethics for social scientists: Between ethical conduct and regulatory compliance*. Thousand Oaks, CA: Sage.

Ivankova, N. V. (2015). *Mixed methods applications in action research: From methods to community action*. Thousand Oaks, CA: Sage.

Ivankova, N. V., & Stick, S. L. (2007). Students' persistence in a distributed doctoral program in educational leadership in higher education. *Research in Higher Education, 48*(1), 93–135.

Janovec, T. (2001). *Procedural justice in organizations: A literature map*. Unpublished manuscript, University of Nebraska-Lincoln.

Janz, N. K., Zimmerman, M. A., Wren, P. A., Israel, B. A., Freudenberg, N., & Carter, R. J. (1996). Evaluation of 37 AIDS prevention projects: Successful approaches and barriers to program effectiveness. *Health Education Quarterly, 23*(1), 80–97.

Jick, T. D. (1979, December). Mixing qualitative and quantitative methods: Triangulation in action. *Administrative Science Quarterly, 24*, 602–611.

Johnson, R. B., Onwuegbuzie, A. J., & Turner, L. A. (2007). Toward a definition of mixed methods research. *Journal of Mixed Methods Research, 1*(2), 112–133.

Jungnickel, P. W. (1990). *Workplace correlates and scholarly performance of pharmacy clinical faculty members.* Unpublished manuscript, University of Nebraska-Lincoln.

Kalof, L. (2000). Vulnerability to sexual coercion among college women: A longitudinal study. *Gender Issues, 18*(4), 47–58.

Keeves, J. P. (Ed.). (1988). *Educational research, methodology, and measurement: An international handbook.* Oxford, UK: Pergamon.

Kemmis, S., & McTaggart, R. (2000). Participatory action research. In N. K. Denzin & Y. S. Lincoln (Eds.), *Handbook of qualitative research* (2nd ed., pp. 567–605). Thousand Oaks, CA: Sage.

Kemmis, S., & Wilkinson, M. (1998). Participatory action research and the study of practice. In B. Atweh, S. Kemmis, & P. Weeks (Eds.), *Action research in practice: Partnerships for social justice in education* (pp. 21–36). New York: Routledge.

Kennett, D. J., O'Hagan, F. T., & Cezer, D. (2008). Learned resourcefulness and the long-term benefits of a chronic pain management program. *Journal of Mixed Methods Research, 2*(4), 317–339.

Keppel, G. (1991). *Design and analysis: A researcher's handbook* (3rd ed.). Englewood Cliffs, NJ: Prentice Hall.

Keppel, G., & Wickens, T. D. (2003). *Design and analysis: A researcher's handbook* (4th ed.). Englewood Cliffs, NJ: Prentice Hall.

Kerlinger, F. N. (1979). *Behavioral research: A conceptual approach.* New York: Holt, Rinehart & Winston.

King, S. (2000). *On writing: A memoir of the craft.* New York: Scribner.

Kline, R. B. (1998). *Principles and practice of structural equation modeling.* New York: Guilford.

Kos, R. (1991). Persistence of reading disabilities: The voices of four middle school students. *American Educational Research Journal, 28*(4), 875–895.

Kraemer, H. C., & Blasey, C. (2016). *How many subjects? Statistical power analysis in research.* Thousand Oaks, CA: Sage.

Krueger, R. A., & Casey, M. A. (2014). *Focus groups: A practical guide for applied research* (5th ed.). Thousand Oaks, CA: Sage.

Kvale, S. (2007). Doing interviews. In U. Flick (Ed.), *The Sage qualitative research kit.* London: Sage.

Labovitz, S., & Hagedorn, R. (1971). *Introduction to social research.* New York: McGraw-Hill.

Ladson-Billings, G. (2000). Racialized discourses and ethnic epistemologies. In N. K. Denzin & Y. S. Lincoln (Eds.), *Handbook on qualitative research* (pp. 257–277). Thousand Oaks, CA: Sage.

LaFrance, J., & Crazy Bull, C. (2009). Researching ourselves back to life: Taking control of the research agenda in Indian Country. In D. M. Mertens & P. E. Ginsburg (Eds.), The handbook of social research ethics (pp. 135–149). Thousand Oaks, CA: Sage.

Lather, P. (1986). Research as praxis. *Harvard Educational Review, 56,* 257–277.

Lauterbach, S. S. (1993). In another world: A phenomenological perspective and discovery of meaning in mothers' experience with death of a wished-for baby: Doing phenomenology. In P. L. Munhall & C. O. Boyd (Eds.), *Nursing research: A qualitative perspective* (pp. 133–179). New York: National League for Nursing Press.

Lee, Y. J., & Greene, J. (2007). The predictive validity of an ESL placement test: A mixed methods approach. *Journal of Mixed Methods Research, 1*(4), 366–389.

Leslie, L. L. (1972). Are high response rates essential to valid surveys? *Social Science Research, 1,* 323–334.

Levitt, H., Bamberg, M., Creswell, J. W., Frost, D. M., Josselson, R., & Suarez-Orozco, C. (in press). Journal article reporting standards for qualitative research in psychology. *American Psychologist.*

Li, S., Marquart, J. M., & Zercher, C. (2000). Conceptual issues and analytic strategies in mixed-methods studies of preschool inclusion. *Journal of Early Intervention, 23*(2), 116–132.

Lincoln, Y. S. (2009). Ethical practices in qualitative research. In D. M. Mertens & P. E. Ginsberg (Ed.), *The handbook of social research ethics* (pp. 150–169). Thousand Oaks, CA: Sage.

Lincoln, Y. S., & Guba, E. G. (1985). *Naturalistic inquiry.* Beverly Hills, CA: Sage.

Lincoln, Y. S., Lynham, S. A., & Guba, E. G. (2011). Paradigmatic controversies, contradictions, and emerging confluences revisited. In N. K. Denzin & Y. S. Lincoln, *The SAGE handbook of qualitative research* (4th ed., pp. 97–128). Thousand Oaks, CA: Sage.

Lipsey, M. W. (1990). *Design sensitivity: Statistical power for experimental research.* Newbury Park, CA: Sage.

Locke, L. F., Spirduso, W. W., & Silverman, S. J. (2013). *Proposals that work: A guide for planning dissertations and grant proposals* (6th ed.). Thousand Oaks, CA: Sage.

Lysack, C. L., & Krefting, L. (1994). Qualitative methods in field research: An Indonesian experience in community based practice. *The Occupational Therapy Journal of Research, 14*(20), 93–110.

Mac an Ghaill, M., & Haywood, C. (2015). British-born Pakistani and Bangladeshi young men: Exploring unstable concepts of Muslim, Islamophobia and racialization. *Critical Sociology, 41,* 97–114.

MacKinnon, D. P., Fairchild, A. J., & Fritz, M.S. (2007). Mediation analysis. *Annual Review of Psychology, 58,* 593–614.

Marshall, C., & Rossman, G. B. (2016). *Designing qualitative research* (6th ed.). Thousand Oaks, CA: Sage.

Mascarenhas, B. (1989). Domains of state-owned, privately held, and publicly traded firms in international competition. *Administrative Science Quarterly, 34,* 582–597.

Maxwell, J. A. (2013). *Qualitative research design: An interactive approach* (3rd ed.). Thousand Oaks, CA: Sage.

McCracken, G. (1988). *The long interview.* Newbury Park, CA: Sage.

Megel, M. E., Langston, N. F., & Creswell, J. W. (1987). Scholarly productivity: A survey of nursing faculty researchers. *Journal of Professional Nursing, 4,* 45–54.

Merriam, S. B. (1998). *Qualitative research and case study applications in education.* San Francisco: Jossey-Bass.

Mertens, D. M. (2003). Mixed methods and the politics of human research: The transformative-emancipatory perspective. In A. Tashakkori & C. Teddlie (Eds.), *SAGE handbook of mixed methods in social & behavioral research* (pp. 135–164). Thousand Oaks, CA: Sage.

Mertens, D. M. (2007). Transformative paradigm: Mixed methods and social justice. *Journal of Mixed Methods Research, 1*(3), 212–225.

Mertens, D. M. (2009). *Transformative research and evaluation.* New York: Guilford.

Mertens, D. M. (2010). *Research and evaluation in education and psychology: Integrating diversity with quantitative, qualitative, and mixed methods* (3rd ed.). Thousand Oaks, CA: Sage.

Mertens, D. M., & Ginsberg, P. E. (2009). *The handbook of social research ethics.* Thousand Oaks, CA: Sage.

Miles, M. B., & Huberman, A. M. (1994). *Qualitative data analysis: A sourcebook of new methods.* Thousand Oaks, CA: Sage.

Miller, D. (1992). *The experiences of a first-year college president: An ethnography.* Unpublished doctoral dissertation, University of Nebraska-Lincoln.

Miller, D. C., & Salkind, N. J. (2002). *Handbook of research design and social measurement* (6th ed.). Thousand Oaks, CA: Sage.

Moore, D. (2000). Gender identity, nationalism, and social action among Jewish and Arab women in Israel: Redefining the social order? *Gender Issues, 18*(2), 3–28.

Morgan, D. (2007). Paradigms lost and pragmatism regained: Methodological implications of combining qualitative and quantitative methods. *Journal of Mixed Methods Research, 1*(1), 48–76.

Morse, J. M. (1991). Approaches to qualitative-quantitative methodological triangulation. *Nursing Research, 40*(1), 120–123.

Morse, J. M. (1994). Designing funded qualitative research. In N. K. Denzin & Y. S. Lincoln (Eds.), *Handbook of qualitative research* (pp. 220–235). Thousand Oaks, CA: Sage.

Morse, J. M., & Niehaus, L. (2009). *Mixed methods design: Principles and procedures.* Walnut Creek, CA: Left Coast Press.

Moustakas, C. (1994). *Phenomenological research methods.* Thousand Oaks, CA: Sage.

Murguia, E., Padilla, R. V., & Pavel, M. (1991, September). Ethnicity and the concept of social integration in Tinto's model of institutional departure. *Journal of College Student Development, 32,* 433–439.

Murphy, J. P. (1990). *Pragmatism: From Peirce to Davidson.* Boulder, CO: Westview.

Nastasi, B. K., & Hitchcock, J. (2016). *Mixed methods research and culture-specific interventions.* Los Angeles, CA: Sage.

Nastasi, B. K., Hitchcock, J., Sarkar, S., Burkholder, G., Varjas, K., & Jayasena, A. (2007). Mixed methods in intervention research: Theory to adaptation. *Journal of Mixed Methods Research, 1*(2), 164–182.

Nesbary, D. K. (2000). *Survey research and the world wide web.* Boston: Allyn & Bacon.

Neuman, S. B., & McCormick, S. (Eds.). (1995). *Single-subject experimental research: Applications for literacy.* Newark, DE: International Reading Association.

Neuman, W. L. (2009). *Social research methods: Qualitative and quantitative approaches* (7th ed.). Boston: Allyn & Bacon.

Newman, I., & Benz, C. R. (1998). *Qualitative-quantitative research methodology: Exploring the interactive continuum.* Carbondale and Edwardsville: Southern Illinois University Press.

Nieswiadomy, R. M. (1993). *Foundations of nursing research* (2nd ed.). New York: Appleton & Lange.

O'Cathain, A., Murphy, E., & Nicholl, J. (2007). Integration and publications as indicators of "yield" from mixed methods studies. *Journal of Mixed Methods Research, 1*(2), 147–163.

Olesen, V. L. (2000). Feminism and qualitative research at and into the millennium. In N. L. Denzin & Y. S. Lincoln, *Handbook of qualitative research* (pp. 215–255). Thousand Oaks, CA: Sage.

Onwuegbuzie, A. J., & Leech, N. L. (2006). Linking research questions to mixed methods data analysis procedures. *The Qualitative Report, 11*(3), 474–498. Retrieved from www.nova.edu/ssss/QR/QR11-3/onwuegbuzie.pdf.

Padula, M. A., & Miller, D. (1999). Understanding graduate women's reentry experiences. *Psychology of Women Quarterly, 23,* 327–343.

Plano Clark, V. L., & Ivankova, N. V. (2016). *Mixed Methods Research: A Guide to the Field.* Thousand Oaks, CA: Sage.

Patton, M. Q. (1990). *Qualitative evaluation and research methods* (2nd ed.). Newbury Park, CA: Sage.

Patton, M. Q. (2002). *Qualitative research and evaluation methods* (3rd ed.). Thousand Oaks, CA: Sage.

Phillips, D. C., & Burbules, N. C. (2000). *Postpositivism and educational research.* Lanham, MD: Rowman & Littlefield.

Pink, S. (2001). *Doing visual ethnography.* Thousand Oaks, CA: Sage.

Plano Clark, V. L. (2005). Cross-Disciplinary Analysis of the Use of Mixed Methods in Physics Education Research, Counseling Psychology, and Primary Care (Doctoral dissertation, University of Nebraska–Lincoln, 2005). *Dissertation Abstracts International, 66,* 02A.

Plano Clark, V. L., & Creswell, J. W. (2008). *The mixed methods reader.* Thousand Oaks, CA: Sage.

Punch, K. F. (2014). *Introduction to social research: Quantitative and qualitative approaches* (3rd ed.). Thousand Oaks, CA: Sage.

Rhoads, R. A. (1997). Implications of the growing visibility of gay and bisexual male students on campus. *NASPA Journal, 34*(4), 275–286.

Richardson, L. (1990). *Writing strategies: Reaching diverse audiences.* Newbury Park, CA: Sage.

Richie, B. S., Fassinger, R. E., Linn, S. G., Johnson, J., Prosser, J., & Robinson, S. (1997). Persistence, connection, and passion: A qualitative study of the career development of highly achieving African American-Black and White women. *Journal of Counseling Psychology, 44*(2), 133–148.

Riemen, D. J. (1986). The essential structure of a caring interaction: Doing phenomenology. In P. M. Munhall & C. J. Oiler (Eds.), *Nursing research: A qualitative perspective* (pp. 85–105). New York: Appleton & Lange.

Riessman, C. K. (2008). *Narrative methods for the human sciences.* Thousand Oaks, CA: Sage.

Rogers, A., Day, J., Randall, F., & Bentall, R. P. (2003). Patients' understanding and participation in a trial designed to improve the management of anti-psychotic medication: A qualitative study. *Social Psychiatry and Psychiatric Epidemiology, 38,* 720–727.

Rorty, R. (1990). Pragmatism as anti-representationalism. In J. P. Murphy, *Pragmatism: From Peirce to Davison* (pp. 1–6). Boulder, CO: Westview.

Rosenthal, R., & Rosnow, R. L. (1991). *Essentials of behavioral research: Methods and data analysis.* New York: McGraw-Hill.

Ross-Larson, B. (1982). *Edit yourself: A manual for everyone who works with words.* New York: Norton.

Rossman, G.B., & Rallis, S. F. (2012). *Learning in the field: An introduction to qualitative research* (3rd ed.). Thousand Oaks, CA: Sage.

Rossman, G.B., & Rallis, S. F. (2017). *An introduction to qualitative research: Learning in the field:* (4th ed.). Los Angeles, CA: Sage.

Rossman, G. B., & Wilson, B. L. (1985, October). Numbers and words: Combining quantitative and qualitative methods in a single large-scale evaluation study. *Evaluation Review, 9*(5), 627–643.

Rudestam, K. E., & Newton, R. R. (2014). *Surviving your dissertation* (4th ed.). Thousand Oaks, CA: Sage.

Salant, P., & Dillman, D. A. (1994). *How to conduct your own survey.* New York: John Wiley.

Salkind, N. (1990). *Exploring research.* New York: MacMillan.

Salmons, J. (2010). *Online interviews in real time.* Thousand Oaks, CA: Sage.

Sandelowski, M. (1996). Using qualitative methods in intervention studies. *Research in Nursing & Health, 19*(4), 359–364.

Sarantakos, S. (2005). *Social research* (3rd ed.). New York: Palgrave Macmillan.

Schafer, J. L., & Graham, J. W. (2002). Missing data: Our view of the state of the art. *Psychological Methods, 7*(2), 147–177.

Schwandt, T. A. (2014). *Dictionary of qualitative inquiry* (5th ed.). Thousand Oaks, CA: Sage.

Shadish, W. R., Cook, T. D., & Campbell, D. T. (2001). *Experimental and quasi-experimental designs for generalized causal inference.* Boston: Houghton Mifflin.

Shaw, E. K., Ohman-Strickland, P. A., Piasecki, A., et al. (2013). Effects of facilitated team meetings and learning collaboratives on colorectal cancer screening rates in primary care practices: A cluster randomized trial. *Annals of Family Medicine, 11*(3), 220–228.

Sieber, J. E. (1998). Planning ethically responsible research. In L. Bickman & D. J. Rog (Eds.), *Handbook of applied social research methods* (pp. 127–156). Thousand Oaks, CA: Sage.

Sieber, S. D. (1973). The integration of field work and survey methods. *American Journal of Sociology, 78,* 1335–1359.

Slife, B. D., & Williams, R. N. (1995). *What's behind the research? Discovering hidden assumptions in the behavioral sciences.* Thousand Oaks, CA: Sage.

Smith, J. K. (1983, March). Quantitative versus qualitative research: An attempt to clarify the issue. *Educational Researcher,* 6–13.

Spradley, J. P. (1980). *Participant observation.* New York: Holt, Rinehart & Winston.

Stake, R. E. (1995). *The art of case study research.* Thousand Oaks, CA: Sage.

Steinbeck, J. (1969). *Journal of a novel: The East of Eden letters.* New York: Viking.

Strauss, A., & Corbin, J. (1990). *Basics of qualitative research: Grounded theory procedures and techniques.* Newbury Park, CA: Sage.

Strauss, A., & Corbin, J. (1998). *Basics of qualitative research: Grounded theory procedures and techniques* (2nd ed.). Thousand Oaks, CA: Sage.

Sudduth, A. G. (1992). *Rural hospitals' use of strategic adaptation in a changing health care environment.* Unpublished doctoral dissertation, University of Nebraska-Lincoln.

Sue, V. M., & Ritter, L. A. (2012). *Conducting online surveys* (2nd ed.). Thousand Oaks, CA: Sage.

Sweetman, D. (2008). *Use of the transformative-emancipatory perspective in mixed methods studies: A review and recommendations.* Unpublished manuscript.

Sweetman, D., Badiee, M., & Creswell, J. W. (2010). Use of the transformative framework in mixed methods studies. *Qualitative Inquiry, 16*(6), 441–454.

Szmitko, P. E., & Verma, S. (2005). Red wine and your heart. *Circulation, 111,* e10–e11.

Tarshis, B. (1982). *How to write like a pro: A guide to effective nonfiction writing.* New York: New American Library.

Tashakkori, A., & Creswell, J. W. (2007). Exploring the nature of research questions in mixed methods research [Editorial]. *Journal of Mixed Methods Research, 1*(3), 207–211.

Tashakkori, A., & Teddlie, C. (1998). *Mixed methodology: Combining qualitative and quantitative approaches.* Thousand Oaks, CA: Sage.

Tashakkori, A., & Teddlie, C. (Eds.). (2003). *SAGE handbook of mixed methods in social & behavioral research.* Thousand Oaks, CA: Sage.

Tashakkori, A., & Teddlie, C. (Eds.). (2010). *SAGE handbook of mixed methods in social & behavioral research* (2nd ed.). Thousand Oaks, CA: Sage.

Teddlie, C., & Tashakkori, A. (2009). *Foundations of mixed methods research: Integrating quantitative and qualitative approaches in the social and behavioral sciences.* Thousand Oaks, CA: Sage.

Terenzini, P. T., Cabrera, A. F., Colbeck, C. L., Bjorklund, S. A., & Parente, J. M. (2001). Racial and ethnic diversity in the classroom. *The Journal of Higher Education, 72*(5), 509–531.

Tesch, R. (1990). *Qualitative research: Analysis types and software tools.* New York: Falmer.

Thomas, G. (1997). What's the use of theory? *Harvard Educational Review, 67*(1), 75–104.

Thomas, J. (1993). *Doing critical ethnography.* Newbury Park, CA: Sage.

Thompson, B. (2006). *Foundations of behavioral statistics: An insight-based approach.* New York: Guilford.

Thorndike, R. M. (1997). *Measurement and evaluation in psychology and education* (6th ed.). New York: Macmillan.

Trujillo, N. (1992). Interpreting (the work and the talk of) baseball: Perspectives on ballpark culture. *Western Journal of Communication, 56,* 350–371.

Tuckman, B. W. (1999). *Conducting educational research* (5th ed.). Fort Worth, TX: Harcourt Brace.

University of Chicago Press. (2010). *The Chicago manual of style* (16th ed.). Chicago: Author.

University Microfilms. (1938–). *Dissertation abstracts international.* Ann Arbor, MI: Author.

VanHorn-Grassmeyer, K. (1998). *Enhancing practice: New professional in student affairs.* Unpublished doctoral dissertation, University of Nebraska-Lincoln.

Van Maanen, J. (1988). *Tales of the field: On writing ethnography.* Chicago: University of Chicago Press.

Vernon, J. E. (1992). *The impact of divorce on the grandparent/grandchild relationship when the parent generation divorces.* Unpublished doctoral dissertation, University of Nebraska-Lincoln.

Vogt, W. P. & Johnson, R.B. (2015). *The Sage dictionary of statistics and methodology: A nontechnical guide for the social sciences* (4th ed.). Thousand Oaks, CA: Sage.

Webb, R. B., & Glesne, C. (1992). Teaching qualitative research. In M. D. LeCompte, W. L. Millroy & J. Preissle (Eds.), *The Handbook of qualitative research in education* (pp. 771–814). San Diego, CA: Academic Press.

Webb, W. H., Beals, A. R., & White, C. M. (1986). *Sources of information in the social sciences: A guide to the literature* (3rd ed.). Chicago: American Library Association.

Weitzman, P. F., & Levkoff, S. E. (2000). Combining qualitative and quantitative methods in health research with minority elders: Lessons from a study of dementia caregiving. *Field Methods, 12*(3), 195–208.

Wilkinson, A. M. (1991). *The scientist's handbook for writing papers and dissertations.* Englewood Cliffs, NJ: Prentice Hall.

Wittink, M. N., Barg, F. K., & Gallo, J. J. (2006). Unwritten rules of talking to doctors about depression: Integrating qualitative and quantitative methods. *Annals of Family Medicine, 4*(4), 302–309.

Wolcott, H. T. (1994). *Transforming qualitative data: Description, analysis, and interpretation.* Thousand Oaks, CA: Sage.

Wolcott, H. T. (2008). *Ethnography: A way of seeing* (2nd ed.). Walnut Creek, CA: AltaMira.

Wolcott, H. T. (2009). *Writing up qualitative research* (3rd ed.). Thousand Oaks, CA: Sage.

Yin, R. K. (2009). *Case study research: Design and methods* (4th ed.). Thousand Oaks, CA: Sage.

Yin, R. K. (2012). *Applications of case study research* (3rd ed.). Thousand Oaks, CA: Sage.

Yin, R. K. (2014). *Case study research* (5th ed.). Thousand Oaks, CA: Sage.

Ziller, R. C. (1990). *Photographing the self: Methods for observing personal orientations.* Newbury Park, CA: Sage.

Zinsser, W. (1983). *Writing with a word processor.* New York: Harper Colophon.

Author Index

Subject Index